People and Organizations Interacting

Edited by
Aat Brakel

Consultant
Formerly with Shell International Petroleum Company

JOHN WILEY & SONS

Chichester · New York · Brisbane · Toronto · Singapore

Library of Congress Cataloging in Publication Data:
Main entry under title:
People and organizations interacting.
Includes index.
1. Organizational change—Addresses, essays, lectures.
I. Brakel, Aat.
HD58.8.P46 1984   658.4'06   84-5212
ISBN 0 471 90476 7

British Library Cataloguing in Publication Data:
People and organizations interacting.
1. Royal Dutch/Shell Group of Companies
2. Organizational change
I. Brakel, Aat
338.7'6223382   HD9575.N64R6

ISBN 0 471 90476 7

Phototypeset by C. R. Barber & Partners (Highlands) Ltd,
Fort William, Scotland.
Printed by St Edmundsbury Press, Bury St Edmunds,
Suffolk.

List of Contributors

Mr J. E. M. Boezeman
c/o Shell Gabon
Boîte Postale 224
Libreville
Gabon

Dr A. Brakel (editor)
Achterdijk 18
3161 EC Rhoon
The Netherlands

Mr D. Cormack
c/o Shell International Petroleum
    Company Ltd, LP/4
Shell Centre
London SE1 7NA
U.K.

Mr L. V. Gjemdal
A/S Norske Shell
Tullingsgt. 2
Oslo 1
Norway

Mr C. T. Greeve
c/o Shell Nederland Raffinaderij
    (DOE)
Postbox 7000
3000 HA Rotterdam
The Netherlands

Dr N. Halpern
Consultant Organisation Effectiveness
c/o Shell Canada Ltd
Box 400
Terminal 'A'
Ontario M5W 1E1
Canada

Mr O. Hattori
c/o Shell Sekiyu Kabushiki Kaisha
Central P.O. Box 1239
Tokyo
Japan

Dr G. H. Hofstede
c/o Institute for Research on
    Intercultural Cooperation
Velperweg 95
6824 HH Arnhem
The Netherlands

Mr A. Langstraat
c/o Shell Nederland (PTR)
Floris Grijpstraat 2
2596 XE The Hague
The Netherlands

Mr D. K. Mungall
c/o Shell U.K. Ltd, PRL/4
Shell-Mex House
Strand
London WC2R 0DX
U.K.

Ms W. Pritchard
c/o Shell International Petroleum
   Company Ltd, PNRL/3
Shell Centre
London SE1 7NA
U.K.

Dr J. Roggema
Oosterweg 17
9995 VJ Kantens
The Netherlands

Mr P. Sadler
c/o Ashridge Management College
Berkhamsted
Hertfordshire HP4 1NS
U.K.

Mr J. van der Veer
c/o Shell U.K. Oil
Shell-Mex House, UOMK/35
Strand
London WC2R 0DX
U.K.

Mr Th. Voors
c/o Petromin Shell Refinery Coy
P.O. Box 10088
Al-Jubail
Kingdom of Saudi Arabia

Mr B. A. Wallace
c/o Organisation Dynamics Ltd
85 Knutsford Road
Wilmslow
Cheshire SK9 6JH
U.K.

Mr J. N. Watson
13 Clovelly Avenue
Warlingham
Surrey CR3 9HZ
U.K.

Table of Contents

Foreword

Faced with rapidly changing technologies and with new and uncertain economic and social conditions, the advanced industrial societies are having to tackle the extremely difficult yet inescapable process of changing organizations and institutions so as to adapt to environmental pressures. This process can be seen as occurring at two levels—the level of people as individuals or members of face-to-face groups and the level of organizations seen as complex structures of relationships. Change makes its impact on people by changing their lives—often radically. They may have to learn new skills, change jobs, change employer, move house; in the process they often lose—if only temporarily—security, status, even their sense of personal identity. Change makes its impact on organizations by changing their objectives, policies, processes, and structures. Organizational change profoundly affects people and people's response to change strongly influences organizational effectiveness.

This interactive process between people and organizations is explored in this book. Aat Brakel, who was seconded from Shell International Petroleum Company to Ashridge Management College during 1980–1981 as a Visiting Lecturer, has brought together a collection of case histories and put them in a framework which adds greatly to our knowledge of and insight into the complex patterns of human activity involved in changing organizations. His selection of material illustrates his chosen theme very well, particularly in the context of the hugely complex organization represented by the world's second largest oil company.

At the same time, the content of the book also provides an illuminating demonstration of another interaction—that between theory and practice. The 'theory' running through the contributions, sometimes explicitly sometimes implicitly present, is organization theory (and in particular socio-technical systems theory) which is perhaps potentially the single most important contribution of the social sciences to solving the practical problems of human existence in modern society. (The qualification 'potentially' must be used here since relatively few among those reponsible for managing complex organizations make use of such theoretical knowledge.) The 'practice' dealt with in the book is, of course, that of managing organizations like oil refineries or projects such as developing an offshore oilfield.

ix

The encouraging thing is that in a highly successful organization like Shell and in cultural settings as diverse as Europe, North America, and Japan, organization theory *has* been made use of, *is* being made use of, and is above all *being useful*. In the process of being used in this way the theory is itself being greatly enriched. This is the interaction which in the social science field is vital to the advancement of knowledge. Thinking managers and organizational theorists alike are therefore indebted to Aat Brakel for publishing this material and in so doing making a significant contribution to the growing stock of evidence that we *are* able to achieve a better understanding of human behaviour in organizations and can use that understanding to manage more effectively.

Philip Sadler
Ashridge Management College

Introduction

Today Shell companies* make up the second largest enterprise in the world's oil industry. They handle about 8% of the non-communist world's oil and natural gas, exploring and producing, purchasing, processing, and selling it. They operate in over 100 countries and employ more than 165,000 people worldwide.

Since the formation of the Royal Dutch/Shell Group in 1907, Shell companies' activities have continued to expand. Besides being involved in all aspects of the oil and natural gas business, they are major chemical producers. They also produce and trade in coal and metals. Each Shell company around the world runs its own day-to-day business in one or more of these areas of activity, according to local conditions and opportunities. At the same time, each one can also take advantage of being part of a larger group of companies, with a broad geographical and technical spread of interests. Even the smallest Shell company, therefore, can have access to the experience and expertise which highly skilled people have developed and built up over many years of activity in a multitude of world-wide operations.

The continued success of Shell companies' operations will, in part, be determined by their ability to adapt to an environment radically different from the one in which they attained their present size and structure. The subject-matter of this book is in this sphere of activity: adaptation of organizations to changing environments, shown in a number of case histories from Shell companies in various countries around the world.

The variety of experience recorded makes for a kaleidoscopic picture. How do we look at this picture? It depends on our viewpoint, which is affected by our attitude to the future. The editor takes the presupposition that a desirable future depends on our being able to build the kind of world that represents our choices, which we cannot do alone. People have to consider other people's viewpoints; organizations have to take the purposes of other organizations into account. The preferred way to look at things is therefore an *interactive* way, as expressed in the title of this book.

---

*Shell companies have their own separate identities, but in this book the collective expressions 'Shell' or 'Group' are sometimes used for convenience in contexts where reference is made to the companies of the Royal Dutch/Shell Group in general. These expressions are also used when no useful purpose is served by identifying the particular company or companies.

An organization—seen as people trying to reach objectives within a particular framework—is man-made. The history of every organization starts with: Once upon a time . . . Once upon a time somebody had an idea and started something that became an organization. This man-made entity can also be re-made and that is what we see in our day; this book gives an account of this and tries to discover a pathway to the future.

An important message of the book is that culture is an organizational variable. With Hofstede we define culture as 'the collective programming of the mind which distinguishes the members of one human group from another'. Until recently these aspects hardly came to the fore and it was supposed that what worked in one part of the world would also work in another. Geert Hofstede has kindly agreed to write a chapter for this book which is based on material presented in the various chapters.

An interesting feature is that in a number of cases the general executive officer or one of the senior managers of the companies concerned have provided an epilogue to the chapter in question which places the development as described in an actual context and gives us a viewpoint from the top man. It also gives a view *of* him: it shows how he uses and commits himself to organizational change to reach his objectives.

An overview of the 12 chapters is as follows. Chapter 1 presents 'A way to look at things' in order to see the wood for the trees and to find some common ground. Our viewpoint is expressed in what is called the skating analogy. The remarkable thing about a skater is that he is obliged to make movements to and fro in order to move forward. An organization progresses (and changes) in a similar way: two strokes are imperative, one related to the tasks and one related to the people. This skating model is not only a very Dutch model, it is also a Western model that expresses a particular way of looking at things. In the final paragraph of Chapter 1 the bias of the model is discussed by posing the question of contexts.

Chapters 2–7 originate from a variety of activities: Chapter 2—tanker transport; Chapter 3—oil exploration (North Sea); Chapter 4—oil refining; Chapter 5—research; Chapter 6—engineering; and Chapter 7—chemicals.

Chapters 8–10 concern processes of change, over a certain period of time, with regard to Canada, Norway, and Japan.

In Chapter 11 an overall view is taken related to the changed character and its implications for the Shell Group of Companies.

Chapter 12 presents an interpretation of previous chapters from a cultural perspective.

Finally, in Chapter 13, entitled 'Managing diversity', the question is addressed as to the message emanating from the material presented. What have we learned? What about organizations and managers for the future? In order to find a common vantage-point to examine the data, a framework is presented that allows information from various sources to be combined. Among other distinctions both evolutionary and revolutionary changes become apparent.

In total this book shows and explains *why* and *how* organizations adapt, referring both to *content* and *context*. It is intended for all those concerned with or interested in organizations so that they may better understand their own experiences and develop their own or their organization's ability to adapt.

As editor it is my privilege to thank all authors, most of them within Shell and a few outside, who contributed with so much enthusiasm and competence. I am also indebted to a number of general managers and senior managers of Shell for their willingness to write an epilogue at the end of some of the case studies.

My thanks are due to Philip Sadler, Principal of Ashridge Management College, for writing the Foreword. I wish to thank Marja Hirschfeld, who did the typing. I also want to mention the constructive co-operation of the publisher, John Wiley & Sons Ltd, who had to put up with an editor and several authors whose first language is not English.

Finally, I express my thanks to the Management of the Royal Dutch/Shell Group who agreed to have the material from within Shell published. Although I greatly benefited from all support given to me by friends and colleagues, the responsibility for the final content of the book must be mine.

Aat Brakel

'Accordingly, we decided to take a look at management excellence itself. We had put that item on the agenda early in our project, but the real impetus came when the managing directors of Royal Dutch/Shell Group asked us to help them with a one-day seminar on innovation. To fit what we had to offer with Shell's request, we chose a double meaning for the word "innovation." In addition to what might normally be thought of—creative people developing marketable new products and services—we added a twist that is central to our concern with change in big institutions. We asserted that innovative companies not only are unusually good at producing commercially viable new widgets; *innovative companies are especially adroit at continually responding to change of any sort in their environment.'* T. J. Peters and R. H. Waterman: *In Search of Excellence.*

People and Organizations Interacting
Edited by A. Brakel
© 1985, John Wiley & Sons Ltd.

Chapter 1

A Way to Look at Things

Aat Brakel

Starting point

There is an old story from India about a village the inhabitants of which had never seen an elephant before in all their lives. On a certain day an elephant is transported into the village in a large wooden crate. The crate is put in the middle of the village and one of the elders of the village invites the people to go into the crate one by one and subsequently recount what they have seen. The first to go into the crate touches the trunk of the elephant, comes outside and says that an elephant looks like a water hose. The second one finds an ear and tells a story about an elephant looking like a fan. Number three touches a leg and is reminded of a pillar. The fourth touches the back of the animal and maintains that an elephant is built as a throne. In short everyone sees an elephant based on what occurred to him when touching something in the dark crate. Everybody

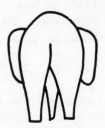

1

expressed a certain truth—so continues our story—but nobody knew the total truth. If they had discovered the real elephant in the light of a lamp they would have found that they said the same thing with different words. They were all right and at the same time not right. The story finishes with the moral that we only understand that which we have in our own fingers (Gelpke, 1957, p. 65).

My being right is determined to a large extent by my own world and my own biography. Your being right as a reader will be different from mine. If both of us were to look at the same thing the chances are that each of us would experience something different. People do not always see the same things: they have unique perspectives. In fact, most of the time we are both right and not right at the same time, just like those looking at the elephant.

Now we could also talk about being equal. It is interesting that in other languages 'being right' and 'being equal' are expressed with the same word. Whenever I look around me I see that people are not equal. Is that correct? Is it not our experience that in our society we are continuously told that we are equal? My experience is rather that in order to be able to communicate with people and live with them I have to adopt their roles and put myself in their shoes. We have to make each other, as it were, equal.

In summary, we can say we are both equal and unequal, right and not right. People living together and working together assumes the ability to handle both being equal and unequal, right and not right. It appears that this is not a simple problem. How often do we see very competent people in enterprises, hospitals, churches, governments, and other organizations get stuck because of insufficient ability to communicate and work together? In many of these cases the individual remains convinced of his own right which means for him that his opponent is not right. It hardly ever occurs to him that he may be right and not right at the same time. Multiple perspectives mean that there is no single 'right' in all places and times.

In Western society people work normally with '*either* one *or* the other' and hardly ever with '*both* one *and* the other'. This last aspect, however, is more related to an interactive attitude than the first one. Interaction of people and organisations involves the ability to handle both being right and not right, equal and not equal. In this book an organization seen as a total of people and their work will be approached from this basic perspective, in particular an organization in a changing environment. It will be shown that developments and uncertainties in society require extension of the repertory concerning forms of organization as well as forms of individual behaviour in the organization. We have to be able to take a number of different looks.

On realities

If we want to think in terms of *both* the one *and* the other we have, as it were, to look with our two eyes at two different things at the same time, which is a rather difficult thing to do. We now explain what we mean by giving some thought to the concept of 'reality'.

We live in different realities (Schutz, 1962, pp. 207, 340; Berger and Luckmann, 1967, p. 21). My wife and my boss are not only different people, but they also represent different realities. The reality of a chemical plant is a different one from the reality of a hospital. As it turns out, realities are relative. What is considered as normal or as abnormal is determined by the surrounding society. In a report on an investigation with three different peoples, Benedict (1971, p. 198) found the tendency to identify normality with the statistically average; deviations from it were defined as abnormal. (See also M. Mead, 1928/54.)

One of the most important realities is that of daily life. Every reality, not least the everyday, humdrum one, has a number of implicit assumptions that are taken for granted, e.g. unwritten precepts of behaviour, language, recipes of all sorts as a matter of course. That is how you do things, it has always been that way: water comes from the tap; on the road you keep left (or right); the train goes at a certain time; you can use the telephone; the letter I put in the mail will arrive; you dress in a certain way; we are not hungry; etc. These assumptions become clear as soon as one of them stagnates: then we panic, or at least get into trouble. The current meanings and assumptions that are taken for granted form the *social stock of knowledge*. It is a series of assumptions concerning accepted and proper behaviour in different circumstances or environments, the correctness of which appears from the activities of other people. The social stock of knowledge makes our environment trustworthy: things have meaning and fit together. The social stock of knowledge belongs to our culture as though it were a second nature. Without this *umwelt* that presents itself as an objective reality, chaos would reign.

This stock of knowledge is carried over by our parents and/or those who accompanied our first steps in life. Every individual is born in an objective social structure in which he meets those that guide his societal education. The child takes the role, the attitude, and the world from his parents, they are for him the significant others. What else would there be to take over? The world of the parent is originally the only available world; it is *the* world, within which the rules of the game are determined by these others. In this first societal education the first world of the individual is being constructed in an irreversible way. But this is not everything.

What the significant others do and say for the child develops into what 'people' do and say. By 'people' we mean society, the group, the people in the street, the generalized other (G. H. Mead, 1972, p. 154). A series of attitudes of this generalized other is taken over by the individual. This series is determined by tradition, convention, and societal environment. It is a social construction carried over by others, which I experience as an objective reality, that is to say, as if this reality were an objective one. If I had been born in a primitive tribe I would have been educated in a different way and my reality would have been a different one. I would experience a different objectivity and I would handle different meanings and different assumptions. It may be remarked here as an aside that this would also be the case in a counter- or sub-culture.

The objective reality also and at the same time manifests itself as a subjective reality. When taking things over from others the objective reality obtains subjective meaning, and in my dealings with things I am going to confirm that meaning and take part in defining it. I react as a subject to the transferred attitudes of others. From my own 'I' as a creative element, I react to the tradition and convention that accumulated within myself; this is the way changes and innovations take place.

In the literature (Berger and Luckmann, 1967, p. 129), the relationship between objective and subjective reality is described by the word 'dialectics', which is used to express the fact that we are dealing with *two* aspects of *one* problem. We try to project a total by continuously keeping our eye on both composing parts. We are, as it were, engaged in a movement to and fro. In the framework of our problem concerning active adaptation of an organization in an unpredictable environment, this dialectic movement is essential since it provides us with the possibility of effectively looking at an organization and its parts, basically people and tasks. We shall work this out in the following sections that deal with man and his work, and man in relation to others. In another section we combine the views in a coupled system, while in the final section we shall pay attention to the context.

Forms of organization

The traditional build-up

Why do most organizations have a bureaucratic and hierarchical build-up? The development of big steam engines at the end of the nineteenth century led to the question of how a relatively large group of people could work in a productive way. Scientific management was the answer (Emery, 1977, p. 26). Scientific management has as its principle the exchange of parts, the thinking that organizations can be built in the same way as an engine, with people as replaceable parts.

Within the framework of a bureaucratic, hierarchical structure, tasks are split up and subsequently allocated to a person or unit. In such an organization the hierarchy is characterized by uniform relationships between people. The decisions regarding task execution are taken by the higher levels on behalf of lower levels, who take, in their turn, decisions for still lower levels. In this way decision-making and co-ordination are separated from the execution of tasks at all levels. This separation requires external control; the means of control is determined by the way co-ordination has been organized.

This bureaucratic model is logical and coherent, but it is based on a principle of organizations that has become less applicable in practice. Traditional hierarchy works when obedience works. As long as individuals grew up believing that some people had the right to order others about, particularly if they paid them, then it made sense to give the power of command to those who were first in the decision-making sequence (Handy, 1980, p. 118). The model dates from the social stock of knowledge of Taylor's time: a mechanical time that produced mechanical images, also in the field of organizations. During the greater part of the nineteenth century, things in life had their own place and were there once and for all. The established social order was accepted as ordained by God and therefore unchangeable. This view gave the growing industry no other point of contact but its own mechanical one to think about the social organization.

The social stock of knowledge seen as a fabric of assumptions by which a society obtains cohesion has been changing drastically since Taylor. In particular we think of developments in education. Also, the view on the social organization has changed. The end of the twentieth century will produce a different type of social organization as compared to the beginning of the twentieth century. Since many organizations originated at the beginning of the twentieth century, there is a fair chance of short-circuiting between the traditional forms of organization and forms that fit in with the actual stock of knowledge. This short-circuiting may become even stronger between the traditional forms and those that fit in with the future stock of knowledge. This is an important consideration for the continuity of the organization, which might become determined to a larger extent by the social system than by technical and economic criteria.

Future forms of organization are coming into view by raising the question concerning the quality of the work situation.

A different build-up

The quality of the work situation is the quality of the contents of the relationship between man and his work situation in which the nature of the task design plays a central role (van Beinum, 1976, p. 1). Emery and Thorsrud (1976, p. 15) give the following summing up of principles of task design:

(1) Sufficient elbow room—the feeling of being one's own boss without continuous control. On the other hand, not so much elbow room that one does not know where to start work.

(2) The chance to learn on the job—the job has to have a reasonable challenge. Feed-back of results should allow correction.

(3) A certain amount of variation preventing boredom and tiredness so that a satisfactory tempo of work can be maintained.

(4) A climate with conditions such that one can receive help and respect from colleagues, preventing situations in which mutual assistance is to nobody's avail, where people are set up against each other so that the gain of one means loss to the other, where group strivings and interests negate individual possibilities.

(5) The feeling that one's own work has meaning and has a contribution to make. That is, not something that could also be done by a trained ape or a robot.

(6) A desirable future, not a dead-end job, but one that allows for personal growth, which is not necessarily the same as promotion in the job. (See also Hill, 1976, p. 4.)

These criteria do not fit in the model of the traditional hierarchical organization. They may even be at odds with it. The fundamental assumption resulting in a vertical organization is, as we saw, that every individual is limited to a single specialized and fragmented task. In this way a structure of hierarchical relationships develops within which job execution at a certain level is controlled by the next higher level. In this ideal type of organization aspects of the quality of work are in fact denied.

Whenever the consequent splitting up of work is left behind and with it the one-man/one-task principle, the need for an exclusive vertical build-up disappears. A view on alternative forms of build-up comes to the fore that offer possibilities for a larger measure of independent activities that still fit in a larger total. Such alternative forms of organization are found in models like the relative autonomous group, the matrix structure, and the network (Herbst, 1976, p. 29).

In the ideal type of autonomous group all members can replace each other to a large extent. There is no need for an outspoken leadership role. The structure is fluid, the members of the group determine the most suitable structure for a specific task. The main requirement is that the activities of the different group members are directed towards reaching a common goal. The responsibility for co-ordination is within the group, which means with those whose work requires co-ordination in order to reach the common objectives.

This is also true for the matrix structure. In a matrix each group member has a specialized function resulting in a multi-functional group. Also, in this instance, the structures are not fixed, but are dependent upon the task to be executed.

The network is the reverse of the autonomous group: the group members work more or less geographically divided and come together quite regularly. Members have the largest measure of autonomy and are dedicated to a common goal. In daily life they could be working in conventional institutions, like scientific workers in different countries. They could become centres of a network of organizations that work in their own culture on behalf of certain change processes.

The alternative forms of organization make active adaptations possible because these forms, contrary to the original ones, have a certain built-in flexibility. Flexibility is based on some mesure of overcapacity or redundancy. There are two basic ways that redundancy can be realized (Emery, 1977, p. 91).

(1) Redundancy *of* people. This means hiring and firing, dependent upon circumstances. People are considered as replaceable tools, which is the principle of the traditional hierarchical organization in its pure form.

(2) Redundancy *within* people. The principle here is that an individual has

more possibilities than a specific skill for a fragmented task. People are most of the time capable of learning, not only the details of a specific job or craft but also aspects that represent some overview such as preparation, planning, and control. This second design principle is based on the multi-skilled individual, some of whose skills are at any time redundant to the task in hand (Emery, 1 J i ι, p. 27). The optimum level of organizations that have been based on this principle is at a point 'where undermanning stretches their joint resources and challenges them to frequently reallocate functions' (Emery, 1977, p. 99).

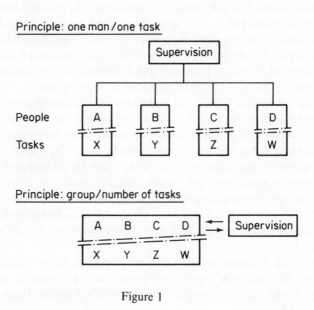

Figure 1

The above-mentioned principles of organization can be summarized as shown in Figure 1. The various forms have been described as ideal types. In everyday reality all sorts of intermediate forms occur, although an organization is usually presented in a hierarchical way. If somebody were asked about the set up of his organization, in most instances a hierarchically drawn scheme would be produced. Alternative, intermediate forms are then presented as informal organizations. The distance between the formal and informal organization can now be such that, as it were, conflicting work designs present themselves. If a formal organization has a vertical build-up and, for instance, independent forms of organization were developing based on certain change processes, there may be in fact two conflicting task designs prevailing in that organization, which can result in ineffectiveness or apathy.

Forms of behaviour

The previous section dealt with people and tasks in a framework of interaction and led up to a view on more autonomous forms of organization. The subject of this section is behaviour in the organization.

We can distinguish some form of personal contact which gives freedom to our words: a contact in which we know beforehand that we have a hearing. We can be silent in the presence of the other without necessarily creating tension or unrest. We only need a few words to make ourselves clear.

We are also familiar with contacts in which this is not the case. The presence of the other is then a barrier which our words must constantly break down. Our partner in the dialogue is, as it were, interposed between us and our words.

When listening to and enjoying a piece of music, I am somewhat taken aback when the person sitting next to me asks, 'Don't you think that is an awful noise?' I do not know what to say, I am speechless. However, if my neighbour indicates that he enjoyed the music too there would be scarcely any need for words, and words might even have a disturbing effect on a shared experience. We rely on the other person adding extra meaning which we wish to express, but cannot find the words for. We say the music is beautiful, but we mean more than that; we mean that something is explicitly communicated to us by the music.

This 'more' is the hidden factor which can be understood as a form of fundamental redundancy and which determines the quality of the human contact. Our words circle around this quality and are fed by it, but never filled out by it. The thing we are speaking about always seems to be infinitely more than we are able to express in words. This then is dialogue when it is more than merely reporting.

All dialogues between people are more than that. Even in the most technical discussion the speaker's own world shines through, starting with his use of language. In the case of dialogue, too, the whole is greater than the sum of the parts.

There is evidently something akin to a 'social intelligence' which can be distinguished from other forms of intelligent behaviour. We have all met highly intelligent people who yet do not appear to be well adjusted to society, or children capable of unusually high intellectual performance who are ill at ease in dealing with people. The distinctive terms 'general' and 'life' intelligence have been coined to describe this—terms which are vague as concepts, but are useful in that they combine many behavioural observations. Despite this 'observational' evidence social intelligence lacks 'statistical' evidence: social intelligence is evidently difficult to measure (Berger, 1972, pp. 1–3).

Social intelligence is defined as the ability to open up oneself to day-to-day interpersonal behaviour. We regard someone as socially intelligent if he demonstrates in day-to-day life that he understands people in their involvement in the reality which surrounds them. The socially intelligent person appraises more than he reasons and discovers for himself opportunities to use his social intelligence rather than selecting from alternatives offered to him by someone else.

In order to appraise someone's intentions one must be able to put oneself in his role in a given situation. In social psychology 'taking the role or attitude of the other' is an important concept (G. H. Mead, 1972, p. 76). For our purposes we consider it permissible to use the terms 'role-taking' and 'social intelligence' as synonymous.

We have described that what the significant others (the parents) do and say in the course of socialization develops itself into what 'people' do and say. By 'people' we mean society, the group, the generalized other. The generalized other is society compressed into a single person whom I meet in the street. Social intelligence not only encompasses the ability to take the role or attitude of an individual, but also the ability to internalize developments and processes in society.

What can we say in this context about an organization? Within an organization two kinds of knowledge function in parallel, or rather are intermingled. In the first place we have the general stock of knowledge made up of things we take for granted: assumptions, prevailing standards of right and wrong, justice or injustice, what one should or should not do. In the second place the specific knowledge related to the purpose and dominant processes of the organization. The general stock of knowledge is the vehicle for the specific knowledge. An organization can be regarded as a segment of the social stock of knowledge within which is diffused a certain amount of specific meaning. The discussions in the social field within organizations are therefore essentially societal discussions.

This is a new phenomenon in the development of organizations. The early form of company was a closed system with a labour organization which reflected a mechanical design principle. Workers with muscles came into the organization, but were by no means generalized—also to be called societal—others. The modern form of organization can be regarded as an open system. The transactions between organization and environment concern not only resources such as raw materials and end products, but also people with their backgrounds, definitions of the situation, and expectations. There is a world of difference between the complete dependence, lack of political weight, and the concept of labour as merchandise at the end of the nineteenth century and the current views. Nor is there any reason to assume that this difference will remain constant from now on: it may be that the organization, as an open system, will become increasingly open. Every day the environment plays a part in the organization in many different forms. People not only play the role allotted to them, they also play themselves, their 'societal selves'. 'Individuals have a propensity to resist depersonalization, to spill over the boundaries of their segmentary roles to participate as wholes' (Selznick, 1969/1972, p. 263). The social system of an organization acquires therefore characteristics that correspond with those of the surrounding society. If the surrounding society is complex, turbulent, and unpredictable, so is the social system of the organization embedded in that environment. Interaction in such situations demands a form of behaviour which makes it possible to handle varying and complex relationships with the other, on the one hand as a unique individual and on the other as representing a society or culture with values that may be different from my own. This demands role-taking, the ability to adopt the role and attitude of the other, i.e. social intelligence.

A coupled system: the skating model

In the earliest Chinese cults man's life upon earth was made possible by magical forces maintaining the harmonious balance of the cosmos. This concept was formulated as the doctrine of the Yin and the Yang, the alternating forces expressive of light and darkness, negative and positive, male and female. These powers in their combined operation are the mainspring of every activity, the mechanism of constant change and balance; they are represented by the illustrated symbol of the circle equally divided by a curved line (Figure 2), indicating equilibrium maintained by the ceaseless flux of two balanced forces (Fitzgerald, 1935/1950, pp. 35, 220).

Figure 2

The Yin and the Yang provide an example of a coupled system (Trist, 1980), that indicates the interdependence of the parts and the whole. Another example is to be found in the skating analogy, which we shall explain in the following.

Discussing forms of organization and forms of behaviour in the third and fourth section of this chapter the general focus of both sections has been on *men* and their *work*. Referring to the dialectic relation between two elements we explained in the second section we now assume such a relation to exist between 'people' on one side and 'work' or 'tasks' on the other. In an organization they belong together as two sides of a coin. Both elements, like the Yin and the Yang, are seen as complementary; it means that

(a) for each of the elements the presence of the other is required in order to give it its true value, and

(b) conversely, each of the two elements deteriorates in the absence of the other. This idea to describe an organization in terms of complementary elements is expressed in the *skating analogy*.

On inspection the skating movement is a complicated one. A remarkable thing is that we are originally moving in a direction A and subsequently in a direction B, in neither direction we want to be; eventually we make progress in a third direction, C (see Figure 3).

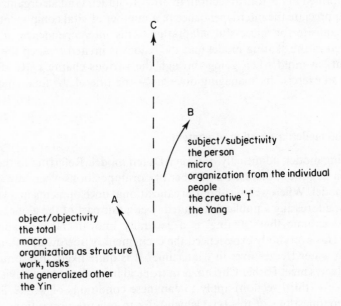

Figure 3

In an organizational context we are dealing with one stroke related to work, the tasks, and one stroke related to the people. Just as with any comparison, ours too is rather inaccurate: the skater moves forward on qualitatively different legs; primarily, though, we are concerned with the type of movement: progress is not in direction A, nor B, but in the third direction, C. This also holds for change or adaptation which thus involves both vital categories.

The start of the change process can be with either one of the composing elements, the category people, or the category tasks. But a *complete* change only occurs when complementary activities take place, irrespective of the starting point.

Whenever an activity limits itself either to people or to tasks, then no change develops according to our model. In this instance we are only concerned with a passive or pseudo adaptation. For instance, certain training activities in an organization may relate to working as a team rather than on an individual basis. But when the communication between people remains based on hierarchical ways of working there is a good chance that everything remains in the old mould. The training activity then does not relate to the everyday work traditions. The strokes are only single ones and a change process cannot come off the ground.

'People and tasks' form only one 'doublestroke' of quite a number that occur in work organizations. Another is 'organization and environment', and on the individual level 'general intelligence and social intelligence', components that were mentioned in the fourth section. In order to understand an organization we have to appreciate the interdependence of a number of vital components, which is a prerequisite for successful adaptation. This interdependence of parts is symbolized in the skating model and the reader is invited to keep the skater's movements in mind when going through the various chapters. Reading thus becomes an exercise in 'managing diversity'—the title of the final chapter.

Bias of the model: a question of context

The skating model, admittedly, is a very Dutch model. Referring to the second section on 'realities', there are a number of presuppositions when introducing a skating model. When writing about organizational developments in a variety of countries, addressing a public distributed over a fair part of the globe, is it then correct to assume that 'skating' is a generally known and well understood practice? Has everybody experienced the excitement or sorrow of a thing called 'ice' when water freezes over in wintertime? It is quite likely that a number of readers always meet Father Christmas in tropical heat. Would the Tavistock job requirements (third section) apply to Japanese conditions of work? There are many more questions of this type which refer to our presuppositions. Bateson (1979, p. 26) observes a lack of knowledge of the presuppositions of everyday life and comments on the phenomenon that people are notably rigid in their presuppositions.

As indicated in the second section we assume that each person carries a certain amount of mental programming which is stable over time and leads to the same person showing more or less the same behaviour in similar situations. Our prediction may never prove true: Mrs X may not turn up, the taxi driver may take me to the wrong destination, family member Y may refuse to come for dinner. But the more accurately we know a person's mental programming and the situation, the more sure our prediction will be (Hofstede, 1980, p. 14). Hofstede broadly distinguishes three levels of uniqueness in mental programmes. The least unique but most basic is the universal level of mental programming which is shared by all, or almost all, mankind. This is the biological 'operating system' of the human body, but it includes a range of expressive behaviours, such as laughing and weeping, and associate and aggressive behaviours which are also found in higher animals.

The collective level of mental programming is shared with some but not all other people; it is common to people belonging to a certain group or category, but different among people belonging to other groups or categories. The whole area of human culture belongs to this level. It includes the language in which we express ourselves, the deference we show to our elders, the physical distance from other people we maintain in order to feel comfortable, and the way we perceive general human activities like eating, making love, and the like. Also included is the way we organize ourselves to reach certain goals and maintain perceptions of, for example, work, power, and profit.

The individual level of human programming is the truly unique part—no two people are programmed exactly alike, even if they are identical twins raised together. This is the level of individual personality, and it provides for a wide range of alternative behaviours within the same collective culture (Hofstede, 1980, pp. 15–16).

The skating model is at the collective level of mental programming, it is a culturally determined model and we should therefore exercise restraint in applying it to other spheres of mental programming than Western ones. There is also the following. The cultural dimension may not only become manifest when going from one culture to another, but also when values and beliefs *within one culture* change. If we say the world is round, it would constitute a true description of reality. But such a statement would once have been false, foolish, and heretical (Schwartz and Ogilvy, 1979). There are many more phenomena which were self-evident at one moment in time and refuted at another, the Newtonian physics and the new physics are further examples. Apparently our beliefs about what is true and real undergo fundamental shifts from time to time; at the individual level this would constitute a matter of mental *re*programming.

Are such shifts taking place now? We will leave this question unanswered here, but will return to it at the end of the book when reviewing the data presented.

References

Bateson, G. (1979) *Mind and Nature* (London).
Benedict, R. (1971) *Patterns of Culture* (London).
Berger, H. J. C. (1972) *Kijk op de werkelijkheid van alledag, Het meten van sociale intelligentie* (Amsterdam).
Berger, P. and Luckmann, T. (1967) *The Social Construction of Reality, a Treatise in the Sociology of Knowledge* (New York).
Emery, F. (1977) *Futures We Are In* (Leiden).
Emery, F. and Thorsrud, E. (1976) *Democracy at Work*, Report of the Norwegian Industrial Democracy Program. Appendix 1A: Participative approach to the democratization of the workplace (Leiden).

Fitzgerald, C. P. (1935/1950) *China. A Short Cultural History* (The Cresset Press Ltd, London).

Gelpké, R. (1957) *Persisches Schatzkästlein, Geschichten des Orients, den Quellen nacherzählt und illustriert mit acht bisher unveröffentlichen Miniaturen* (Basel, 1957).

Handy, C. (1980) Through the organizational looking glass, *Harvard Business Review*, Jan./Feb. 1980, 118.

Herbst, P. G. (1976) *Alternatives to Hierarchies* (Leiden).

Hill, P. (1976) *Towards a New Philosophy of Management* (London).

Hofstede, G. (1980) *Culture's Consequences* (Beverly Hills/London).

Mead, G. H. (1972) *Mind, Self and Society* (London).

Mead, M. (1928/1954) *Coming of Age in Samoa* (New York).

Schutz, A. (1962) *Collected Papers, Volume 1: The Problem of Social Reality* (The Hague).

Schwartz, P. and Ogilvy, J. (1979) *The Emergent Paradigm: Changing Patterns of Thought and Belief* (Stanford Research Institute, Values and Lifestyles Program).

Selznick, P. (1969/1972) Foundations of the theory of organizations, in: Emery, F. E. (ed.), *Systems Thinking* (Harmondsworth).

Trist, E. (1980) The environment and system-response capability, *Futures*, April 1980, 113–127.

van Beinum, H. J. J. (1976) *On the Strategic Importance of the Quality of Working Life* (European Institute for Advanced Studies in Management, Brussels).

People and Organizations Interacting
Edited by A. Brakel
© 1985, John Wiley & Sons Ltd.

Chapter 2

The 'Project with the Long Breath': Organizational Change in a Tanker Company

Jacques Roggema and Theo Voors

Introduction

In 1976 Shell Tankers B.V. (STBV) (Rotterdam, The Netherlands) started a project which later became known in Dutch as the 'project met de lange adem' (PLA, 'project with the long breath'). Management of STBV, being convinced that something had to be done about organizational conditions onboard, sought advice from training and O.D. consultants within the personnel department of Shell Nederland N.V. The original problem definition was phrased in terms of a growing discrepancy between social values in society at large and the more traditional ones onboard ship. This discrepancy was assumed to strain the relationship between senior officers and the junior officers and ratings. In order to improve the man-management skills of senior officers, a course to that effect was asked for. To assess the validity of the problem definition and in order to be able to outline the contents of an eventual training course, some exploratory interviewing was done onboard a number of ships and in the shore office. Except for some cases of rather idiosyncratic leadership behaviour, the impression from these interviews was that relations onboard went smoothly, given the constraints posed by the traditional organizational structures and practices. The team, by now consisting of an internal Shell consultant and a contracted consultant,* having been involved in the Norwegian shipping industry, suggested to STBV's management a more fundamental reappraisal of both the existing shipboard organization and the relations between ship and shore office. It was argued that the existing shipboard organization would become increasingly antiquated due, for example, to economic pressures, technological change, and changes in the educational system. In order to remain competitive it was felt necessary to embark upon a process of organizational change that would lead to an economically viable shipboard organization, being compatible with the social trends indicated at the beginning of this introduction.

Before elaborating upon content and process of this change programme, a short description of the context in which it took place might be helpful to the general reader.

The traditional shipboard organization

The advent of steam propulsion created a whole new breed of seafarers: the seagoing engineer. Slowly and after intense rivalry a separate engineroom department emerged, more or less being a mirror image of the rank and status structure of the deck department.

On the conventional cargo ship, once a nearly universal standard ship but now a shrinking minority, the departmental structure functioned rather well. On this type of ship deck and engine department could meet the majority of its task requirements from manpower and skill resources within its own ranks with minimal need for interdepartmental co-ordination. In both departments existed a relatively balanced task structure and, despite regular skirmishes about the relative importance of the departments, there was no doubt that each made an important contribution to the whole.

The organization that originated on the conventional cargo liner has been copied on all kinds of specialized types of ships, including tankers. Up to about 1960 the complement of a tanker counted some 50 men, divided among three (including catering) separate departments. Not only officers but also the lower ranks and the ratings belonged to a specific department. Below the rank of officer both the deck and engine departments knew a fairly differentiated role structure, consisting of at least five different job titles.

During the 1960s there was a strong drive to reduce the number of men onboard in order to cut manning costs. Especially on tankers and bulk carriers the concept of a 'general purpose' crew was introduced. This concept implied that ratings would work in both deck and engine departments. They no longer belonged exclusively to either of the two departments. After experimenting since

---

*The writers of this chapter.

1965 Shell Tankers B.V. introduced the concept in its fleet under the name 'integrated crew'. The introduction of the integrated crew concept was successful in terms of the original aim, i.e. the reduction of crew. In other respects it was a rather traumatic experience for those involved onboard.

In the first place, the introduction of the GP concept more or less emphasized and reinforced a gradual process of de-skilling among the ratings caused by the use of new technology and materials. Within the departmental logic of the shipboard organization, being defined as a general work force meant a loss of identity for the ratings.

In the second place, the reduction of crew that resulted from the introduction of the GP concept had profound effects on the manner in which deck and engine departments related to each other. No longer being able to meet all task requirements from 'own' manpower resources, an integrated form of work planning became necessary. Beside uneasiness about having to hold meetings, latent rivalry between the departments was revived through discussions about priorities.

Thirdly, the way in which the GP concept was implemented had very harmful effects. After some successful try-outs on a few ships the change was more or less implemented 'by decree'. Not only Shell Tankers B.V. but many other shipping companies implemented the GP concept in such a way. The reaction of seafarers was generally negative and it reinforced their already present resistance to change.

In economic terms the introduction of the GP concept was a sound step, but what this concept unintentionally did was to put a question mark against the appropriateness of the departmental logic in the conventional shipboard organization.

Factors pressing for change

A number of economic, technological, and social factors press for organizational change within the shipping industry (Herbst, 1974; Moreby, 1976). We shall discuss these below before turning to the PLA project.

Economic pressures

The economic viability of shipping in general is threatened by a number of factors such as the collapse of freight rates after the oil crisis and the dramatically increasing fuel and capital costs. In the Western world the shipping industry is faced with increasing competition from developing countries, which are able to operate their ships with much lower manning costs. The Comecon countries have built up their fleets considerably and tend to undercut established freight rates in their attempts to 'sail in' as much hard currency as possible.

Technological changes

A variety of technological changes have considerably altered the task structure onboard. Space does not allow us to elaborate on these technological changes in detail, but their effects can be summarized by the following trends.

(1) Technological changes, such as new cargo-handling methods, automation, use of new maintenance equipment and materials, have widened rather then closed the gap between officers and ratings in terms of qualifications needed in order to do the job. The traditional rating had a semi-skilled task; nowadays most of his work is of an unskilled nature.

(2) The importance of engineering and instrumentation skills in all aspects of ship operation has considerably expanded. At the same time changes in technology and trade patterns have reduced the need for traditional cargo-handling skills. Also, the introduction of advanced navigational equipment may have an adverse effect on the job content of the deck officer. Both changes in skill requirements and the introduction of the unmanned engineroom* make the right of existence of the traditional departmental structure increasingly questionable.

Social change

A number of changes in society at large impinge, more or less tangibly, upon the traditional shipboard organization. Values develop which are increasingly incompatible with the traditional assumptions of life at sea. Without trying to be exhaustive, we present a few examples.

(1) The present rank structure onboard is based on a craft-like way of acquiring skills and knowledge. In order to achieve the highest rank, periods at sea have to be interchanged with periods at school. In the educational system there is a strong tendency to qualify future seafarers up to the highest rank before they go to sea. This tendency, which can be seen in many European countries, makes it increasingly difficult to uphold the traditional task division among the various ranks onboard ships.

(2) Evolving values concerning job content and 'quality of working life' make it increasingly doubtful that suitably qualified men can be attracted to do the work of a rating. In many of the European shipboard projects explicit attempts have therefore been made to improve the job content of the ratings.

(3) The autocratic leadership style onboard and the caste-like division between officers and ratings are at odds with societal values around consultation and participation.

The combination of economic, technological, and social values demand significant changes in the traditional shipboard organization. In order to be

---

*Automation has freed engineers from their traditional watchkeeping task—the engineroom is now unmanned during the night.

viable in economic terms productivity has to be increased by choosing organizational options that allow for a smaller crew. At the same time the change in skill requirements brought about by technology and the social trends indicated above have to be taken into account when attempting to develop a new shipboard organization.

Change strategy

After further reflection, STBV's management felt that devising a man-management course might alleviate some of the discomforts experienced, but that a more fundamental approach would be needed to develop a shipboard organization that would be compatible with the changes indicated in the foregoing paragraphs.

The realization that fundamental organizational change was necessary brought into focus the central issue of how to bring it about.

In addressing this issue it was clear that much could be learned from the experiences of shipping companies in other countries who have introduced organizational change. An examination of the strengths and weaknesses of the various approaches already tried confirmed the ideas that were developing with regard to the appropriate strategy (Roggema and Smith, 1981).

If we look briefly at experiences in the United Kingdom up to the early 1970s we see that conventional attitude surveys and in-depth interviewing studies were carried out. This work produced a complex mass of detailed data which was extremely difficult to translate into any coherent plan for change. By reinforcing the belief that there were significant problems, and then failing to offer solutions, the approach created a feeling that the problems were intractable.

In Germany and Japan a different approach was adopted. Teams of experts in research institutes were given the task to systematically investigate the task requirements of ships and the possible matrices of skills and responsibilities required by the present and future technologies. But by conducting highly sophisticated research in a remote academic manner, the industry did not become involved in the thought processes behind the models. This has resulted in a widespread estrangement, even an active hostility, within the industry which set back the progress of change by several years at least.

In Sweden a similar team was set up to investigate the manning of technically advanced vessels and a similar outcome is apparent. In these cases it is clear that a coherent model of a future shipboard organization was not enough. Two fundamental weaknesses emerge: the lack of a shared ownership of the model and the process whereby it is arrived at; and the lack of a coherent view of how to go about implementing the model.

In Norway some of these difficulties were recognized and were taken into account in the strategic approach adopted. The collaborative learning of the action research approach proved potent in bringing about organizational change in individual project ships. The viability of new organizational concepts was clearly demonstrated by these field experiments.

The weakness of the strategy adopted in Norway lay in the exclusion of two key groups in the concentration on single project ships. Middle management in the shore office was not involved in the critical initial design and objective setting stages, and they actively resisted the implications of the experiments for the ship–shore interface. The seafarers in the rest of the fleet were informed about the aims of the experiments but were in no way actively involved in the process, nor were they in active contact with the project participants. As a result they simply did not accept the validity or relevance of the experiments.

By the creation of a special project group within the company to conduct field experiments the climate of opinion in the remainder of the enterprise seems to be vaccinated against the results of the project.

This vaccination phenomenon has also occurred in other industries and in all cases it has severely hampered the diffusion of the new organizational principles being demonstrated. If we review these experiences the following emerge as fundamental strategic requirements for the design of successful organizational change within a company.

(1) Collaborative learning. All sectors of the organization have to be involved in the analysis of the organizational problems and the design of new organization alternatives. This is a necessary condition for the shared ownership of the process and objectives of change and the development of shared organizational concepts.

(2) Senior management involvement. Senior management as a group should be directly involved in guiding the change process in order to continuously assess and articulate the wider implications of the changes for the company's policies.

(3) Comprehensive implementation. The process of change must be planned from the beginning to encompass the entire organization. This is a necessary condition to avoid the pitfalls of vaccination and encapsulation of the pilot projects.

The workshop approach

Acknowledging the importance of creating a collaborative learning process, management of STBV did not unilaterally define a concept of a future shipboard organization. In order to get a learning process under way, three residential workshops were organized. At each workshop there were individuals from all departments and levels of both the ship and office organization.

The terms of reference given to each workshop were:

(1) 'What form of organization shall we need in the future to optimize the operation of our ships and give everyone a satisfactory job and career situation, in the light of technology and social change?'

(2) 'If organizational changes are deemed necessary, on board and ashore,

how should the changes be implemented, what problems can we expect to encounter in doing so, and how do we propose to solve them?'

Each workshop was opened by the managing director of STBV, who expressed management's commitment to a fundamental reappraisal of organizational effectiveness in human and operational terms. In doing so he underlined the desirability of a scenario that would serve as a guideline for further action.

The workshops were then conducted by the present authors. Our role was essentially to monitor the proceedings in accordance with the following rules:
● Each point of view must be accepted for what it is; no point of view can be immediately rejected.
● Every individual must have an equal opportunity to speak and no individual should monopolize the discussion.
● The value of any point is assessed purely on its merits, not on the hierarchical position of the person proposing it.

The procedure was straightforward, the eighteen participants of each seminar divided themselves into two discussion groups and worked on the following themes:
● The shortcomings of the present shipboard organization.
● What should the shipboard organization look like in about twenty years time?
● The steps to be taken following the workshop to implement the desired changes.

After working on each theme the two groups came together to share their ideas. At the end of each workshop the participants reported their views to management. The output of each workshop was minuted in order to prepare a summary report on the three sessions. Much to the surprise of both participants and management there was a marked convergence in the assessment of the shortcomings of the present shipboard organization and in the views of a desirable shipboard organization for the future. The participants' feelings about the workshops are worth noting: after an initial skirmish, they were surprised to find shore-staff and sea-staff holding similar views. A common basis of understanding quickly developed.

The participants reported a definite shift in their thinking about organizational problems during the course of the workshop. They felt that the free exchange of opinion resulted in ideas which none of the participants felt he would have produced on his own without attending the workshop.

They displayed a strong sense of ownership of the ideas produced and outlined an action plan for the immediate steps to be taken.

The outlines of a future shipboard organization as produced during these workshops can be summarized as follows.

(1) From two distinct training and career paths to a more common basic training. The existing separate education of deck and engineer officers to be replaced by a common basic training which would include all facets of shipboard

activities, such as navigation, mechanical engineering, and electronics. After an initial basic training, individuals should further specialize in one or more subjects in accordance with their own abilities and interest. In this way, breadth as well as depth of competence would be secured in the shipboard establishment. This would, furthermore, provide on the one hand a basis for shared occupational values, whilst on the other hand give opportunity to acquire distinctive competence in a trade of their own choice. The rigid hierarchical structuring of work relations should be replaced by a structure that would place more emphasis on co-operation and consultation between the various specialists. The nature of the task, rather than age and rank, will determine who will act as the leader of a temporary taskforce.

(2) In the proposed model every individual may ultimately have an opportunity to become the 'ship manager'.

(3) From a social dichotomy between officers and ratings to a more homogeneous crew. Obviously there will be gradations of status levels but these would not constitute the significant gaps existing in the present organization.

(4) By taking away the strict delineations between deck and engineroom and those between officers and ratings a less segmented structure will be created which is more capable of managing tension and conflict. This transition entails recruitment right across the educational spectrum, and a career structure in which the individual, wherever he starts, can progress as far as his abilities and ambition will take him.

(5) From an acceptance of a high proportion of unskilled, and often less desirable, manual work to a deliberate policy of minimizing the menial tasks by means of design, new work methods, and better equipment. This is a prerequisite condition both to create a more homogeneous crew and to optimize the size of a shipboard crew.

(6) From a high degree of central decision-making in the shore office to a much greater degree of decision-making on board ship. This will require better management information and planning systems on board ship. Wherever it is possible for the ship to contribute to better performance, it should do so.

(7) From a high turnover of individuals from ship to ship to increased crew stability. This is seen as one of the fundamental conditions for the realization of any of the other changes; and also an aim in itself, because of its positive effect on organization performance and teambuilding.

'Project with the long breath'

It was realized that the changes outlined could not be brought about over night. The editor of Shell Tankers' in-house magazine commented during an interview with one of the workshop participants that one needed a 'long breath' to achieve the shipboard organization outlined. Since this remark succinctly described the developmental nature of the exercise, it was quickly adopted as the catch phrase: 'The project with the long breath', abbreviated in Dutch to 'PLA'.

Much of the project would depend on the co-operation of various official bodies, training possibilities, and the attitude of the unions involved.

During the workshops it was proposed to establish a project group in order to work out the details of the suggested changes, implement project work on several ships, and inform and involve the whole organization on a continuing basis. Bearing in mind the strategic considerations outlined above, senior management decided to set up two groups: a steering group consisting of top and middle management, and a working group consisting of a full-time project co-ordinator supported by two fleet officers. These fleet officers would only stay ashore for limited periods and serve regularly on board project vessels.

Knowing that only a small proportion of the shore and seagoing staff had been involved in the original workshops, the project group organized a number of one-day conferences in order to discuss the project. It became apparent that the articles published about the project had raised severe suspicion and resistance. These one-day conferences were only partly successful in creating some understanding and acceptance of the project.

Before describing in more detail some of the changes that were implemented, we shall indicate the rate of progress in terms of the number of ships involved. The first two project ships (modern product carriers of 32,000 tons) got under way in January 1977. Minor modifications were made to facilitate the development of the project. The ships' conference rooms were refitted in such a way that they became a central office, where the senior officers could work as a team. All files and planning/information systems were concentrated in this office. The central office could also have been—and was in fact—used for workplanning meetings with junior officers and ratings.

The crew of each of these two ships was reduced from 34 to 22 men. During 1978 two more vessels of the same type were added to the project. In 1979 another four ships were integrated into the project. At present ten ships 'sail PLA', which is about a third of the total fleet. The older ships in the fleet are not particularly suited to sail PLA in the full sense, but elements of the projects have been spread to these ships. A number of ships are being built in which PLA concepts will be easily applied.

From the beginning it was realized that concentration on one or two ships would be dangerous, because of the encapsulation or vaccination effect this would have on the rest of the fleet. It was decided to increase the number of ships involved in the project rather quickly in order to prevent the original project ships developing too far ahead of the rest of the fleet. Organizational changes, as the Norwegian shipping projects have shown, cannot be diffused by rational example. Organizational change is a learning process for those involved and to have a ready-made model available seems to destroy this learning opportunity for others.

On the substance of change

In reviewing many of the shipping projects in North-West Europe (Smith and Roggema, 1979a, 1979b, 1980a, 1980b) four common change directions have emerged.

(1) Towards *crew stability*. From a high turnover of personnel on board the ship to a greater stability; more individuals return to the same ship after leave.

(2) Towards *decentralization*. From a centralized control exercised by shore management to a more decentralized shipboard management structure.

(3) Towards a *multiple skill* organization. From a hierarchical and departmentalized organizational structure onboard to a more flexible division of tasks based on a greater versatility of the individual seafarer.

(4) Towards a *redistribution of responsibility* onboard. From a caste-like division between officers and ratings towards a more complex differentiation of responsibilities and tasks.

The nature of these changes indicate a shift from a role-oriented command bureaucracy towards a more task-oriented managerial organization. The PLA project reflects all these change directions, and we will take these as starting points to describe the actual content of the changes.

Crew stability

Two decades ago it was quite common for seafarers to serve continuously on a ship for periods exceeding 12 months. In more recent times the service period has been reduced to approximately 4 months and the actual amount of leave has been substantially increased. Normal practice is to allocate a seafarer who has finished his leave to any vacant position in the fleet. This implies that he only very rarely will return to the ship he served on before his leave. A single position in the shipboard organization will therefore have a minimum of three occupants in a 12-month period. Since the individuals onboard are not relieved at the same time there is a constant turnover of personnel onboard one ship.

Seafarers generally perceive variety of experience as a major attraction of their occupation. They define this variety in terms of new faces met and new places visited, and the acquisition of technical experience on different types of ships. On the other hand, the constant turnover of personnel combined with other factors, such as the value placed upon impersonality and respect for formal position, boundaries imposed by department and rank, and the segmentation of time by the watch-keeping system, have a number of negative consequences.

First of all lack of continuity constrains the formation of personalized relationships. Because individual seafarers are very unlikely to meet again, they tend to invest little in each other for the short time they are together. Onboard there is a definite emphasis on being sociable but at the same time the interactive style is of a superficial nature. The cultural norm is to avoid intensity of feeling in interaction, mainly in order to avoid conflict.

Secondly, the lack of continuity in the relationship between an individual and a specific ship leads to a dominance of short-term objectives. There is no perceivable benefit in adopting a long-term orientation. The individual will not gain the benefit of the long-term consequences of his actions, nor suffer the costs. Senior officers in particular are affected by this situation. Their job supposes a long-term orientation in managing a ship, but the short duration of their affiliation with a specific ship tends to limit their managerial scope to the 4 months they are onboard.

Thirdly, the short duration of affiliation between individual seafarer and a specific ship makes centralized control from the shore office necessary. Since there is no continuity of care onboard the ship, care must be the responsibility of the shore office.

Fourthly, the levels of continuity also reinforce the rigid role structure onboard. In order to accommodate a high degree of turnover, roles must be precisely defined and adhered to.

Finally, lack of continuity creates a situation in which little benefit is seen in training or delegating tasks to junior officers or ratings—they simply will disappear and the effort put into training is pure cost in the short term.

During the first workshops in which the PLA project took its form, it soon became evident that achieving a certain level of continuity was an important objective. First of all continuity was seen as a prerequisite to bring about and maintain the change process. The normal rate of turnover would lead to a constant dissipation of newly acquired skills and values. It would even be unreasonable to expect individual seafarers to invest in changed role relationships on the basis of a short-term assignment to a project ship, followed by an assignment to another, conventionally organized ship. Without continuity the constant influx of newcomers would quickly exhaust the willingness and ability of the senior officers to induct them into the new organization.

Secondly, continuity coupled with a greater degree of decision-making power onboard ship was seen as an end in itself. The longer-term perspective would provide senior officers in particular with an opportunity to take a more active role in the management of the ship. Besides an improvement of the job content of the senior officers, continuity was valued as a positive contribution to the climate onboard in interpersonal terms.

At the initial stage of the project it was accepted as a policy to send the senior officers back to the same ship after their leave. People in other ranks would be sent back to the same ship whenever possible. They would in any case be employed in the pool of project ships. During the development of the PLA project there has been a continuously increasing demand for more continuity. Also, junior officers and ratings wished to go back to the same ship.

From a personnel planning point of view continuity is difficult for logistical reasons. It involves extra costs because periods of unattached service have to be accepted in order to achieve continuity.

Certainly, in periods of personnel shortages the personnel department has found it difficult to satisfy the demand for continuity. Nevertheless, the level of continuity has improved considerably over the years.

The latest development in the quest for continuity is the so-called ship internal relief (SIR) project. Except for the top four ranks, all ranks are manned with seafarers having dual qualifications, which means that they are certified to work both on the bridge and in the engineroom. Given these dual qualifications there is a greater flexibility in the crew and the whole relief system is organized onboard the ship.

That continuity does create a longer time perspective may be illustrated by 'complaints' from some of the captains and chief engineers involved that when on leave they cannot stop thinking of 'their' ship.

Decentralization

The theme of decentralization runs through virtually every change project in shipping that we know of. Nevertheless, it is very difficult to pin down what is actually meant by decentralization. The decentralization issue is often phrased in terms of moving decision-making power down the line, from the shore office to the senior officers onboard. The corresponding increase in accountability is hardly ever mentioned. Since decentralization not only requires the restructuring of organizational relationships between ship and office, but also within the office itself, the crude notion of decentralization as moving power down the line is both dangerous and misleading.

Both the physical separation of the ship from its fleet headquarters and the ease with which it is seen as a self-contained unit with its own Master, give rise to an impression of a high degree of autonomy. This impression of independence is only true in a very limited sense. Despite the geographical dispersion of ships, a highly centralized control is exercised by shipping companies. Companies lay down elaborate rules and procedures for the operation and maintenance of their vessels and require detailed reporting so that decisions can be made and control exercised by head office staff. The frequent transfer of personnel from ship to ship does not have the explicit purpose of inhibiting commitment to a particular ship, but it unintentionally has this effect. The traditional structure in shipping company offices is a departmental one based upon functional specializations, e.g. marine, technical, chartering, accounts, and personnel. The advantages of such a structure are several, but there are two main problems associated with a functional structure relevant to the issue of decentralization. First, the problem of lateral co-ordination, and secondly the assumption that universal rules can be formulated that are applicable to the variety of circumstances encountered at the periphery. Despite efforts at top management level to formulate policies and to set priorities, lateral co-ordination remains a problem in a functional organization.

In a functional organization each department will tend to make decisions and issue policies in accordance with its departmental objectives, which do not necessarily correlate with the objectives of other departments. Certainly, when central co-ordination is weak this will imply that the senior officers onboard are subject to separate, often unco-ordinated and sometimes conflicting, directives from the shore office.

To enable decentralized shipboard management a single line of accountability between ship and shore is necessary. To achieve this a structure in the office can be introduced in which a manager is made responsible for a particular group of ships covering all technical, operational, and personnel aspects, so that a co-ordinated set of performance objectives can be formulated for these ships. By giving such a manager a group of ships which are alike in terms of trading conditions or technology, the second problem referred to, namely the functional structure, is circumvented. Instead of formulating universal rules and policies, policy and decision-making can become more sensitive to the particular conditions under which certain ships operate.

The notion of putting 'power back to the ship' recognizes that decentralization involves greater discretionary responsibility for senior officers onboard, but fails to acknowledge the greater degree of accountability involved. In fact, decentralization implies a much higher and more effective control of ship performance. The crude notion of decentralization also fails to recognize that decentralization does not involve a simple transfer of authority from office to ship, but the development of a joint problem-solving approach and/or mutually consultative relationship.

In order to give the shipboard management team discretionary responsibility, new information and budgeting systems are necessary. When the first PLA ships got underway it was decided to provide each ship with cost information about stores and spares and to send copies of bills on any expenditure made by the ship. The provision of cost information proved to be beneficial, in the sense that for the first time in their life ships' officers were confronted with the price of what went through their hands. A more careful use of stores and spares was the result.

Gradually, the shipboard management teams have become more responsible for the financial aspects of ships' operation. To begin with, the management team was made responsible for the food budget; more recently they have been more involved in budgeting for maintenance and repair.

As a follow-up to the first three workshops, which were primarily concerned with shipboard organization, three other workshops were held to discuss the structure of the shore office and the relationship between shore office and ships. The concept emerged of 'ship management groups', covering all operation, maintenance, and personnel aspects of particular segments of the fleet. Various criteria were worked out to divide the fleet into a number of groups of ships. The model aimed at better co-ordination in the shore office *viz-à-viz* the ships and the creation of a single line of communication and accountability. For various reasons, the management of STBV did not want to implement the proposed model because it was thought that the model would lead to higher manpower costs in the shore office; that the advantage of economy of scale would be lost; and that divergent policies would evolve. Recent developments do suggest that the whole issue of accountability will trigger a new discussion which will help clarify the relationship between shore office and ships. Cost overruns during dockings have led to a drive from fleet management to monitor shipboard performance in terms of planning and budgeting for repairs. In this process the objective setting and monitoring role of the office will be emphasized, and at the same time it will be stressed that greater discretionary power onboard also implies a greater degree of accountability *viz-à-viz* the shore organization. The crude notion of decentralization is dangerous in the sense that it leads to strong resistance and anxiety in the shore organization. The expression 'putting power back to the ship' defines the management of ships as an either/or process: 'Either we do it in the shore office or they do it onboard.' Besides disbelief that it is possible to run ships in this way, this notion of decentralization implies a threat to job security for office staff. Decentralization formulated in terms of moving decision-making down the line obscures the fact that a far more complex restructuring of relations is implied. Recent developments as indicated above may give the discussion a new impetus.

Multiple skill organization

Various approaches to the redesign of the shipboard organization in relation to technological developments in shipping converge upon a multiple skill type of organization—commonly referred to as a matrix organization. This matrix consists of an array of tasks on one dimension and an array of skills on the other. Although there are similarities, it is in fact a different concept to the matrix organization as discussed by Galbraith (1973) and others. The main objective of developing a multiple skill concept is to reduce manning in the context of advanced technology. The greater versatility of individuals enables peak variations in workload to be dealt with by fewer men (Roggema, 1977). The various approaches to organizational design in the context of advanced ship technology have included the multidisciplinary research referred to earlier, action research projects, and participative planning workshops with seafarers.

During the initial PLA workshops the multiple skill organization emerged as an 'horizon' model. All but one of the discussion groups developed this model in response to the problems experienced in the existing rank and departmental structure.

The present departmental structure is based upon two distinct career paths with different training programmes. In each department there is a progression of ranks, at each step of which there are distinct tasks allocated so that the officer gains experience in progressively more complex aspects of his department's work. The assumption of the progression of experience is that the man at the top has experience of all aspects of his department. This traditional system of learning and career development presupposes a stable technology and is not capable of accommodating new entrants with higher levels of education. Both the changes in shipboard technology and in the level of education and training in society suggest the need for change in both the departmental and rank structure aboard ship.

Before describing the actual changes implemented in the PLA project, we shall outline the principle characteristics of a multiple skill organization.

In a multiple skill organization the officers work in both a *primary and secondary role*. Each officer has in-depth training in a major area of expertise for his primary role and future career development. He also receives a basic training in other areas of expertise to enable him to assist other specialists. In his primary role each officer is responsible for all aspects of a part of the ship's operation. Normally he will perform the tasks himself, but where workload and skill requirements demand it, he will call upon others for assistance. In this way each officer exercises a *task-based leadership* over a domain of work. This is in contrast to the conventional organization where leadership is based upon rank. The primary and secondary role structure and task-based leadership enable the formation of a variety of task groups. It is this *task-based group formation* which gives the organization flexibility in meeting fluctuating workloads.

The responsibility built into the primary roles of the officers amounts to a *redistribution of managerial control*. The senior officer's role is considerably altered in this new organization. Instead of directly planning and supervising the work of his subordinates, he now co-ordinates the scheduling of tasks and group formation and monitors the work being done in relation to the budgetary targets and administrative systems of the company. In order to bring about the change in task and skill allocation for both officers and ratings, this type of change in the senior officer's role is a necessary supporting condition.

The basic arguments in favour of this type of organization are that it enables reduced manning in the context of advanced technology, it is adaptive to a changing technological environment, it makes the shipboard organization compatible with changes in the educational system, and provides new entrants with a work situation that is more congruent with their level of education and their social values.

However, a multiple skill organization is a radical departure from the conventional organization. It is contrary to existing occupational values and cuts across almost every institutional boundary in the shipping industry. Even though individual shipping companies can experiment with the model, and introduce it on a fairly wide scale, they face considerable resistance in doing so because the change implies considerable restructuring of institutional boundaries at the industry level; e.g. union and professional association boundaries, the reframing of government and international regulations covering the manning of ships, and the structure and resources of training establishments.

As an example of work system design the introduction of a multiple skill organization is relatively straightforward; it is the problem of implementation which is complex because of the array of institutional forces surrounding the shipboard system.

When the first new PLA ship got underway only traditionally trained officers were available. Nevertheless, a start was made to realize elements of the proposed multiple skill structure. Each of the junior officers was assigned to a particular area or system of the ship for which he was made responsible in terms of operation, planning and execution of maintenance, and administrative back-up. Concerning their area of responsibility, all the junior officers report directly to the chief engineer, who is responsible for the overall co-ordination of maintenance work. Work planning meetings are held on a weekly basis.

In line with the multiple skill concept, deck officers are given the maintenance responsibility for technical systems within the deck department. They are trained to carry out work normally done by engineers.

At the initial stages of the project some deck officers and engineers were asked to go back to school and qualify in the 'opposite' department. Since this way of providing officers with dual qualifications proved to be very costly indeed, it was decided to offer a number of students studying for their nautical or engineering certificate the opportunity to obtain a 'plus certificate'. In 1983 some 60 officers with basic qualifications in both navigation and engineering have entered the organization.

This double certification should—from a training point of view—be considered as an interim step leading towards some form of common basic training, encompassing all aspects of shipboard operations, such as navigation, mechanical engineering, and electronics. After this initial common training, individuals should further specialize in one or more subjects in accordance with their own abilities and interests.

The dual training of officers is a lengthy process and really demands a long breath. After more than five years of experimentation and intensive negotiations with unions and governmental authorities, STBV is now in the position to man one ship with doubly qualified junior officers. On board this ship the potential benefits of the multiple skill model will be more fully explored. In principle each of the officers on this special project ship will have one bridge watch of 4 hours per day. The rest of the day he will be working in his particular area of responsibility or he will assist others with their tasks. Experiences so far confirm the idea that a multiple skill organization increases the internal flexiblity of the organization and that some manpower efficiencies can be achieved.

The job content of the ratings

The difference between officers and ratings is a fundamental aspect of the conventional shipboard organization, and has the quality of a caste-like division. The two groups are in a rigid hierarchical relation to each other, with a strictly delineated division of tasks, little or no mobility between the two groups, marked segregation during non-working hours, and marked differences in privilege and status. Both groups have norms which restrict relationships between them, and members of each group tend to maintain their self-esteem by using the other as a negative reference group. Elsewhere (Smith and Roggema, 1979b), the differences between the two groups have been mapped out on a set of variables concerned with social background and orientation, employment conditions, and work-related attitudes. The two groups are in polar opposition to each other on all of these variables, but in terms of the shipboard organization, the division between the groups can only be understood in terms of an all-or-none distribution of responsibility.

Historically, the military character of the shipboard organization came about as a response to the internal threat of mutiny and external threat of piracy. Given the recruitment practices in shipping over the centuries, the need for legally constituted authority on board, with powerful sanctions available, is obvious. Both the large numbers of crew involved and the fact that many, if not all, were not on board by virtue of their own choice, made coercive authority necessary.

The codification by law over the centuries defines the officer as being responsible and makes him personally accountable for failing to meet defined standards. The rating not being accountable, is not held to be responsible. Responsibility then tends to be defined in terms of personal attributes. In the dynamics of the situation, the rating becomes defined as an irresponsible being. This all-or-none distribution of responsibility as a personal attribute is a core value of the system and the individuals in it; and is the major source of resistance to changes in the work organization.

In fact, the all-or-none division of responsibility is exacerbated by the growing divergence of the skill content in officers' and ratings' tasks. Technological change demands a higher skill level on the part of the officers, whilst at the same time it reduces the demand for the semi-skilled type of work traditionally done by the ratings. Many projects in shipping have had the explicit objective of enhancing the job content of the rating and his degree of participation in the planning of the work. Given the impoverishment of the ratings' job and the higher degree of formal education of entrants, it was feared that only a very poor calibre of man would be retained by this kind of job.

In the context of the PLA project a number of steps have been taken to improve the standing of the ratings within the shipboard organization.

(1) Ratings on board the PLA ships are entrusted with more responsible work

of a technical nature. Attempts are being made to reduce the amount of unskilled and repetitive work like washing and painting.

(2) Ratings are being given technical training at the training school of the Shell Pernis refinery.

(3) Petty officers have been eliminated in the shipboard organization, which gives the ratings greater freedom and responsibility.

(4) Each of the ratings has been assigned his own area of responsibility.

(5) Ratings have regular work planning meetings with the chief engineer. During these meetings tasks are distributed.

(6) During non-working hours there is a degree of social integration between officers and ratings. Same bars and messrooms are used by both groups.

Conclusion

This chapter has described what is essentially an ongoing process. The 'Project with the Long Breath' started in 1976 with a number of workshops in which the features of a future shipboard organization were outlined. The relevance of the title 'Long Breath' is demonstrated by the fact that some of the ideas developed at the outset are only in the process of being implemented in 1983. Only after years of negotiating with official bodies was it possible to start training officer cadets along new lines. These cadets then needed seatime in order to get their certificates. It is only recently that some of the fundamental changes could be implemented. PLA is a long and slow process in which some of the basic assumptions of the conventional shipboard organization are being changed.

References

Galbraith, J. (1973) *Designing Complex Organizations* (Addison-Wesley, Mass.).

Herbst, P. G. (1974) *Socio-technical Design: Strategies in multidisciplinary research* (Tavistock, London).

Jackson, J. and Wilkie, R. (1975) General purpose manning. A case study in organisation change (in 3 parts), *Marit. Pol. & Mgmt*, **2,** 132–137, 215–220; **3,** 21–26.

Moreby, J. (1976) *The Human Element in Shipping* (Seatrade Publications, London).

Roggema, J. (1977) The design of shipboard organisation. Some experiences with a matrix-type of organisation in Norway, *Marit. Pol. & Mgmt*, **4,** no. 5, 265.

Roggema, J. and Smith, M. H. (1981) On the process of change in shipping, ERGOSA '81 Conference paper, Nautical Institute, London.

Smith, M. H. and Roggema, J. (1979a) Emerging organisational values in shipping. Part 1: Crew stability, *Marit. Pol. & Mgmt*, **6,** no. 2, 129–143.

Smith, M. H. and Roggema, J. (1979b) Part 2: Towards a redistribution of responsibility on board ship, *Marit. Pol. & Mgmt*, **6,** no. 2, 145–156.

Smith, M. H. and Roggema, J. (1980a) Part 3: The matrix concept—towards a multiple skill structure, *Marit. Pol. & Mgmt*, **7,** no. 4, 241–254.

Smith, M. H. and Roggema, J. (1980b) Part 4: Decentralisation, *Marit. Pol. & Mgmt*, **7,** no. 4, 255–269.

Manager's epilogue

Five years after the Company started the project 'with the long breath' (PLA), management decided that it was time to take an inventory, not only of what had been achieved, but above all of those things which had not worked out as well as originally foreseen. Efforts should be made to establish the reasons for the successes and failures as honestly as possible. Finally, the question should be answered whether the Company was still on the right track, also given foreseen future external economic, technical, and social developments.

This review took place during the first half of 1982. It was decided that, while this review took place, no new initiatives should be taken, but that existing and already planned projects should be carried out normally. In this respect 1982 can probably be best described as a year of consolidation. The opinion of the fleet staff is of course invaluable for such a review. However, it was felt best not to organize another series of workshops as this might give cause to expectations and speculation. Instead, fleet officers whenever visiting the head office for their normal briefing and de-briefing discussions, met senior management to discuss the PLA project.

From these discussions a number of points emerged, of which the most important were:

(1) the misconceptions among fleet staff as to what the PLA project was all about were more widespread than expected;

(2) the PLA project was seen as a goal in itself and not as a means to achieve a goal;

(3) a strong sense of uneasiness between the PLA and non-PLA officers in the fleet;

(4) only part of the head office organization was directly involved in, and thus committed to, the PLA project.

A summary will be given below of the measures taken. Because of the limited space available the most important of these measures will be mentioned, while it is only possible to hint at their rationale.

First of all, the PLA project was re-defined: PLA aims to maximize the shipboard operations, with due regard to what is possible from technical, desirable from social, and essential from economic points of view. It was furthermore stated that, whilst it was recognized that ships might be technically different, have crews of a different nationality, or be engaged in a different trade, it was the task of each unit in the fleet to maximize its shipboard operations. As a consequence of this new definition all non-PLA ships were now included in the PLA project. At the same time there was a substantial number of cross-postings of senior fleet staff from the PLA vessels to the non-PLA vessels. It was furthermore emphasized that PLA is an ongoing process: that there is a continuing need for the organization to adapt itself to the ever-changing external environment.

The head office organization was changed: all aspects of the fleet's operations were combined into one single fleet operations department. The direct responsibility for the PLA project, which hitherto had rested solely with an interdepartmental project group, was transferred to the newly formed fleet operations department. The responsibility for the PLA project has now become a line responsibility. The Company's management team continues to act as Steering Committee.

Considerable emphasis was put on improved communications. To that end a series of in-house work consultation courses were held.

Probably the most important decision has been to set targets which cover all aspects of the ships' operations. These vary from ship to ship, with the type of trade, etc. The targets are discussed with the master, chief engineer, and chief officer prior to their tour of duty, whilst the actual performance is discussed with them afterwards. At the same time there has been a move away from detailed instructions. These have been replaced by guidelines. It is felt that the shipboard organization has become more task oriented as opposed to a procedural orientation. There is a direct incentive for the ship's management team to make maximum use of the human resources available on board their ships, irrespective of rank.

In this context it is worth while to mention one PLA project which was started in 1982. One of the key elements of the PLA project is the 'dual-purpose' officer concept. During 1982 one of the PLA vessels sailed with an officer complement half of which had dual qualifications. The objective of this project was to ascertain whether such an officer complement would indeed result in a more flexible shipboard organization, in which the tasks performed by the individual officers were dependent on their expertise, as opposed to the traditional approach based upon rank. This project was a success and during 1983 the first vessel sailed with a (reduced) complement of seven officers.

Early in 1983 the first two of a series of workshops were held. The objective of these workshops was to start a discussion on the shipboard organization for the last decade of this century. These workshops were attended by senior fleet staff, but junior fleet staff will also be nominated for future similar workshops.

The discussions in these two workshops have demonstrated that the organization is fully committed to the PLA concept and is aware of the need for continuous change.

Rotterdam,   A. L. Rasterhoff
The Netherlands   Managing Director of
April, 1983   Shell Tankers

People and Organizations Interacting
Edited by A. Brakel

Chapter 3

Organization Change on a North Sea Project

Donald Mungall

Introduction

The focus of this chapter is on an 8-month period, during 1979/1980, in the life of one of Shell Exploration and Production's major North Sea projects. These months covered a particularly traumatic period in the project's already problem-stricken existence. The intent is to try and give a flavour of the situation in which project members found themselves and how this changed over time. We do this by using some of the actual comments and diagrams which were part of the 'change for improvement' process, as well as outlining the key project organization changes that took place and the principles behind them. The nature of the change support given to project personnel through the organization development contribution will also be highlighted.

Before delving into the colourful life and action-oriented existence of North Sea projects, it is worth standing back and developing some sense of the geographical and organization backcloths against which the projects are set.

Background and organizational setting

In the Northern North Sea, 100 miles from the nearest land and 300 miles from the British mainland, lies Shell–Esso's Brent Field (see Figure 1). It is

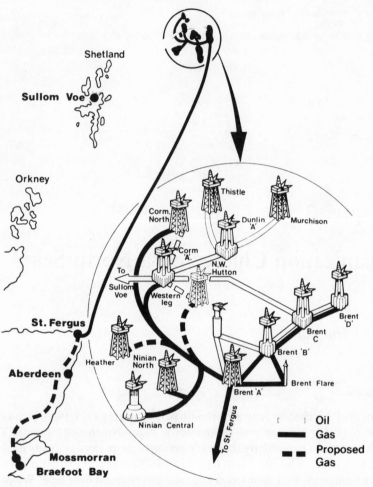

Figure 1   Shell operated and associated oil and gas systems in the northern
North Sea

approximately 2 miles by 10 miles long, containing 2.2 million barrels of crude oil
and natural gas liquids at a pressure of some 6000 pounds per square inch and
combined with some 3.5 trillion cubic feet of natural gas (methane). It lies under
10,000 feet of rock, which in turn is covered by 450 feet of often stormy and
hostile water. Brent was discovered in the summer of 1971 and throughout the
next decade and until the present day, Shell U.K. Exploration and Production
(which operates in the North Sea on behalf of Shell and Esso, and other partners)
has been involved in the development and management of a complex, highly
integrated technological and organizational system to effectively extract and
transport these resources.

Each part of this system (be it a platform, a pipeline, or an onshore plant) is being created within a project organization setting.[1] Once the go-ahead has been given and a project has been deemed both technically feasible and economically worthwhile, a project will follow a predictable and sequential organizational development path through the phases outlined in Figure 2. During the initial phases of design, fabrication and offshore installation, the organization ownership of the project lies within the Engineering Function[2] sited in Shell Expro's London Office. This custody is then transferred to the Construction Department based in Aberdeen when the project (in the case of a platform) reaches the offshore phase of hook-up and commissioning. On completion of this phase the finished asset is then transferred to the ownership of the Operations

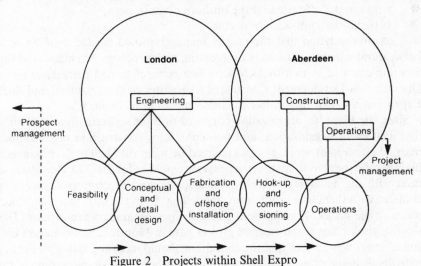

Figure 2   Projects within Shell Expro

Department in Aberdeen until the end of its working life. In the case of a pipeline or an onshore plant, the organization ownership remains with Engineering until commissioning is complete, whereupon it transfers directly to Aberdeen Operations.

Entry into Brent 'Charlie'

In the summer of 1979 the platform Brent 'C' had been in the offshore 'hook-up' phase for 12 months. The project was already 6 years old and, like many of the earlier platforms in the Brent field, had suffered from delays and cost escalations.[3] In the initial schedule, 'first oil' had been planned for 1976 and the final cost was now estimated to be ten times the original estimate (only 50% of this being due to inflation).

Delay and cost escalation and a general sense of 'out of control' through regular failure to meet short-term target dates was still the order of the day. In an attempt to understand the inherent problems in the hook-up and to recommend what actions might be taken to overcome these difficulties, a study team from outside of the project and instigated from the top had been working over the summer months. One of its main findings was that many of the difficulties experiences in the Brent 'C' hook-up were to do with organizational and people characteristics such as:

(a) a lack of clarity in the minds of many people as to what their role was;

(b) poor, adversarial relationships and negative attitudes and feelings between sections of the project organization, e.g.

● between the client and the contractor organization,

● between the offshore and the onshore organizations,

● between the joint-venture partners.

A recommendation that the project manager should engage the help of 'a behavioural scientist' to assist in overcoming such problems was made[4] and this was implemented so that by October a first connection had been made by an Organization Development Consultant (the writer of this chapter), and Shell Expro management responsible for the completion of Brent 'C'.

Since the Brent 'C' organization consisted of three separate organizations—the Shell client organization, and two contractor construction organizations married into a joint venture—it was agreed between the Shell project manager, his boss, and the consultant that the next step would be for the O.D. consultant to meet with the managers of each of these parts, and to develop a consulting contract with them as a group, thus 'modelling' from the start that the project was a single project organization[5] and not three separate organizations. This meeting took place at the onshore project base in Montrose on Scotland's east coast, and it was agreed[6] that the consultant should meet and talk with the key individuals in the project, both onshore and offshore, and sit in on some of the planned meetings as they occurred as well as any *ad hoc* meetings that came about, in order to observe the nature and type of interactions that took place within the project. The purpose of the discussions would be to determine how each individual perceived his own situation and the state of the project in general, and through this to identify some of the key factors inhibiting the effective progress of the project. The role of the consultant was to capture each of these 'as is' states and attempt to represent them in a meaningful way, so as to produce an organizational diagnosis reflecting the generally held view of Brent 'C'. All the contributors would then be asked to come together at a 'feedback meeting' to hear the results of this process and to validate (or not) the diagnosis together.

Two other goals were also aimed at by the O.D. consultant during each of the discussions. The first was to take the opportunity to build a credible, effective, and trusting working relationship with each person. The second was to attempt to convey to each person the type of contribution that an O.D. consultant might make to a project such as Brent 'C'. On all but a few instances the diagram (as in

Figure 3) was constructed in front of each person to help them understand a simple organization framework that the consultant found useful in helping him understand how organizations work, and into which (or the like) would be placed the collective comments and perceptions of those interviewed. Needless to say, maintaining the confidentiality of individual statements is crucial in such a task.

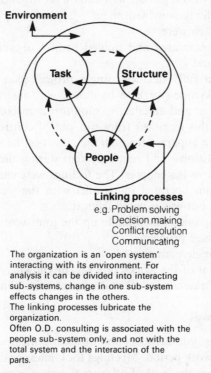

Linking processes
e.g. Problem solving
Decision making
Conflict resolution
Communicating

The organization is an 'open system' interacting with its environment. For analysis it can be divided into interacting sub-systems, change in one sub-system effects changes in the others.
The linking processes lubricate the organization.
Often O.D. consulting is associated with the people sub-system only, and not with the total system and the interaction of the parts.

Figure 3   Simple view of an organization as an open system

Figure 3 diagramatically represents the view of an organization as an 'open system' interacting with its environment, being influenced by it and in turn having an influence on it. The three sub-systems of task, people, and structure were the three chosen for illustration in the discussions (there are, of course, numerous sub-systems). It was suggested that, for the sake of an organization analysis, these can be isolated from each other, but that in reality they are highly interdependent and that a change in one of these sub-systems will have an impact on the others. Similarly, the linking processes of organizational life, such as problem-solving, decision-making, priority-setting, conflict resolution, and communications, can also be observed and described for the purpose of analysis. It is the linking processes which lubricate, or not, the day-to-day functionings of the organization.

Parallel actions

During the entry phase[7] of the O.D. consultant's involvement, the O.D. consultant helped project management agree in principle two key decisions which they then started to implement. The impact of these decisions and actions had a major effect both on project staff and on the organization diagnosis which resulted from the discussions with them.

The decisions taken were:

(a) to form an integrated and unified project organization under a Shell Project Manager, and

(b) to develop a fully detailed, single project plan based on a realistic assessment of workscope (work to be done), with realistic milestones (target dates for completion) and an effective monitoring mechanism.

The need to do this stemmed from the 'out of control' feelings mentioned above. They became apparent through the report of the study team mentioned earlier, entry discussions, and reinforcement during the diagnostic interview phase detailed later in the chapter. The feelings were characterized by:

● The Shell team operated in parallel with the joint-venture contractor organization, but was isolated from it.

● The two companies which made up the joint-venture organization were having 'marriage problems'.

● No shared, single plan existed.

● The true extent of the workscope was unknown.

● Reporting of measured work status was undisciplined and hence chaotic.

Organization diagnosis

Discussions with project members and observing them working together took place over a three-week period. Meetings took place onshore and offshore and included people from the level of offshore foreman to project manager. Those who participated made up the key influencers and, in essence, the power base of the project.

In such a short chapter (and even through the written word) it is not easy to convey 'what actually goes on' during an O.D. intervention, and certainly it is difficult to communicate to anyone not associated with actual events their potency and meaningfulness (or otherwise) to those who were involved. However, by using the actual diagnostic diagrams used during the feedback session, the reader has the opportunity to sense the flavour of what the organization at that time must have been like to work in, and also what it might have felt like to be at the feedback meeting. Remember, the organization characteristics outlined in the previous section were still prominent. These manifested themselves at the individual and interpersonal levels in the form of personal conflicts and negative attitudes and emotions.

The goals of the feedback meeting were:

● For all the contributors to hear at the same time a diagnosis of their situation as they saw it, but put into a meaningful framework for understanding.
● To validate (or not) this diagnosis.
● To determine the next steps (if any) to be taken.

Some of the characteristics of this meeting were:

● It reinforced the involving and participative process already started during the discussion phase.
● It was confronting in nature: confronting both the contributor's own perceptions (individual and collective) and confronting each other.
● The feedback was handled by the O.D. consultant in a manner which was designed to empower and motivate rather than to criticize or alienate.
● In a negative work world it made public to all in the room the knowledge that 'you know that I know that you know!'.

The diagnosis (or 'present situation') fed back for validation appears in Figure 4. It uses an 'open systems' model as used during the discussions, and it attempts to reflect the important factors as determined by the contributors. It is a problem-oriented diagnosis mirroring the almost universally negative states of mind of the contributors. It was displayed using an overhead projector and more detailed illustrative quotes supporting the diagnosis were handed out at the end of the meeting.

The essence of the diagnosis was that the main change thrust of the move towards an integrated organization structure and the introduction of two fundamentally different 'ways of doing' the task from what had gone on before (i.e. the use of a 'project model' approach as the basic management control tool, and moving from a 'discipline' to a 'systems' approach to planning, organizing, and executing work) had disoriented many of the project staff. Things were 'up in the air', as exemplified by the characteristics highlighted in the roles/jobs and people boxes in Figure 4. The 'linking processes' that caused greatest concern were those to do with communications and the way that changes were being handled, with the factors identified in these boxes exacerbating the problems felt by project staff in coming to terms with new roles and new ways of working and relating.

The diagnosis of the present situation was generally validated by those present, and there was general agreement that the 'desired situation' (Figure 5) was the target to be achieved. This, too, had been developed from the discussions. Although it appears somewhat 'motherhood' in nature, it was agreed to be realistically achievable.

Principles and consequences behind the planned changes

At the time of this first diagnosis, the principles behind the two main change thrusts had been made clear to project staff, but few had, as yet, directly

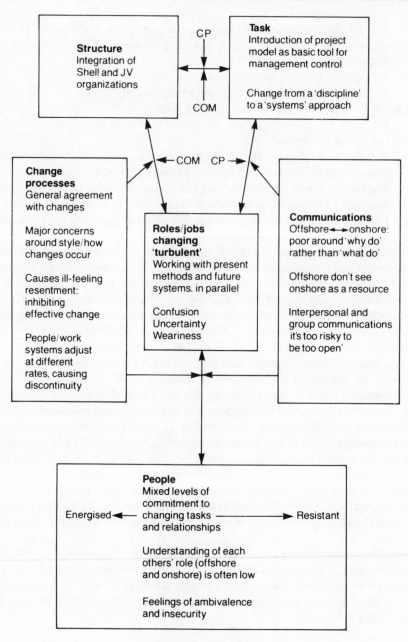

Figure 4   Brent C organization diagnosis (November, 1979)

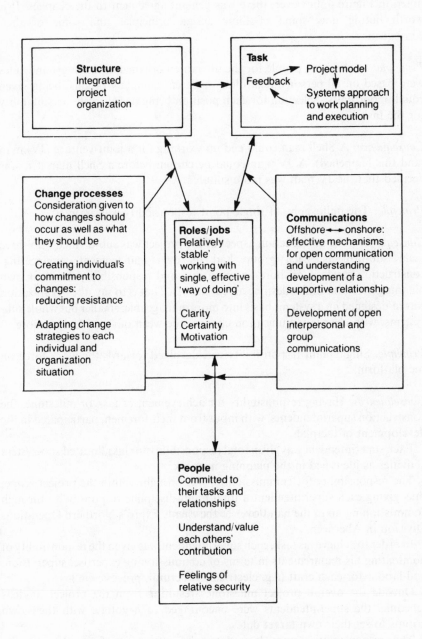

Figure 5   Desired situation

experienced their impact. This was to take place over the months to come. As noted in Figure 4, however, there was general agreement to the changes. It is worth noting now some of these design principles and some of their consequences.

Principle: In choosing people for the integrated organization, the ground rules were based on all persons, regardless of parent company origins, being given equal opportunity. Selection for each position being based solely on suitability for the task.

Consequence: A Shell man could end up working for a joint-venture (JV) man (and this happened). A JV man could be chosen before a Shell man if it was deemed that the JV man was more suitable.

Principle: The philosophy of single-point responsibility was adopted.

Consequence: The construction aspect of the project was sub-divided into three main sub-projects, each group had its own management, engineering, construction services, offshore organization, and responsibility for their own planning networks and milestone achievements. That is to say, the organization was re-designed on a systems basis into more manageable, smaller but whole sub-systems, with clear communication channels between offshore and onshore.

Principle: Single-point responsibility was devolved towards the work-force on the platform.

Consequences: Having responsibility for achievement of task or milestone, the construction superintendents, with input from their foremen, participated in the development of the plan.

Each superintendent was given total responsibility for his allocated sub-system activities as identified in the planning network.

The responsibility for commissioning was brought within the project scope, thus giving each superintendent a total multi-discipline responsibility through commissioning up to the hand-over to the client, Expro's Northern Operations Division in Aberdeen.

In order to achieve his task, each superintendent was given the responsibility of nominating his requirements in terms of commissioning expertise, supervision, and labour for each craft (e.g. electrical, structural, process, etc.).

Outside the overall project milestones resulting from the project model's schedule, the superintendents were encouraged to negotiate with their own groups to set their own target dates.

The responsibilities were legitimated by a message from the top, by reinforcement by the three managers of Production, Water Injection, and Gas

Handling groups, and by designing the planning and work execution system to support these devolved responsibilities.

Principle: The move from a 'discipline' to a 'systems' organization design was reflected in *the design of the work packs* sent offshore as the basis for construction activity.

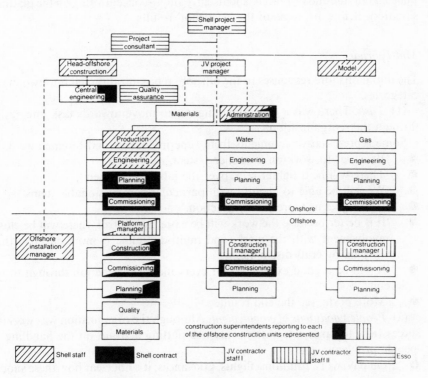

Figure 6 Brent C—simplified organization chart

Figure 6 shows the resultant integrated Brent 'C' project organization, made up from five different employer sources. This was finally achieved in March 1980, 4–5 months after its initial conception, the three sub-groupings of the project being the Production Project Group (PPG) this being the largest, the Water Injection Group (WIG), and the Gas Handling Group (GHG).

The platform manager was part of the PPG group (because it was the largest and the most advanced in terms of work definition) but he was also deemed the most senior construction representative on the platform. Whilst each of the WIG and GHG construction managers answered directly to their own onshore management, the platform manager controlled shared construction activities, safety, administration, bed allocation in emergency situations, and was responsible for the review of group interfacing.

Working with the changes

Three further 'sensing' diagnoses were made by the O.D. consultant—in mid-February, at the end of March, and in early July—concentrating on the platform situation. Below are some of the 'snapshot' results.

Mid-February

The initial offshore responses to the offshore reorganization fell into two major categories.

(1) *Task.* There was a general willingness to move towards task integration through the reorganization.

Some representative comments from superintendents and foremen were:
- 'Its easier to work on a smaller system.'
- 'There will be a tighter rein, over the job and the men.'
- 'We will be able to identify with particular commissionable items.'
- 'It will give us more job satisfaction.'
- 'It is better because the work will be easier to control, there will be closer involvement with the work, and multi-discipline is more effective than working by craft discipline.'
- 'It will be a good experience for everyone, seeing the job through to the end.'
- 'More pride, see the end result.'

(2) *People/conditions of employment.* Although the organization was working successfully towards integration, this was putting a strain on the handling of 'people problems', e.g.
- 'On pay, work rotations, flights, grievances; it's not clear how these should be handled.'
- 'There's uncertainty around who chooses the work-force around each foreman; the foreman or ?'
- 'There are two laws between the joint-venture organizations—we work different hours, different start and stop times, and get paid different rates.'

Also, at this time there were three offshore work rotations practised by the JV partners and Shell. One JV partner worked two weeks offshore to one week's leave, the other worked two weeks offshore to two weeks' leave while Shell worked one week offshore to one week's leave. These conditions of work differences obviously caused concern in themselves, particularly for those working '2 and 1'; specific additional comments regarding the '2 and 1' system included:

- '1 week is not long enough to recharge the batteries.'
- 'I am tired after a few days offshore.'
- 'It's stress-inducing and leads to ineffectiveness.'

Mid-March

After some weeks of actually working the new offshore organization, attitudes were mixed, and there was no cohesive or generally agreed statements regarding the new way of working.

The organization was still in a state of flux, with people and different work groups responding to the organization changes at different rates, resulting in three main groupings: the adjusted, the flexible adaptors, and the resistors. Most seemed to fall in the first two categories.

Both the positive comments and the concerns made in mid-February were reinforced, but in the area of planning/job packaging onshore and the links to offshore, increasing frustration was being felt in some quarters.

- 'There are still job cards arriving on completed work.' (A job card is an administrative tool for executing bits of work still to be done or still to be completed.)
- 'The beach keep holding us back—we know what needs to be done, let's do it!'

However others were saying:

- 'Generally the beach is more responsive, they're listening to us more and adjusting to incorporating our comments more quickly.'

Early July

By this time, individuals were talking much more positively and confidently about the project and there was little negative feeling regarding other groups and the 'beach'. Offshore management were spending much less time 'firefighting' and more time thinking through their work and influencing it rather than being influenced by it. In general, a sense of control and confidence was expressed.

Regarding the reorganization, statements were generally positive. For example:

- 'It produced an effective splitting of priorities.'
- 'It allowed for better work definition and estimating.'
- 'Labour has been used much more effectively.'

The success of the reorganization was perhaps best expressed by members of the Water Injection Group. Reasons given by them for this success were:

- Involvement of offshore superintendents and foremen in designing the plan for work—they saw it as their plan and were committed to it.
- Individual identity with the task.
- Better supervisory control.

● WIG is a small group and a team spirit has been created.
● The group can see the results of its labour.

Finally, there were two opinions given as the main strength of Brent 'C' at this time.

(1) Splitting into three responsibility areas has:

(a) given direction for an overall attack on the job without sacrificing short-term priorities;

(b) generated more productive-type attitudes; and

(c) allowed each group to set short-term (rational) goals.

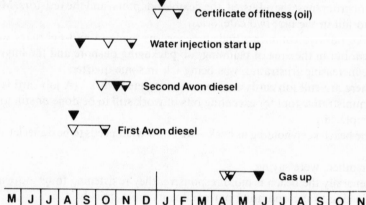

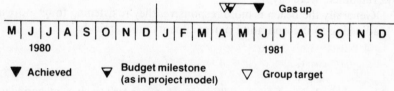

Figure 7   Milestone achievements

(2) Confidence—the project is basically OK and I'm confident we're on course.

This confidence expressed in early July 1980 was confirmed by the target/milestone dates achieved throughout 1980 and 1981. Figure 7 demonstrates some examples of targets achieved.

(1) *1st Diesel Avon:* Group target achieved to the day—2 months ahead of project milestone.

(2) Water Injection: Beat the group target by 6 weeks and the project milestone by 3 months.

(3) *2nd Diesel Avon:* Did not achieve group target but beat project milestone by 3 weeks.

(4) Certificate of Fitness to Produce: Missed group target by 4 days but beat project milestone by 5 weeks.

(5) 1st Oil Production: Failed to achieve group target and project milestone by 6 weeks.

Normally (5) would have been achieved in a matter of days after (4). However, two major set-backs hit the project both of which were beyond the control of the offshore management and labour. A supply boat hit a platform leg in October 1980 and prevented the power supply to the Booster pumps being connected. When the leg was sealed in February 1981 and the power re-connected, a design problem was found that caused further delay.

Some O.D. contributions

The O.D. contribution took various forms, most of them not obvious to, or seen by, many of the project personnel on Brent 'C'. The most obvious contribution, however, took the form of the organization diagnosis process outlined above:

● Individual discussions discovering current perceptions of situations and observing members of an organization working together.
● Create a diagnosis/framework for understanding.
● Feedback to all contributors at the same time, to have a rational review of the situation.
● Agree on action options.
● Implementation by project staff.
● Evaluate.
● Data collect (and repeat the stages).

Other contributions included:

● Consulting to the project manager on the design principles, implementation, and review of the reorganization.
● Consulting to individual managers within the project on problems facing them, planning for action, and exploring different 'ways of doing' and their consequences on behaviour, on systems, and on structure.
● Process consulting at numerous project meetings, either planned or *ad hoc*.
● Organizing and running an intergroup workshop between onshore and offshore staff to determine better ways of communicating between the 'beach' and the platform through improved use of technology, procedures, and face-to-face meetings.
● Preparing the ground for co-operative working between individuals, between groups, and within groups. This mainly occurred on the boundaries between planning and construction, between offshore and onshore managements, and at the interface between the three task groups.
● Jointly working with managers to help them manage their 'boundaries', including the boundary between the project and their parent organizations.
● Bringing issues into focus before they reached crisis point.
● Acting as a 'catalyst', e.g. in providing opportunities for project staff to raise and tackle 'real' but difficult issues.

In summary, the O.D. contribution was geared to help technically dominated and highly task-centred project personnel to increase their awareness and their ability to manage the interaction and inter-dependences between the technical and the social systems which made up their project, and to effectively manage both the people and the task together.

Notes

1. A 'project organization setting' is a temporary work organization set up under a project manager to design and construct through to commissioning, a particular piece of 'hardware'—be it an offshore platform, a pipeline, or an onshore plant. It has a clear, observable, and unambiguous 'boundary' around it. The project is made up from members of the client organization, Shell, and members from various contractor and sub-contractor organizations.

Some of the technical competences represented are project management, engineering, materials, project services (contracts, planning, cost engineering), operations, administration, quality assurance, field development, and third parties.

In a successful project, responsibilities and authorities tend to be clear and written down. It is the policy of Shell Expro to give the project manager as much freedom as he needs to meet corporate as well as project objectives. He has 'single-point responsibility' for the management of his project.

2. The Central Engineering department acts as a centre of expertise and specialist resource to Expro as a company, and to individual projects within Expro. These resources are supplied at all phases of a project's life and include all of the engineering specialism such as structural, process, facilities, and instrumentation, as well as project support services such as project planning, cost control, quality assurance, and contract management.

The construction department completes new projects from the hook-up phase through to commissioning and carries out any construction work needed on existing platforms. Operations manages the day-to-day workings of each platform, the main activities being in the areas of drilling, production, maintenance, and transport, supply, and services.

3. A substantial escalation in real terms took place betwen 1974 and 1976. This was the result of (a) the lead time required to implement the revised development plan, in terms of design and cost estimating, and (b) slippage in the construction programme.

During hook-up, cost escalation occurred due to:
  (a) the 'knock-on' effect of the above;
  (b) the need to optimize Brent field profitability; and
  (c) problems caused by lack of quality assurance.
This resulted in a significant offshore construction element in the basic workscope for offshore hook-up, where labour costs are highest.

4. A recommendation was made by the study team to the project manager and to Shell's top management.

● This was followed up by the project manager's line boss and the project manager. The former played an important connecting role in approaching Shell for the appropriate resources. The project manager played the indispensable role of being an 'excellent' client.

● A behavioural scientist was chosen because of the nature of the problems diagnosed (i.e. they were deemed as 'behavioural').

5. Single is emphasized because the project (on entry) was divided into a client organization and a contractor organization, and this division was proving extremely harmful. I also wanted to reinforce the point that I was an outside consultant working to the whole enterprise, not to just one segment of it (be it the client or the contractor segment).

6. The parties involved were the Shell project manager and the two top managers on the contractor side of the organization. This group effectively became a steering group for the O.D. contribution (I believe this 'jointness' in learning and problem-solving is essential to an effective O.D. intervention).

7. On arrival, first discussions between the three individuals mentioned in note 6 had taken place on (a) new organization structures and (b) developing a single, project plan. I acted as consultant to them during this decision-making process and so was instrumental in helping them to move towards a unified and integrated planning and work execution process in harmony with a 'systems' approach and organization. However, philosophically, the three men 'were already there'.

Epilogue

The application of organizational development (O.D.) to a specific department in Shell Expro was, in my opinion, a step that was taken in the hope that it might do some good. It was viewed by most people, inside as well as outside the Brent 'C' project team, with a good deal of scepticism. That attitude in itself was an indication of the problems which had to be overcome.

There is still an unresolved question about the real value of the O.D. contribution to the Brent 'C' project's ultimate success. It is not possible to identify where O.D. has been specifically effective, but my impression is that the major contribution was the identification of problem areas in such a manner that they became evident to most of the people in the project team. It also helped to show that the same problem area is perceived differently by different people and that in areas of conflict there are usually not a number of black knights on the one side and white knights on the other side.

The fact is that the Brent 'C' project team changed from a 'divided house' into a coherent and task-oriented group.

At times, I had the impression that the team had become too independent and single task orientated and thus overlooked the wider responsibilities in the total of Shell Expro's Northern North Sea development. Internal conflicts appeared to have been resolved, but for some members of the team the 'outside world', i.e. other Shell departments, had become the substitute common enemy. I must add that the 'outside world', which was very much organized along the lines of functional responsibilities in a matrix organization, very often had difficulties understanding the strict organizational system of Project Management as practised by the Brent 'C' project team. Eventually it became the task of Senior Management to ensure that relations with other departments improved and that the handover of the platform to the Operations department was a well-managed activity. In retrospect, I believe that organizational development could have made a contribution in this area as well.

Finally, the Brent 'C' experience has taught us many lessons and made us aware of the fact that basic principles of Project Management should be applied as soon as a Project Team is formed. I believe that it is very worthwhile to involve an O.D. consultant at the beginning of a project's life, in order to avoid the traumatic exercise of setting a project on its proper course after it has run out of control.

London,
U.K.
May, 1983

P. A. Kouwenhoven
Head of Projects
Shell U.K. Exploration and Production

People and Organizations Interacting
Edited by A. Brakel
© 1985, John Wiley & Sons Ltd.

Chapter 4

From Vertical to Horizontal: New Organizational Principles in a Refinery

Arie Langstraat and Jacques Roggema

Introduction and summary

In 1977 the management of Shell Netherlands Refinery (SNR) concluded, as the result of a workshop, that there were major problems in their organization. A reorganization plan was developed and implemented. This chapter describes the reorganization and how it was carried through during 1978/1979 until the beginning of 1980.

The main feature of the reorganization was the introduction of a number of relatively independent production units (PUs). The management team of each unit is multi-functional. It consists of operational, maintenance, and technological personnel. Besides the PUs there are a number of functional departments providing specialist service. The PUs and the central service departments relate to each other in a matrix structure.

After the new organization had been functioning for over a year, interview and questionnaire studies were conducted to evaluate the reorganization.

The reorganization

Management workshop

In 1977, at a workshop lasting a few days, the SNR management team reviewed the organizational structure of SNR against the background of their corporate objectives. The reason for this review was their concern about the manageability of such a large and complex organization under conditions of fairly rapid commercial change. Changes in world energy production, decreasing economic growth, and increased environmental concern, were all factors which were seen as pressing for a more efficient organization capable of a faster and effective response to changing circumstances.

The objective of the workshop was to develop a common philosophy concerning the future of the refinery organization. The workshop began with a thorough scrutiny of the shortcomings of the existing organization. The main conclusions from this scrutiny were the following:

(1) There was over-emphasis on the vertical structure of the organization, including long communication lines, many hierarchical levels, and narrow spans of control.

(2) Related to the vertical emphasis was the laborious horizontal co-ordination of job performance and a sense that the different departments seemed to strive after their own ends at the expense of the overall unity of purpose of the organization.

SNR's main objective was described as 'being permanently capable of exporting outside the Benelux'. Such a capability demands a high standard of operational efficiency and flexibility. The organization structure therefore must have the capacity for flexible adaptation to fluctuating economic circumstances.

From this objective, and based upon their analysis of shortcomings, the management team outlined a new organization with the following features:

- division of the refinery into eight production units, relatively autonomous and each managed by a multi-functional team consisting of operational, maintenance, and technical staff;
- improvement of the relationship between the central technical services and the production units;
- reduced number of hierarchical levels.

In particular, the creation of production units was intended to give much stronger emphasis to the primary purpose of the organization, i.e. production.

Workshops 'down the line'

As a follow-up to the management workshop, a number of additional workshops, attended by lower management levels, were organized. The objective of these workshops was to develop a detailed specification of the structure outlined by the management team.

Joint consultation council

The final proposal for reorganization was then laid before the Joint Consultation Council. The members of the Council assented to the proposed reorganization provided that the following conditions were met:

- the development of the proposed changes, and any further changes, to be in consultation with those directly affected by the changes and the Council;
- carefully designed implementation process that should actively involve staff in the changes;
- sensitive handling of situations where long-serving staff members are involved.
- provision of adequate information to those staff not directly involved in the reorganization;
- continuing evaluation of the progress made in reorganization, and discussion of the results with the Council.

Following the acceptance of the proposal by the JCC, and management's full acceptance of their conditions, an immediate start was made to implement the production units according to a fixed timetable.

The new organization

In this subsection we describe in more detail the new organizational set-up. To help understand the overall structure of the operational process, Figure 1 shows the hierarchy of the co-ordinating teams. First, we describe the most important features of the production units (PUs), and then describe the relationship between these PUs and the supporting functions.

Eight production units. The total operational process within the refinery is divided between eight PUs. Each PU consists of a set of refinery installations. The different plants that make up the refinery are highly interdependent, the output of one installation often forming the input of one or more other plants. In forming the PUs the following factors were considered: process relations, geographic proximity, the possibility of combining control rooms, and plans for possible expansion or dismantling of installations.

Features of the PU. At the head of each PU is a manager who is responsible for all the unit activities. He is not only responsible for operational activities, but also for the maintenance of the plant and technological aspects of the production process. The PU manager is head of a so-called co-ordination team. This team has a multi-functional nature and consists of a PU engineer in charge of maintenance, a process engineer whose task is to optimize the process operations, and one or more operational assistants taking care of the day-to-day co-ordination of operations. Brief job descriptions of these functions are given in Appendix A.

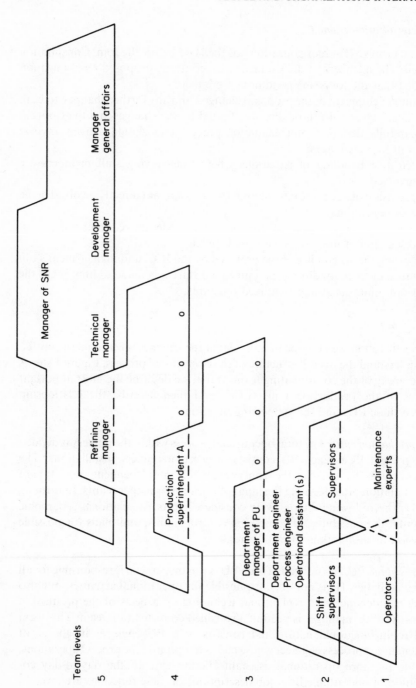

Figure 1 Team hierarchy of SNR organization

Before the reorganization operations, maintenance, and process technology were the responsibility of their respective departments. In the PU, these responsibilities now belong to the co-ordination team in order to maintain the optimal balance between maintenance and other needs, and the production process.

The PU also contains a number of shift supervisors and operators working on a continuous shift basis. There are also supervisors and craftsmen with skills in civil, mechanical, and electrical/instrumentation engineering who carry out maintenance tasks. These craftsmen report to a PU engineer. Before the reorganization these craftsmen belonged to a central maintenance organization. Furthermore, each PU has a small administrative unit charged with work planning and scheduling. The organization of a PU is illustrated in Figure 2.

Location. Previously, the various members who now belong to a PU worked in separate locations. To encourage better co-operation they are now accommodated in the PU area. Whilst permanent PU office buildings are being constructed, they are using portacabins. It is also intended to provide each PU with a small workshop, and changing and rest-room facilities. It is hoped that these measures will strengthen the cohesion of each PU and thereby contribute to increased efficiency.

Relative autonomy. The composition of the PUs and their location close to their installations was meant to make them highly self-supporting in all aspects of their task. To further this autonomy greater authority for committing expenditure was introduced. The PU can call upon central service departments only in cases of high workload, or the need for specialist resources.

PU and service department relationships. The aim of introducing the PU concept was to establish a number of decentralized, multi-functional, and relatively self-supporting organizational units. The PU is typically a product organization. However, to offset the main disadvantage of the product organization, i.e. the loss of specialist expertise, the central technical and services departments were retained in the reorganization. The task of these departments is to maintain and extend technical standards and knowledge.

The PU manager has the final line responsibility for all staff members within the PU. Some PU members, e.g. the process technologist and the maintenance supervisors, have a secondary accountability to their respective resource managers for the maintenance of technical standards within the PU. The resource manager is also responsible for the career planning and professional development of the specialist staff in the PUs. This type of PU member reports to two managers concerning the different aspects of his work. As it has been said: 'they are wearing two hats'.

In summary, the new organization consists of eight relatively autonomous

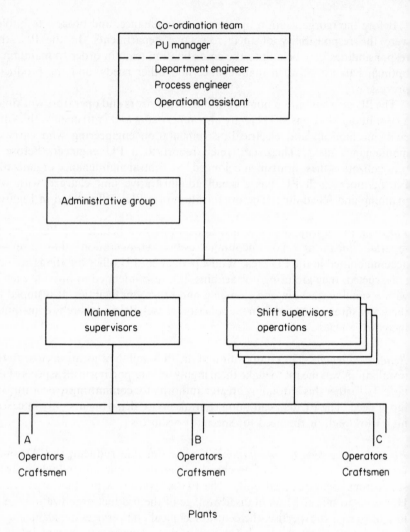

Figure 2   Production unit

production units on the one hand, and central resource departments on the other, related in an overall matrix structure (Figure 3). Some issues involved in reorganization from a general point of view are presented in Appendix B.

Evaluation

Aims and method

A year or more after the reorganization an evaluation was carried out to discover
the extent to which the purpose of the reorganization was being achieved, and to

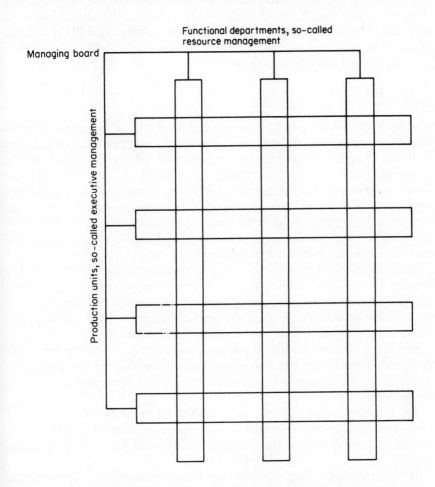

The eight production units are to be looked
upon as executive management, and the
functional departments as resource management;
together they form a matrix structure

Figure 3   Matrix organization

establish what kind of bottlenecks existed. From this evaluation a fine-tuning of the organization could then be made.

Information was gathered by means of semi-structured interviews. Senior managers and heads of resource departments were interviewed individually. In each PU, group interviews were conducted separately for the co-ordination team and a mixed group of operations and maintenance supervisors. The interview information was complemented by data from a short questionnaire. The areas covered by both methods were (a) the internal functioning of the PU as a whole, particularly the functioning of the co-ordination team, and (b) the relation between PU and resource management.

Advantages of the new organization

The particular advantage of the new organization can be seen in the internal functioning of the PUs. To bring out the nature of this advantage, a comparison with the functioning of the old organization is helpful. Prior to the reorganization, separate operational, technological, and maintenance departments existed. Each department laid down its own priorities for the daily progress of its work, and then had to engage in consultations and negotiations with other departments to relate the various priorities to each other. When this co-ordination was not successful at the lower and middle management levels, then 'co-ordination over the top' was necessary.

However, it is now possible to decide on priorities within the PU, precisely because the process technologist, maintenance engineer, and operational assistants belong to the same co-ordinating team, and the PU team has at its disposal its own maintenance crew. In fact the PU is much less dependent upon external activities in determining priorities. In practice, this co-ordination is achieved at a morning meeting of the multi-functional co-ordinating team, with or without maintenance and shift supervisors. At this meeting they discuss the problems that have arisen, decide on priorities, and make arrangements to tackle the problems.

The common location of team members has led to greater accessibility and contact within the team, compared to before the reorganization when they were separately located all over the refinery area. This has led to faster decision-making.

The internal functioning of the PU has been optimized and in this sense the primary objective of the reorganization has been achieved. However, when old demarcation lines are removed, new ones will be created. The new demarcation lines can give rise to bottlenecks in the functioning of the new organization.

Since the concept of matrix organization is attracting much interest in general, we emphasize the problems in the new organization as they have emerged in the evaluation studies.

Bottlenecks in the new organization

Contact between the PUs. In the old situation, the PU managers were located in the main building of Shell Pernis, where their immediate managers superintendents) also have their offices. As a result of the on-site location of each PU manager, the contact between PU managers and the superintendents has been substantially decreased. Since the PUs are very interdependent in processing operations, it is not surprising that the PU managers, whilst recognizing the improved co-ordination within the PU, complain about the difficulties of co-ordination between the PUs.

Co-ordination between the PUs is, therefore, a main objective to pursue, without however sacrificing the improved internal functioning. This objective is given added importance by the observation of the tendency within the PUs to attach overriding importance to the interests of the PU. This over-emphasis has arisen either from lack of information about what is happening in other PUs, or from an over-identification by people with their own PU.

Arrangement of the PUs. The creation of the PUs was mainly prompted by the desire to make the complexity of the overall refinery activities more controllable by the formation of more manageable units which integrated the operational, maintenance, and process aspects for a section of the refinery. However, in order for these smaller units to function properly, it is necessary that each PU has a degree of control of its own boundary conditions, or that these conditions are predictable to a certain extent. If two PUs are highly interdependent in processing operations, the risk can arise that, willingly or unwillingly, they can have a negative influence on each other's functioning by pursuing divergent policies concerning the production programme.

In two PUs the question arose in the group interviews of whether or not it was desirable to shift the demarcation line between them because of their interdependence in processing operations. In the other PUs the interdependence of process operations is limited, or sufficiently controllable, so that they can function as independent units. However, the overall refinery activities form one coherent whole, and it is not a question of the presence or absence of dependence between parts of the process. In determining where best to draw the boundaries of the units, it is a question of the degree of dependence between plants, and also the development of procedures to facilitate co-ordination between the units.

Relative autonomy of the PUs. The degree of process dependence partly determines the degree of autonomy of each PU. Apart from the degree of independence in process operations, there are other dimensions to the autonomy of the PUs. For example, the following are all relevant aspects of PU autonomy: staffing levels, assignment of tasks, financial management, administrative procedures, maintenance and new construction policy, and the 'farming out' of work. In the interviews the question that repeatedly came up was: 'How autonomous is autonomous really?' In the PUs as a whole, the opinion was held that the promised degree of autonomy had not been sufficiently realized. For example, in the financial sphere a greater degree of authority is desired than presently exists. Having to have the payment of expenditures authorized, when these were already approved in budgets, was felt to be a retarding factor which also reduced the autonomy of the PU. Greater authority for non-budgeted expenditures was also desired.

How one judges the desired magnitude of the autonomy of the PU will often depend upon the position the person holds in the organization. The desire for increased autonomy in a local PU may conflict with the desire for supervision, uniformity, and controllability in central departments. Particularly in periods of strong cost-control pressures, central departments will seek a tight control of expenditure in the PUs. This intensifies the conflict between the desire for local autonomy and that for central control. Given the overall objective of relatively decentralized and autonomous PUs, it is necessary for management to undertake a periodic adjustment of the competing desires for local autonomy and central control.

It is not possible to define autonomy in absolute terms; however, given the underlying philosophy of the reorganization, a further exploration of the degree of PU autonomy along the various dimensions is required.

Relation between the PUs and central resource departments. The PU concept places a strong emphasis upon the production process perse. The relevant professional skills are combined in one organizational unit to enable quicker and better decision-making in relation to the production process. It is the central resource management's task to develop and maintain professional standards and criteria, as well as the training and career development of technical staff. The tasks, competence, and authorities of the resource management limit the autonomy of the PUs. The tension between resource management and PUs can be illustrated by means of the following simple example.

Most of the PUs have one or more welders assigned to them. Because of their greater involvement in overall PU activities, these welders are motivated to carry out other technical tasks, and can often be assigned to work in a wider sphere than in the old situation. In a certain case a welder had developed into a kind of 'handyman' who was of great importance to the functioning of the PU. Seen from the point of view of the resource management this task enrichment may be at the cost of the further extension of the welding skills of the man concerned. By transferring him to a central technical department, or to a PU where welding of another type is a regular requirement, and sending him on training courses, resource management will endeavour to increase the skills of the welder. However, when the PU was approached by resource management on this subject, the PU tried to keep the welder concerned, arguing that because he was thoroughly conversant with his duties, and could be assigned a wide range of duties, he was of great value within the PU.

The inherent conflicts of interest between the PUs and central resource management in this kind of case must be handled constructively in order to maintain a proper balance. At present the technical departments are generally of the opinion that they are accepted by the PUs, and they can, therefore, fulfil their responsibilities adequately. Nevertheless, they point out that transfers for the career development of professional personnel and the observance of prevailing standards is being increasingly impeded by the independence of the PUs. The PUs, in turn, are of the opinion that the influence of the central resource management is too great. They feel that their autonomy should allow them a greater say in matters that are, to a great extent, presently under the control of the resource management.

The relation between PUs and central technical departments is a potential source of conflict. In itself this can be advantageous, because in a matrix structure both interests are considered legitimate and attention is given to both. It is, however, a matter of creating a situation in which the two interests are well balanced.

Conclusion

In this chapter we have described a reorganization of considerable magnitude. We have been fortunate in that a follow-up evaluation was possible. This has meant that a change initially with a 'top-down' approach has been followed by a period in which adaptation to, and clarification of, the new organization structure was possible.

Appendix A

Staff employees

It may be difficult for someone outside the organization to form an accurate idea of the functions of PU head, technologist, department engineer, and operational assistant. A brief description of each function is given below.

PU head

His task is to guide all the activities within the PU. He is responsible for meeting the requirements of the production programme in terms of quantity and quality of product, and delivery times. He is also responsible for seeing that these objectives are met in a safe, competent, and cost-effective manner. He should have a thorough knowledge of the 'operation' of the plant, and generally have a very extensive experience of running plants. He has to have a high level of technical understanding, and often has a technical education at master's level degree.

Process engineer (technologist)

His task is to optimize the processing operations. This can require solving immediate problems in the processing activities (trouble-shooting), or the development, over the longer term, of new methods or improvements. He should have a thorough theoretical understanding of physics and chemistry at the level of a master's degree at a university.

Department engineer

His main task is the maintenance of the plants within the PU. This may involve mechanical, civil, and electrical/instrumentation engineering work. The work may be carried out by Shell employees or farmed out to contractors. The department engineer should have ample experience in maintenance work for petro-chemical installations. His technical education should be at the level of a bachelor's and preferably a master's degree.

Operational assistant

His task is the execution of the production plan and he keeps in regular touch with shift supervisors during the day. He has first of all a practical approach to problems. His education is at technical high school level. Operational assistants are mostly recruited from the ranks of the shift supervisors.

Appendix B

Some issues involved in reorganization

Reorganization generally evokes criticism and opposition. The validity of particular changes is challenged. People often express the view that this reorganization is precisely the reverse of the reorganization of some years ago. They feel their performance is being unfairly criticized, and they respond by questioning the diagnosis underlying the reorganization. Certainly those who have experienced several reorganizations may feel that what was once put forward as an advantage, is later described as a serious drawback of a particular organization. For example, initially greater centralization may be put forward as a major improvement and its disadvantages made light of. After a few years the advantages of decentralization are being voiced strongly, and in the same way little attention is given to the disadvantages. It is not surprising that many people experience organizational change as another swing of the pendulum. The organization seems to oscillate between the extremes of centralization and decentralization. In fact, these observations may be entirely accurate. However, it is another matter whether such observations must give rise to a negative attitude towards periodic reorganization.

Of course, any type of organization has both advantages and shortcomings. However, the weight attached to these is closely related to the specific circumstances of the organization at a given moment. Changes in the organization's environment, in objectives, or policy may make structural modifications desirable. As well as external factors, the inner dynamics of an organization may also require changes in both the structure and functioning of the organization. For example, if the organization has to face a wave of retirements within a short period, it will be necessary to make changes in order to cope with the effects of this wave of retirements.

Changes in internal and external factors will lead to a reassessment of certain organizational characteristics. In the transition from one type of organization to another, the drawbacks of the old organization are curtailed. However, for a period of time the benefits of the old organization are still present. As these benefits fade out, the disadvantages of the new organization become more conspicuous and consequently further modifications are necessary. It is not a question of whether one type of organization is right or wrong in an absolute sense, but rather which type of organization is appropriate to external and internal circumstances.

Organizational design principles

The changes made in the refinery organization show the choice made out of the options available when grouping tasks into organizational units.

The most common form of organization is the *functional* one, in which tasks requiring similar skills or knowledge are grouped into one department. The organization is composed of a number of departments, each of which concentrates on a particular aspect of the organization's activities. This gives rise to the familiar departmental structure of production, sales, transport, personnel, finance, etc. The advantages of such a functional structure are:

- the growth of expert knowledge;
- promotes specialization;
- the efficient use of experts;
- career opportunities for specialist staff;
- the development and maintenance of professional standards and values.

A functional structure is effective when the co-ordination of tasks can be planned well in advance. As the need for interchange of information during the execution of the task increases, considerable co-ordination problems arise in a functional structure. It is this co-ordination problem, in organizations faced with complex tasks requiring the simultaneous contribution of different specialists, that has led to a departure from the functional organization. A further difficulty within a functional structure is the selective attention to its own objectives that each department develops, thereby increasing the problems of co-ordination. To avoid these disadvantages a *product* organization is created in which the main specialists required for a task, whether it is a specific product, project, or service, are grouped into one organizational unit. The main advantage of such an organization is the facilitation of horizontal co-ordination, which results in a more effective and efficient task performance. However, in the long run, the product organization constrains the development of specialist expertise because it may limit the amount of contact between members of the same functional discipline.

A type of organization which tries to combine the advantages of both the functional and the product organization is the *matrix* organization. Within the matrix organization two lines of accountability can be distinguished. On the one hand there is accountability for the completion of tasks (product or project management) and on the other hand there is accountability for specialist resources (functional or resource management). In a functional structure the departmental head is responsible for both the execution of tasks and the maintenance and development of professional standards. In a matrix structure these responsibilities are split so that sufficient attention can be paid to both.

To survive, the organization must be capable, in the short term, of a rapid and efficient execution of its tasks. In the longer run it must also develop and maintain its distinctive competence. The following two survival needs are the basis for the two axes of the matrix structure:

(1) a project or product manager(s) responsible for the completion of tasks in accordance with time and cost budgets; and

(2) a resource or functional manager(s) responsible for technical policies and standards, technical quality, training and development of specialist staff, etc.

In a matrix structure the principle of a single line of command is dispensed with. Some roles in the matrix structure have a dual accountability, e.g. a man working in a project team reports to the project manager about task progress and reports to his functional manager about the specialist aspects. A matrix structure requires that tasks and responsibilities be clearly defined in order to achieve a well-balanced relationship between these two main lines of accountability in the structure.

References

Brakel, A. (1979) *Gelijk is niet gelijk*. Over het veranderen van organisaties, Doctoral dissertation, Krips Repro B.V., Meppel, The Netherlands.

Davis, S. M. and Lawrence, P. R. (1978) Problems of matrix organizations, *Harvard Business Review*, **May–June 1978.**

Galbraith, J. R. (1973) *Designing Complex Organisations* (Addison-Wesley Publishing Company Inc.).

Kingdom, D. R. (1973) *Matrix organisation* (Tavistock, London).
Knigh, K. (1976) Matrix organisation: Review, *Journal of Management Studies*, **May 1976.**
Veld, J. in't (1978) *Analyse van Organisatieproblemen* (Elsevier, Amsterdam/Brussels).

Manager's epilogue

This chapter provides a concise overview of the developments of the refinery organization from 1977 until 1980. The writers have given an account of activities, which seemed to lead us to achieving the objectives set out at the onset of the endeavour. It was very much a combined effort of management and staff, in which the Works' Council played a critical and constructive role.

All this, though, does not exclude the occurrence of anxieties and problems. Difficulties were expected and are inherent to a process of renewal of sizeable proportions. We proved the point that a number of small-scale units could fruitfully coexist within a large-scale enterprise. As managers we have been pleased with the personal motivation of employees working in the production units. There was clear identification with the objectives of the entity, people showed understanding for priorities of fellow-workers, and there was a constructive dialogue going on between operations and maintenance staff whose traditional loyalty was more with their own functional unit.

Apart from the positive points, a number of shortcomings also became apparent during 1981/1982 which prompted another review of the organization. The weaknesses, which were concentrated on the maintenance engineering side, can be summarized as follows.

(1) The new system did not train people for the job of maintenance engineer, and learning possibilities were limited. Owing to the very short communication lines, there was a relatively large professional gap between the engineer in charge and the levels that supervised the daily maintenance work. The absence of an intermediate level precluded the development of a new generation of engineers with practical experience.

Equally, at the other end of the scale, maintenance engineers with experience in production units were difficult to transfer into jobs elsewhere in Shell, because this type of experience is—so far—not normally required. It should be remembered that transfers of managers in Shell are the rule rather than the exception. The new concept of organization did not fit the conventional career pattern. Our universities show a clear-cut distinction between the education of mechanical engineers and of technologists with a background in chemistry. These distinctions are maintained in Shell's central offices, and anyone with a certain degree of professionalism in both specializations would be considered a hybrid—with few exceptions.

(2) Originally it was the intention and expectation that the manager of a production unit would have either a technological background and experience, or a maintenance engineering background. On reconsideration, however, there

were doubts whether people with a maintenance background would be acceptable as PU managers from an operational point of view. This point may be related to aspects mentioned in the previous paragraph; one might question whether the experiment was carried on long enough, but at a certain point we were faced with the reality that filling the posts of PU managers from the ranks of maintenance personnel was unlikely.

(3) In the chapter the relation between the production units and the central technical resource departments has been described as a potential source of conflict. The original thought was that maintaining the technical standards of work would be the responsibility of the resource departments through their representatives in the PU. In a number of instances, though, it appeared that it hurt these representatives' pride to call on their professional line in order to solve particular problems. The result was the possibility of inferior quality of technical maintenance work. It would have taken a relatively long time to start and finish a process to instil a more constructive attitude in the people concerned, and we considered this phenomenon a distinct risk in the longer term.

Apart from these weaknesses, a development of a different nature required attention. The Shell refinery of Pernis has Shell Chemicals as its neighbour. During 1982 the bleak foreseeable future of Shell Chemicals (see Chapter 7 of this volume) made restructuring a necessity, and it was decided to combine the two technical departments of oil and chemicals into one central technical department for both companies. In this reorganization the reporting line of the maintenance engineer was changed back into the resource department, giving him at the same time an area consisting of more than one PU to supervise. Moreover, the technical professionalism in each area was strengthened by providing the maintenance engineer with technical staff assistants at an intermediate level. In this way the short communication lines were maintained.

Rotterdam,   J. C. D. Boot
The Netherlands   Refinery Operations Manager
May, 1983   Shell Netherlands Refinery

                                    A. L. Gerretsen
                                    Technical Manager
                                    Shell Netherlands Refinery

People and Organizations Interacting
Edited by A. Brakel
© 1985, John Wiley & Sons Ltd.

Chapter 5

Redesign in Research
Participative redesign of a work organization in the Royal/Dutch Shell Laboratory in Amsterdam, The Netherlands

*Cees Th. Greeve**

Introduction

This chapter deals with the participative redesign of a work organization in the Royal Dutch Shell Laboratory in Amsterdam in the period 1975–1978. These redesign activities were part of a broader field of developments which started in 1970 and were directed towards improvement of communication within the Laboratory and a more effective organization. The overall strategy was based on socio-technical principles: the employees concerned would actively be involved in the analysis, evaluation, and re-structuring of their work situation. It was thought that by means of a process of active participative redesign a flexible learning organization would develop.

The research activities of the Laboratory involve the processing of crude oil to yield oil products, and of petroleum derivatives to obtain chemical products. The

*In the period under review, internal O.D. consultant of the Laboratory.

transport and processing of coal and modern process control techniques are also part of the research effort. With a work-force of about 2000 (1981) the Laboratory at Amsterdam is the largest of its kind within the Shell Group.

Participative redesign

An area that required attention from the viewpoint of effective communication was the organization of projects in which more than one department was involved. Projects became to be considered as hinges between research departments and between research and the Technical Services Department of the Laboratory. Moreover, the projects were seen as suitable vehicles to put into practice the ideas of relatively autonomous groups. Management subsequently decided to carry out an investigation with the following objectives:

(a) to describe and analyse the organizational and managerial aspects of a current project;

(b) to investigate if and in which way the development of relatively autonomous groups would be possible; and

(c) to provide guidance for organizational aspects of future research projects.

It was envisaged that the execution of this investigation would positively affect the overall aims of organization development in the Laboratory for the following reasons:

(a) the projects are considered 'leading parts' in the organization of the Laboratory and key points of interest in O.D. in general:

(b) the investigation could make a practical contribution to discussions that had been going on for several years about the way in which research projects should be defined;

(c) the study would link up with management's efforts to give more prominence to actual work to be done in the context of O.D. activities;

(d) the development of relatively autonomous groups would be an important step in the move towards an organization with sufficient flexibility and adaptability.

The main contributors to the first project under study were the Oil Process Research Department and the Technical Services Department. The team that was set up in 1975 to guide and co-ordinate the study consisted of one representative from each of these departments and two members from the Organization Services Department. The main task of the team was to promote organization efficiency. The team was led by Dr H. J. J. van Beinum, who was, in the period under review, Dean of the Foundation for Business Administration at Rotterdam, Holland.*

In the investigation two phases could be distinguished:

*At present Director of the Ontario Quality of Working Life Centre of the Ontario Ministry of Labour, Toronto, Canada.

(1) the orientation phase, and

(2) the redesign phase.

In the orientation phase the team took stock of the characteristics and relevant tasks and activities of the research project under study. The team interviewed 23 persons out of a total of 100 from 14 different organizational units, and asked about their experience and views. The key questions were: How are the tasks divided, what demands does the work make on the participants, and how far does it meet their wishes? What problems and disturbances have come up or have been prevented in time and what effects have these had? Apart from the data collected from these interviews the team studied documents about the project in general and its progress.

The redesign phase was marked by active participation of employees directly involved in the execution of the project. The team's activities in this second phase were confined to introducing, coaching, and providing information. The first step was to return all material collected in the orientation phase to the interviewees for discussion and possible corrections and additions. Secondly, it was considered essential that in advance of the actual redesign sessions the principles of active participation were discussed with and understood by the managers, the works council, and supervisors of the departments concerned, and a number of meetings were held.

The agenda of these meetings dealt with the setting-up and the programme of the investigation, the basic principles and boundary conditions, and the ways to cope with the possible results of the redesign meetings.

The participative redesign meetings

There were three separate redesign meetings, each attended by about 12 people, and each lasting a day and a half. Two meetings were devoted to the relationships between the process design activities in the Oil Process Research Department and the plant design activities in the Technical Services Department. The third meeting was directed to the relationship between plant design and plant construction, both within the Technical Services Department.

The programme of the meetings contained the following items for the first day.

(1) The heads of the Oil Process and the Technical Services Departments gave a short talk expressing their agreement with the participative redesign and their own expectations about these meetings. One boundary condition was given: 'The process design activities should stay within the Oil Process Department'. After having promised their support for implementing the results of the participative redesign, they left the meetings.

(2) Team members then gave an introduction about the importance of the redesign meetings in the context of the whole investigation and summarized their impressions that emerged from the interview data and documents studied. One of the team members elucidated the underlying principles of the investigation,

thereby starting a discussion among the participants on the meaning of redesign. These rather structured discussions led to a first rough harmonization of participants' views and expectations.

(3) The third agenda item consisted of group discussions directed at obtaining a common analysis of the work-streams in which members were engaged. This was done in small groups of 5 or 6 people each.

(4) Building on the expectations as expressed and the common analysis of the existing work-streams, the second day was spent working alternately in groups and plenary sessions on task redesign and proposals and possible consequences.

At each of the three redesign meetings two participants recorded the results and submitted their draft report to all participants prior to writing a combined final report.

Results and proposals

The most important conclusion that emerged from the redesign meetings was that designing and building a research pilot plant involves a work-stream with many parallel, simultaneous activities. It was felt this simultaneous progress of activities forms a characteristic of the realization of pilot plant projects and at the same time represents the most difficult aspect to manage adequately. The participants recommended very strongly that an adaptable work-method be

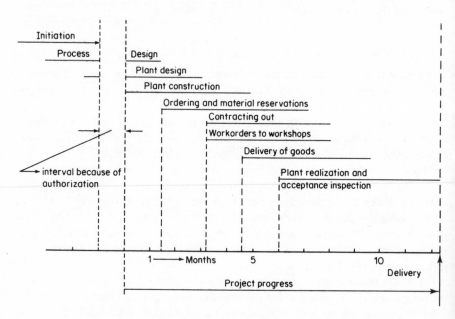

Figure 1   Phases in the realization of a pilot plant

maintained which would allow the researcher to introduce his final ideas at a relatively late point in time. The different phases are presented in Figure 1.

The proposals that came forward from the meetings were aimed at obtaining a smooth and simultaneous progress of the various tasks to be fulfilled within process design and plant design. In the interim report six proposals were formulated which can be summarized as follows.

(1) The management of a pilot plant project should be given to project teams. These teams should have a fair amount of autonomy. While retaining a fixed core, the members of a project team can change, depending on competences required. The fixed core remains active throughout the whole life cycle of the project and consists of a process expert and a process designer from the Research Department and one or more equipment designers from the Technical Services Department. The expertise of the equipment designer(s) would be chosen depending on the scope and nature of the project at hand.

(2) Within the limits of time, money, technical requirements, and quality standards, to be agreed in the initiation phase of the project, a project team should be entrusted the necessary authority for the project realization. The fixed core of a project team should already be set up in this initiation phase.

(3) In cases of large and complex projects the members of a project team should be housed together. The location should be adapted to the scope of the project. The responsibility for the level of expertise and seniority of those who are nominated to a project team rests with their 'home departments'.

(4) As a principle the project team would take care of the project planning, work preparation, and project administration. The team may ask for assistance from an Engineering Services Centre. This centre, still to be formed, could be a combination of the existing Work Preparation Group and Engineering Planning Centre of the Technical Services Department.

(5) With regard to the internal organization of the Technical Services Department, it would be effective to integrate the three independently operating inspection and testing units, namely the mechanical, electrical, and instrumentation units. The participants thought it would be advantageous to combine the electrical and instrumentation specialists groups of the same department.

(6) It would be advisable to set up a 'small projects group' to take care of those activities within the Technical Services Department which only require little or no effort on the design side. Such a group could consist of the present area supervisors of that department.

Follow-up

As a first step the heads of the Oil Process Research Department and the Technical Services Department discussed the proposals with their own director. The main elements of this discussion were as follows.

(a) Both the department heads would proceed with the implementation of the proposals by:

- choosing one or two medium-sized projects within their own jurisdiction to which to apply the proposed organization and management approach;
- initiating the necessary changes in procedures to facilitate the change-over to relatively autonomous project groups; and
- providing relevant information to the other parts of the laboratory organization.

(b) The team that carried out the investigation would remain available for further guidance and evaluation. It would give particular attention to:

- redesigning tasks in the workshops; and
- starting further investigations in other parts of the Laboratory.

(c) As soon as developments may have consequences in a broader context the two department heads concerned would take care of adequate information to the departments involved.

Within one year of the proposals, two relatively autonomous project groups had started work and obtained the authority to carry out their projects according to the proposals.

Conclusion

The members of the investigation team guided the two new projects on a request basis and in mid-1978 made an evaluation of their experiences. The major observation was that the participants of the original redesign meetings did not succeed in jointly developing the proposals. They felt a lack of active support from their managers. The managers appeared to regard the redesign activities as a temporary experiment and not as the start of a self-development of the entire organization. However, some results were achieved; e.g. there was a shift in tasks from supervisors and staff functionaries to members of the project groups.

The conclusion must be that, notwithstanding a promising start in which the staff of the departments directly involved had committed themselves to the redesign experiments and subsequent proposals, the objectives were not reached. The developments became bogged in lengthy discussions and normative statements; they remained exclusively in the *social* system and did not become embedded in one or other new *structural* form based on mutual agreement of the parties concerned. In terms of the skating analogy of Chapter 1: the skater was confined to one leg only and did not get very far.

People and Organizations Interacting
Edited by A. Brakel
© 1985, John Wiley & Sons Ltd.

Chapter 6

Organization Development on the Shop Floor

Jeroen van der Veer and Jan E. M. Boezeman

Introduction and summary

Many reorganizations are undertaken using the basic model of diagnosis by experts, plans, budgets, management approval, and implementation. This is not a necessity and successful reorganizations can be accomplished according to a different model of change. This was done in the workshops of an oil refinery in Rotterdam. The pattern was: limited diagnosis, 'discussion' with the 250 people involved based on a 'framework', and implementation.

The difference was that the work-force played a major role in developing the plans and that management approval was given to the involvement of the work-force before any budget, plan, or guarantee of success was known.

The remarkable facts of the involvement of the work-force were:

● changes came about, whilst some attempts before that failed;
● the impression is that most people were satisfied with the results;
● it is doubted whether this would have been the case if the reorganization had been undertaken according to the 'normal pattern';
● final implementation was very easy and ended up considerably below budget.

But:

- the preparation took substantially longer;
- productive labour hours were lost because people were involved in meetings;
- the development of the plans with involvement of the work-force was emotional and sometimes difficult for management to control.

And:

- senior management was not used to the slow start of this reorganization process; this caused doubts as to whether the long preparation with the involvement of the work-force was the right thing to do;
- the reorganiztion can only be done if senior management is prepared, at the beginning of the process, to give the green light to involve the work-force without knowing plans, budgets, or cost–benefit analysis in detail.
- the quality of middle management is put very much to the test during the process and the weaker ones will not succeed.

To demonstrate the above points a short background of the scene will be given, followed by what happened during the reoganization. The main emphasis after that is to try to evaluate the differences compared with 'normal' patterns of reorganization.

The scene

The Central Workshop of one of the biggest and oldest refineries in Shell is located at Pernis near Rotterdam in the Netherlands. Their task is to repair or to build equipment for the plants on the refinery. The Central Workshop consisted of a Mechanical Workshop, a Fabrication Workshop, and a Transportation Workshop. Furthermore, there are Work Preparation and Expediting departments, which are not relevant to this article (Figure 1).

The Mechanical Workshop (120 men) was organized in a functional way: all lathes together, all drilling machines together, then the 'bank fitters' together but split into a rotating equipment and 'appendages' side.

The Fabrication Workshop (82 men) was organized partly in a functional way as well. All fitters who repaired heat exchangers together, and in another building the metal sheet workers. The welders were spread between the two previous groups.

The Transportation Workshop (30 men) was in fact a kind of garage repairing trucks, rail bogeys, and cranes.

Work Preparation (8 men) was responsible for accepting orders, indicating a delivery time, ordering materials and spares, drawings, and to sub-contract work to outsiders, if necessary. Expedition (10 men) looked after all internal transport.

The problems

For many years prior to 1975 complaints by senior management and by customers of the Central Workshop were:

OLD SITUATION

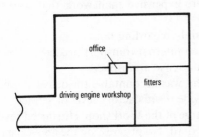

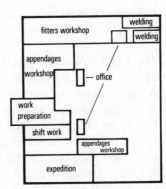

FRAMEWORK

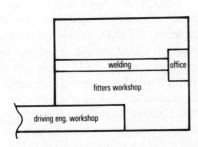

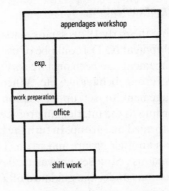

FINAL

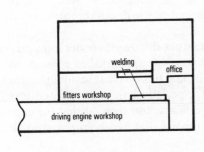

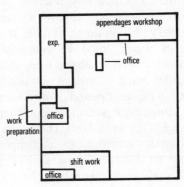

Figure 1

(1) Excessive delivery time and uncertainty whether the delivery time would be met: 'You never knew when your repairs would be ready until they were ready.'

(2) The Central Workshop was more expensive than work that was sub-contracted to outside workshops.

(3) A bad working environment, mainly regarding noise.

(4) A shortage of space and too much internal transport needed.

(5) Bad communications, often with a tense atmosphere.

(6) For outsiders it was not clear who was accountable for delivery times.

In short, the Workshop did not provide a satisfactory level of service.

In 1975 a new manager was put in charge of the Workshop. He started several studies but they all ended up in the cupboard. No progress on the above aspects was made for some years.

The reorganization

During the early 1970s senior management of the refinery felt that organization development (O.D.) could be of use to the refinery. Nearly all senior and middle management had been on a weeks O.D. course. This emphasized communication skills, group behaviour, etc. When completed, the O.D. people tried to help management to set up discussion groups of 10–20 people. This was done according to the interlocking rings of the Likert concept, e.g 15 fitters with their boss formed one group. In turn the boss himself with his peers and their common boss in another group, and so on. This arrangement was called setting up 'work discussions'. So a set-up was made for the Central Workshops for these work discussions under the guidance of a sociologist. Twelve work discussion groups were formed and their first meetings were spent on communication skills.

The attitude towards these work discussions of both management and workers was mixed and, in a way, reserved. Nobody believed at the time that it could contribute significantly towards a solution of the problems of, for example, cost or delivery time, in the short term. It was seen as an effort to try to change the attitudes which could be beneficial in the long term. After the initial communication skill subjects there was a tendency to discuss problems related to the 'coffee machine' instead of work itself.

During the same period of introducing work discussions under some pressure from senior management, a young engineer was appointed as assistant to the manager of the workshops. The reason behind this was that senior management was keen that something should happen, especially in the area of the costs of the Central Workshop. The manager of the Workshop thought that the engineer could best start to summarize the old reports that had been put away in the cupboard.

It appeared that nearly all the old reports suggested a new layout for the workshops. A new layout could contribute to better working conditions and lower costs by having less internal transport; but it was not a solution to get quicker or more definite delivery times, nor to get better communications or accountability and it was unclear whether it was the real cause behind the high costs.

After one month the young engineer reported in a one page note back to the senior management and the managers of the workshops, that only a combined attack on layout *and* organizational structure *and* planning procedures could improve the situation. Thus, a framework plan for layout, organization structure, and procedures was worked out. This framework was very broadbrush. It was suggested that this plan should now be detailed in the work discussions by the work-force themselves.

The initial reaction was one of enthusiasm. However, senior management had reservations and they realized that on the one hand, on the basis of the framework plan, neither costs nor benefits could be quantified. Whilst on the other hand, when the framework was announced to the 250 men in the work-force, and when they had given their input to detail it, it would later be very difficult to stop it. A breakthrough was made by announcing at the same time that whatever came out of the detailing, no more than $400,000 would be made available.

The work discussions to detail the plan took about three months. The discussions were often emotional, accusing others instead of specifying what their own part of the plan should be, and some groups virtually did not want to co-operate at all.

Nevertheless, suggestions and recommendations from the discussion process were so good that even changes in the framework plan were made and in the end a detailed plan existed for layout, planning procedures, and the organization structure. (Note in Figure 1 the difference between 'framework' and 'final'.)

During this period management had a tendency to become sceptical. Phrases like 'progress on the spot', 'the workshop is a talk shop', 'blue collars should not be in meetings but behind their lathes', were voiced.

The plans were frozen and implementation started. As is normal practice in Shell, a network plan and budgets were made, which were controlled by a project manager. To the surprise of many, the implementation needed hardly any management. The changes in the layout were made much quicker than anticipated and the actual costs were substantially lower than budget (approximately 30%). What happened was that everyone knew so well what the final situation should be that a lot of spare moments were spent preparing and arranging things in anticipation of the changes. It was remarkable that the people got on with the job themselves, there were no demarcation problems in the sense of 'this should be done by a mover and not by me'.

After everything had settled down it was clear that the working conditions were improved and that there was less internal transport and congestion. The planning accountability, commitment, and accountability for delivery times were improved. It was more difficult to evaluate how far the costs had come down; an attempt was made to compare them, but no clear results came out. Another poin which was difficult to prove was whether the positive change in the atmosphere on the shop floor was caused by the reorganization or by the process o involvement itself.

Evaluation

It is the usual pattern for reorganization that a limited group of experts make a diagnosis, suggest a preferred alternative, and advocate the proposal to ge management approval. After that usual confidential process an implementatio plan is made. Compared to that pattern it can be said that this reorganization was unusual in the following respects:

(a) a major reorganization was announced that affected many people wher management were not aware of the end-result, cost/benefits, and time frame;

(b) senior management had to approve an open-ended plan;

(c) to detail a plan with about 250 people;

(d) the man-hours to prepare the plan were substantially higher, but the man-hours to implement the plan, substantially lower; it could be said that the proces is top-heavy with man-hours, but that savings will result later during the implementation process;

(e) the emotions which are inherent to a reorganization become more visible for management;

(f) (to a certain degree) after the implementation the atmosphere was 'we have done it' with some pride, instead of 'we were done';

(g) the quality of middle management involved will come out very clearly.

The model of change

We now reflect what really happened as compared to the writer's estimate of what could have happened if the model of change had been the classic approach. Of course, the end-result would have been different from the estimate and this cannot be reflected in the model of Figure 2.

Note

(1) For four months after the management approval of an open-ended plan, nothing happened apart from there being a 'talk shop'.

(2) At the time consideration was given to setting up a consultation process by having a representative for every group of 10–15 people. This was rejected because it was felt that the representatives would probably work considerable man-hours in isolation and after that they would have to 'sell' the plan to their colleagues, which might take as many hours as a direct consultation process.

Actual			Classic		
Man-hours estimate	Calendar	Process	Process	Calendar estimate	Man-hours estimate
		diagnosis of problems/ bottlenecks	same		
200	2 months	'framework' based on common-sense principles	alternatives detailed so that a cost/ benefit estimate can be made	3–4 months	500 ?
		management approval to involve the shopfloor	management selection		
1000*	4 months	'work discussion' to detail the plans (specialist support for certain areas)	further detailing and implementation plan	2–3 months	500 ?
fewer than 'classic'	6 months	implementation	implementation	8 months ?	more than 'actual'

*These were recognisable hours, but probably many more hours were spent during coffee breaks, lunches, etc.

Figure 2

With hindsight it was realized that:

(a) not everybody was happy with the outcome;

(b) part of the shop floor 'work discussions' will only be seen as successful by the participants if they get what they ask for;

(c) to indicate to a group that they have to do the work under certain firm constraints, e.g. a budget, is felt as authoritarian;

(d) it is inevitable that during the discussion process additional wishes will slip in which will cost additional money.

What if we had to do it again?

Participants made the following suggestions.

(1) Maintain the principle of making a framework which should be detailed with the involvement of the shop floor.

(2) More background information should be made available for every work discussion group. Part of this information should be tailor-made for the group.

(3) To have a tougher attitude to specify what the constraints are and if people start to discuss outside these constraints, to feed back quickly that this is not the intention.

(4) To bring in the sociologist earlier in the process, e.g. before the framework is made.

People and Organizations Interacting
edited by A. Brakel
© 1985, John Wiley & Sons Ltd.

Chapter 7

Evolution, Revolution, and the Battle for Survival

Dave Cormack and Brian Wallace

Introduction

This chapter gives an account of one organization's attempt to come to terms with radical changes in its business environment. It is also a significant case history of the role of a team of O.D. consultants working with that organization and how the experience changed the views of the management and consultants as to the nature of the change process and the contribution required from O.D. in times when business survival is the main objective of change.

The battle ground

In 1956 the Royal Dutch Shell Group of Companies invested in a major petrochemical complex. The acquisition was to become part of one of the largest downstream developments of any oil major. By 1981 the chemical interests accounted for some 10% of the Shell Companies' turnover and ranked as the eighth largest chemical company in the world with proceeds of over £3,000 million.

In the 1960s the growth of the Shell Companies' Chemical business was rapid, but was paralleled by similar growth in many competitor organizations as companies sought to take advantage of a world market growing at 15% per annum with little forecast change. Programmes to build more capacity were established by the industry in most of the developed countries. In Western Europe in particular capacity for ethylene production doubled in the period 1972–1982 as a result of investment decisions made in earlier years (see Figure 1).

To manage such developments in Shell Companies many high calibre staff were recruited, and in 1970 following a large-scale management philosophy exercise, using resources from the line organization and the Tavistock Institute of Human Relations (Hill, 1970), O.D. consultants were employed to help the

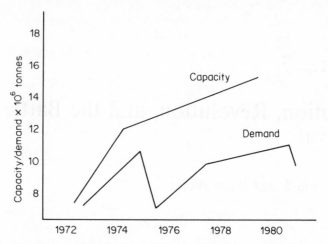

Figure 1   Ethylene capacity in Western Europe, 1972–1982

chemical business cope more effectively with a major new phase of expansion. Their role was to support the planned investment programme with a major educational strategy focused on enhancing managerial capability to create a new management philosophy and foster new employee relations—a more participative and open climate for change. The impact of this training was mixed, some—the younger managers—valuing the new approach, others—the experienced managers—being more conscious of the risks of moving from traditional management practice. An evolutionary approach was underway.

Then in 1973 came the first oil crisis and the future was rewritten.

Forecasts of growth rates were halved, only to be halved again and halved again. By the end of the decade the industrial face of the world had changed beyond recognition and the international petrochemical business, founded and built on double figure annual growth rates, was in a state of disarray. Overproduction, with demand remaining at 60% below capacity, uneconomic plant utilization, tumbling prices, and astronomic losses demanded radical responses at industry and company level.

These difficulties in themselves posed a leadership challenge which demanded a cohesive response. The risks of breaking an established organization culture with a tradition related to growth were all too apparent. At the same time that losses were beginning to hit operating companies, a process of evolutionary adaptation was underway in the Shell Service Companies concerned with the international chemical business (London and The Hague) but progress had been patchy and some managers were beginning to 'go it alone' and introduce radical changes in procedures and methods in response to growing business pressures to rationalize products, plants, and services. Should this be encouraged? If so, how could cohesion and consistency be maintained? Some managers, feeling the constraints of the conservative, evolutionary approach advocated a complete change from the centralized type of approach to a decentralized mode in an attempt to reduce overheads and give more flexibility to the local operating companies. Would such a radical switch be possible? Could commitment be developed rapidly? Would resistance to imposed change and internal conflict slow down progress? These were some of the issues that faced the leadership as the business pressures mounted.

The aims of change—senior management's view

This coincidence of the need for urgent business rationalization linked with a need for a co-ordinated and cohesive approach to change meant that a choice was required—either to persist with evolution or to impose change because of the urgency of the situation. A middle course was chosen; namely, to have an organization study carried out under the direction of the top management team and then to use the proposed reorganization as the vehicle for change.

The recommendations were that, with low growth prospects, the Operating Companies should be freed to respond to local market conditions as much as possible, whilst not threatening to optimization of Shell Companies' business, and the Service Companies should focus on the long-term prospects and strategies.

The existing organization had been product based, in which business strategies were co-ordinated centrally with Operating Companies' input (see Figure 2).

To achieve this distinction of roles the study highlighted that any change of structure should have the following aims:

- To improve co-ordination against overall strategies.
- To create clearer accountability within and between the Service Companies and Operating Companies.
- To reduce the involvement of the Service Companies in the Operating Companies' ongoing chemicals operations.
- To improve mechanisms for conflict resolution across the sector.
- To put more emphasis on advice and services from Service Companies to Operating companies.

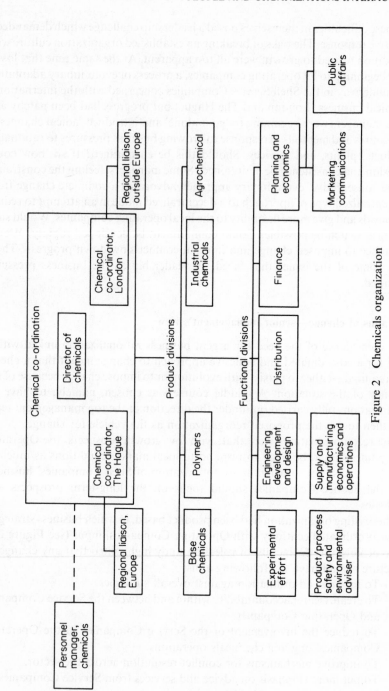

Figure 2 Chemicals organization

These aims reflected the need to change the Service Company role and the elationship with the Operating Companies and represented a clear challenge to he traditional Service Company activity, to become more strategic and less involved in the day-to-day optimization of the business—a breaking of the implicit power base to be paralleled with a run down of Central Office staff of ome 20%.

The revolution had begun!

The changes implied would significantly affect the whole of Shell Companies' Chemical business, with a turnover of £3 billion and over 50 Operating Companies covering a world-wide market.

Figures 2 and 3 illustrate the basic structural changes.

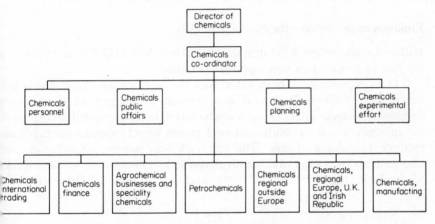

Figure 3   Proposed organization

The sector was run on a matrix principle in which functions and locations were epresented in 'business groups'. This structural device had attempted to create an integrated business process in which all parties contributed, through the matrix organization, to the development of strategies and plans. The matrix aimed to provide vertical and horizontal integration. It utilized a 'bottom-up' process with many levels and stages involved in the formulation of business plans. It was, in consequence, slow, but went a long way to ensuring the epresentation of all major functions, businesses, organizations, and countries with interests in the chemical business in the decision-making process.

The new proposals recommended a major reduction in the level of co-ordination through the matrix and placed the emphasis on functional activity. Thus, for example, 'manufacturing was to manufacture' and not become nvolved in long business co-ordination-type debates; trading was to be broken out from the business units and given a new and separate identity, and strategic planning was to be brought together for the whole of the petrochemical business.

The overall shift within the Service Companies was toward the provision o services to Operating Companies and toward the representation of th shareholders in these operating companies.

Paradoxically, the capacity to change to a new type of organization wa imbedded in the principles and structure of the old organization. To move to a decentralized structure would require careful central co-ordination! To make the revolution work needed an evolutionary approach!

The battleground was defined: the need for a change of strategy from growth to retrenchment; to establish a new leadership philosophy; to devolve the organization; to reduce manpower; to change attitudes and responses; and o course while all this was going on, the business still had to be run!

Evolution or revolution—the challenge to O.D.

Within this revolution, what then should be the role of O.D.? To carry on as in the past or to shift to a new mode of operation?

O.D. in chemicals had been linked with the development of the matrix and hence was 'traditional', in that it attempted to support an evolutionary development mode. The O.D. work was based on the assumption that creation o the appropriate culture, skills, and mechanisms would engender the capacitie required to achieve change. The approach was patient, consultative, and emergent, and was successful in providing a set of fundamental building block which, during the 1970s, enabled many developments to be tackled successfully

Table 1

Evolution	Revolution
'Evolution is not a force but a process, not a cause but a law' (Morley, 1874)	'Revolution is not a dinner party ... i cannot be so refined, so leisurely and gentle ... A revolution is an insurrection, an act o violence ...' (Mao Tse-tung, 1927)
Evolutionary change: ● Follows laws ● Is slow ● Results in casualties ● Is environmentally determined	Revolutionary change: ● Breaks laws ● Is rapid ● Results in casualties ● Breaks constraints
Traditional O.D. values: ● Searching for order ● Planning change ● Valuing individuals ● Emphasizing learning	Today's business needs: ● To survive ● To respond rapidly ● To value contribution ● To emphasize capability

he emphasis was on product strategies, project development, and bottom-up olicy-forming via cross-functional teams, processes which were very relevant to volutionary change—yet, in retrospect, inadequate for radical total system hange.

Table 1 illustrates the emerging challenge for the O.D. consultants as it became pparent that the urgency and route for change would mean a shift from the volutionary approach to supporting and influencing a revolution.

The choice was made to join the revolution, to seek and plan influences, and, hrough time, hopefully to enable management to develop an overall change trategy based on consultation, involvement, and understanding.

The access of O.D. was primarily within the Service Companies at this time. lthough there were significant consequences for Operating Companies, for xample in the method of trading, the focus of this chapter is the London-based ervice Company where the major changes were experienced.

acing the conflict

he complexity of the issues to be faced in the required restructuring of Shell's hemicals business resulted in an unprecedented level of internal tension. onger-term business interests—the need to maintain adequate levels of nvestment—conflicted with the short-term needs for positive cash flow. Healthy ectors of the business, in particular the speciality chemicals and other higher dded value activities, conflicted with those sectors of the business which were in lecline, fighting to maintain distance between themselves and the troubled usinesses in an attempt to differentiate their structures and approaches.

Functions conflicted as to which way the battle should be fought and where avings should be made. Individuals conflicted as the competition for personal urvival increased. Externally the market-place became a battle ground with new llegiances being forged as companies struggled to survive.

At the leadership level in the Service Companies, the conflict focused initially n the change management style to be adopted. A rapid response was required, et most of the organization leaders had been associated with gradual levelopment strategies spanning years rather than weeks.

The service organizations housed the business leaders in terms of professional xpertise and international business experience. These high-quality, high-level taff had become used to a full involvement in organization and business matters. he apparent imposition of 'a solution' was an act which could have been seen to ut across the culture of an organization which had stressed involvement and articipation at all levels.

In addition, the various chemical businesses which formed the biggest part of he service organizations had been run on semi-autonomous lines with lifferences in business and management approach being reflected in the tructures and procedures. To apply standard concepts across the whole business spectrum was felt by many to put at risk some of the unique skills of speciali business approaches.

Also at risk were people. A large number of volunteers would be needed fc early retirement and a larger number of volunteers would be needed fc redeployment in other parts of the Shell Group if the overall objectives were to b met. In order to improve the chances of redeployment a large pool of staf wa offered for transfer. Although this increased the chance of successful selection also increased the number of people faced with uncertainty.

A further source of conflict arose from the fact that developments in th various business divisions were not in phase; for example, the use of moder business methods varied across the organization. For all parts to move forwar together would require a major leap for some and a marking time for others

Finally, there was no consistency of commitment to change. Some lin managers felt that their organizations were adequate to meet the challenge, whil others believed that radical change was just what was required. Table 2 illustrate the dilemma.

Table 2   Leadership dilemma—what style should or can we adopt?

Evolution—let it happen?	OR Revolution—make it happen?
Risks ● Piecemeal evolution ● Pockets of revolution ● Varying levels of awareness of need ● Varying levels of commitment to manage change ● Risk of failure due to slow response	*Risks* ● Breaking traditional norms ● Top-down imposed change with the same top team in place ● Change could be perceived as lacking confidence in staff ● Solution may not be totally valid or supported ● Leadership would need to take risks and inevitably be under close scrutiny
Benefits ● Consultation would lead to commitment and understanding ● Demonstration of value placed on knowledge and experience ● New organization soundly critiqued at planning stage ● Opportunity for building new relationships	*Benefits* ● Sense of urgency would be apparent ● Shake-up could result in questioning of old attitudes/approach ● Top management commitment to change would be demonstrated ● Early achievements in making change could provide a confident basis for next steps

The O.D. team's campaign plan

As part of the planning for the change process it was agreed between th Chemical Co-ordinator (Shell Companies' senior chemical manager) and hi

O.D. adviser (an ex-Shell man but now an external consultant) that the scope of the changes were such that there was a need to establish an O.D. team to support the change programme and that this team should be a mix of external and internal consultants, preferably with knowledge of the Chemical and the Service Company organizations. The mix of the team should provide the benefits of different perspectives on Shell Companies, different approaches, and different access to the various parts of the overall system.

Three senior O.D. consultants were operating within the Service Companies at this time. One, the external, had a long relationship with the Chemical Co-ordinator while the other two internal consultants had clients or ex-clients in the Chemical organization.

This trio met, some two months before the general announcements of the change, to discuss the implications of the pending developments on their own working relationship (they had not previously worked together as a team) and for the client system and O.D. support. The scale of the professional challenge and its complexities was becoming clearer. The team was faced with the need to weld itself quickly into a cohesive unit which maximized the benefit to the client of the different approaches and experiences available.

Discussions were needed to develop trust and understanding of each other and also to establish the ground rules of operation (see Table 3).

Table 3   O.D. operating principles

- A common vision that this assignment would represent a major learning opportunity both for O.D. and the Shell Companies
- Consultants to operate together with business leader (the Chemical Co-ordinator) as a team
- Consultants to build on existing relationships
- Target new clients agreed and responsibilities allocated matching as much as possible experience and acceptability
- Allocation of areas of responsibility to match as closely as possible existing O.D. roles and remits
- Regular joint planning and review meetings
- Team to invest time in maintaining itself and sharing learning
- Maintenance of one master file
- A focal point within the team for written communication with the client system
- Acceptance of the client's plans/proposals/policies as a start position with the O.D. emphasis on process
- Adoption of an enabling strategy for the client based on learning through review

---

The preparation of these principles was no mean feat. Each consultant was in a new position and territories and interests were being protected. Nevertheless, an approach to the Chemical Co-ordinator was agreed and arrangements were made for the O.D. team to meet with him to discuss ideas based on the 'enabling strategy' worked out by the team and described below.

The mine field

At the first meeting with the Co-ordinator some of the challenges and risks became clearer. Owing to the business pressures the management had been forced into a position totally alien to their normal approach and were feeling considerably exposed.

In terms of preparation for the change, the organization study had been carried out by a small elite team which:

(a) due to the need for rapid decisions had not had time to involve more than the top level of management sufficiently to gain full understanding of or commitment to the details of the proposals with the organization;

Table 4   Main targets/objectives

Business/O.D. target areas	Objectives
Overall business strategy	● Immediately after implementing the organizational changes an in-depth business review across the total Chemicals sector would be a priority
Service company roles and organization	● Improved overall business co-ordination ● Accountability for central trading ● Integrated strategy development
Staff levels	● Overhead costs reduction ● Re-allocation of resources
Operating companies relationships	● More independence and local autonomy ● Strengthen appraisal and support mechanisms ● Improved mechanisms for conflict resolution

(b) recommended major changes in philosophy, organization, and resource levels to be implemented simultaneously; and

(c) gave little guidance on implementation in the recommendations.

In terms of change management experience the main observations were that:

(a) no senior manager had been around during the previous major reorganization and rundown some 12 years before;

(b) certain key managers had been in positions for less than two years; and

(c) the O.D. support team had never worked together.

As the meeting with the Co-ordinator progressed, the extent of the risks became apparent as, for the first time, client and consultants shared their understanding of what had to be done. The complete transition to the new organization was to take five months from the first general announcement. Staff with no jobs would have to be retained for up to 13 months while efforts would be made to redeploy them.

All major relationships and systems world-wide would be affected. There were four prime target areas, each with distinct multiple objectives which had to be achieved in varying time frames. Table 4 shows the main targets for the business and hence the O.D. support. Since the targets correlated closely with roles implied in the new organization structure, a consistency was found between the proposals for O.D. support and the above aims of the business. The whole process would be monitored and co-ordinated through client/O.D. team meetings, internal progress reviews within the management team, and by six-monthly overall progress reviews throughout the entire organization.

The basis for these reviews was the enabling strategy which the O.D. team had put together in their earlier discussions. This is reproduced in Figure 4.

This diagram was produced in chart form and the intention had been to take the Co-ordinator through the various streams and levels of activity required for adequate control: Tasks, Processes, Information, Communications, Systems, etc. The plan was accepted in principle; however, it was judged more appropriate to keep it discrete because of a need to get into early action rather than into further consultation on planning. An opportunity would be sought to introduce the plan in response to emerging problems. The first priority, to deal with the staff reduction problem, was already underway. The second priority was to establish an overall communication to the staff who would be affected.

With an unknown number of staff about to lose their jobs (in the event a reduction of 25% in job stock was achieved) and with the bulk of the Service Company roles being changed, the priority was to gear up to handle the displaced staff in as humane, responsible, and professional manner as possible. This preoccupation with staffing matters was to last for about five months. Details of some of the initiatives taken in this key area appear in Appendix A.

Communication to staff in a multinational organization is never easy. In this case the situation was compounded by having major groups based in London and The Hague, in addition to many staff on secondment to Shell Operating Companies around the world (some 50 companies both wholly and jointly owned). It was agreed that senior management should give formal presentations in London and The Hague; the same text and the same handout material would be sent to all Chemicals-based staff around the world. The presentations took place in the Companies' theatres to audiences of 300 plus. The O.D. team contributed to the design of the presentation which dealt with:

- the state of the business;
- the aims of the changes;
- new structure;
- implementation plans;
- staff issues;
- questions and discussion.

These public sessions clearly confirmed staff fears but, as is usual in such large gatherings, most concern remained unvoiced. The frustration and the dismay had to be dealt with by the individual members of the management team. Questions emerged about:

(a) the validity of the new organization in light of the needs of the European Chemical business for central co-ordination;

(b) the 'sell out' (as it was described) of past beliefs by senior management;

(c) the staff selection processes.

The battleground was now visible, the management team was under attack and some were feeling vulnerable. A cohesive and co-ordinated approach was

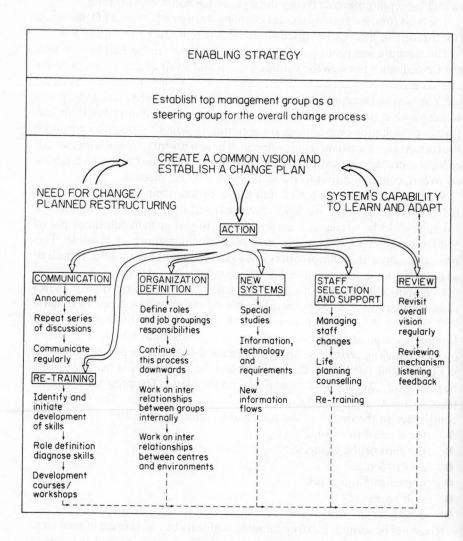

Figure 4   O.D. team's concept of an enabling strategy

eeded—but how was it to be achieved? The main thrust focused on staff matters nd ensuring a consistent approach across the organization. This was not easy, ut was achieved, as described in Appendix A. A consistent approach to the usiness development was to take much longer to achieve.

In order to provide for as much cohesion as possible a Steering Group was set up consisting of the management team, the three O.D. consultants, and the manager with overall responsibility for staff redeployment. Its role is ummarized in Appendix B.

Pre-emptive strike

The initial set of plans for implementation had established February 1982 as the launch date for the new organization. The five-month period from announcement to establishment had been chosen to allow time for detailed organization design to take place and also to enable the personnel agreements with staff and policies to be applied.

Within a few weeks of the announcement of the proposed changes it became clear that the new trading activities would need to be established well before the end of the five-month period. The market-place was changing very rapidly and a long period of internal uncertainty could adversely affect Shell Companies' position and market share.

Setting up the international trading division thus became a priority and its launch was brought forward six weeks.

From a business point of view the decision was clearly correct and the pre-emptive launch became a focal point for the whole change process in relation to the outside world. However, it did also highlight the conflicts existing either openly or covertly. This is illustrated in Table 5.

This situation became apparent through the work of the O.D. team and caused the Chemical Co-ordinator to impose further ground rules. The priorities of managing the staff situation fairly, plus the business priority of establishing the trader organization, were to be maintained.

The need for regular and systematic reviews was established to avoid private frustrations inhibiting the overall plan.

Thus, the need for a pre-emptive launch of the trading organization enabled the O.D. team to demonstrate the need for an overall campaign plan to which the whole leadership team could be committed. This emerging campaign plan (see Table 6) matched closely with the enabling strategy (Figure 4) which had been developed some three months earlier. The emerging plan, however, was seen as being born of the experience of the organization and therefore was readily accepted as being appropriate. Since the content was therefore familiar to management the O.D. consultants took the initiative to move the debate to the level of process.

Campaign process reviews

The emerging campaign plan provided an opportunity for the O.D. and management team to take stock. The original concerns about a revolutionary versus an evolutionary approach were being confirmed; the need for an overall change plan was highlighted; the demands for coherent consistency within the top management team were emerging and the value of review was established.

Table 5   Conflicts

New line management aims	Personnel management aims	Staff aims
● To get on with implementation	● To create a 'felt fair' system for dealing with staff	● To reduce personal uncertainty but still adhere to the voluntary severance scheme
● To secure their own divisions and the best staff possible	● To maintain consistency across divisions	● To understand the direction of the changes
● To design and implement new organizations	● To apply the rules fairly	● To ensure open management
● To minimize the business risk	● To ensure the use of staff consultation machinery	● To be involved in the design work
● To keep their staff plans confidential but deal fairly with the staff	● To achieve redeployment of all staff displaced	● To contribute to the decision-making
Resulting in feelings of:		
● Frustration	● Isolation	● Ambiguity
● Anxiety	● Blame	● Uncertainty
● Responsibility	● Overload	● Fear
● Challenge	● Defensiveness	● Betrayal

As mentioned above, the commitment to systematic reviews was an agreement in principle, it was important to prove the value of review in fact. The original campaign plan had identified that early in the implementation phase leadership would be key, beyond that and further into implementation common understanding and consistency would be tested, and inevitably towards the year end overall sector implications could be significant. Hence, the structuring of the data gathering and the organization of the review conferences was seen to be crucial (see Table 7).

Table 6   Emerging campaign plan

Priorities		
Tasks	Process	
	Management Steering Group	O.D. team
● Overall co-ordination of changes	● Monthly progress reviews ● In-depth reviews scheduled throughout year, post-implementation (1 month/3 months/10 months)	● Sensing progress ● Feedback to client ● Develop review proposals ● Gather data, interpret, and present
● Rigorous application of staff selection process and policies	● Categorization of staff ● Listing of candidates ● Pre-discussions between functional heads	● Support to personnel function on methodology
● Establishing support networks for displaced staff	● Communication to individuals ● Redeployment help ● Counselling	● Process consultation to personnel steering group ● Counselling service network ● Design training for redeployment
● Regular communication to staff and with staff representative structure	● Policy of only communicating decisions and plans ● Staff council role established ● Plan of meetings established	● Guidance on communication and managing feedback
● Establishing trading concept and organization	● Agree trading role/policy/guidelines ● Relationships with Operating Companies—central and direct trading	● New concept development with management team ● Trading ground rules—advice on process ● Understanding/ relationship building with Operating Companies

Table 7   Review process

Months into implementation	Anticipated focus of review	Data-gathering
1 (initial)	Leadership performance	From members of team
4 (interim)	Team cohesion and common understanding and divisional progress	From members of team and next level down
10 (year end)	Total sector implications and critical interfaces	Total Chemicals sector

Initial review

The reviews were special management team events, with no other agenda items. The reviews were held 'off-site'.

Each session was processed by the O.D. team and each session moved the implementation progress forward considerably. Extracts from the first review session are shown in Tables 8 and 9.

The first session, with its emphasis on challenge and questioning of the leadership, provided a jolt to the whole relationship of O.D. to senior management. The discussion focused on two major topics.

(1) The leadership style and behaviour (Table 8).
(2) The overall change strategy and the progress to date (Table 9).

The first item proved to be a priority issue—the pressure for public cohesion being apparent—and yet doubts about the overall direction still prevailed particularly in the context of the business which had to be carried out 'as usual', in a difficult economic climate!

The emphasis on team cohesion reflected clearly the impact on senior management of a period of high uncertainty and conflicting demands. The business required speedy reactions, rapid transitions, and minimum disturbance, while the described reorganization strategy, which included the lengthy

Table 8   The leadership team—how we see ourselves

● Lack of listening
● Low valuing of each other
● Limited trust and mutual respect
● Divisive polarizing of issues
● No challenge/risk-taking
● Superficial co-operation
● Lack of structure and meeting disciplines
● Consisting of individuals who succeeded within the previous organization philosophy
● Coming out of a difficult and demanding period with widely varying aims
● Being pressurized to address significant and different strategic issues

voluntary severence scheme, required a slow transformation. The concept of evolution and revolution is easier to hold in balance in the mind rather than in practice. The situation was recognized, but the pressures on management were still associated with task and getting things done. Thus, although process problems were now 'on the table' the focus was still on task. It was not until the third review, ten months after implementation, that the team faced up to the issues which underpinned the contents of Table 8. These statements are taken from a flip chart used during the review.

Table 9 was produced for the first review by the O.D. team as an overhead projector slide to show the 'credibility gap' which had occurred between what the

Table 9   Two views of a change experience

Desired (evolution)	Actual (revolution)
● Agreeing on the need for change	● The business need $\Big\{$ Prescribed Unco-ordinated Conflicting ● People's needs
● Building a common vision of the future	● Primary effort into gaining acceptance of new organization
● Agreeing the underlying goals of change and communicating these	● Consultation and running the business inhibited by constraints of voluntary severance scheme
● Achieving planned change	● Primary effort into following personnel guidelines
● Agreeing on a consistent leadership approach	● Limited discussion on communication plan
● Gaining commitment and understanding	● Parochial quick selling with mixed quality of consultation down the line
● Implementing in a consistent manner	● Very limited cohesion
● Reviewing progress and building our capacity to manage change and plan for improvement based on experience and learning	● Reviews planned but not implemented
● Learning and improving	● No attempt to learn

leaders had stated would and should happen in change situations (evolution) and what had actually been perceived by them to happen in this current change (revolution).

The difference was clearly recognized as being uncomfortable and inappropriate.

The O.D. team's posture of higher challenge resulted in a vigorous response from the management team questioning both the data and the interpretation. Issues were raised, questions left unanswered. O.D. was at risk, but a stand had been made. The eventual pay-off quickly surfaced as a questioning of the issues began to reinforce the need for team cohesion.

Table 10   Internal functioning—key dynamics

---

1. *Environment*
   There are a number of growing discrepancies between our developing understanding of our role and environmental expectation. Insufficient effort is being dedicated to creating a better match.
2. *Strengths*
   The organization is settling down well and the anticipated advantages are beginning to show. Success is being attributed to quality of staff rather than quality of concept.
3. *Weaknesses*
   Most deficiencies attributable to newness of the operation. Given time and a commitment to monitor and tune the organization the weaknesses can be overcome.
4. *Opportunities*
   The important opportunities are at the interface with operating companies and industry. Currently our energies are directed at systems and procedures and internal operation.

The interim review

Four months after the establishment of the new organization, a second review was held. Building on the experience of the first review, in which some of the contentious issues raised had been challenged, a more systematic approach was followed. The O.D. team gathered data from within all the divisions and functions and designed a two-day review for the Co-ordinator's team. A set of questions was used as the basis for the data collection. This is reproduced in Appendix C.

Table 10 shows a typical summary of the views of one division. Internally, operations were improving rapidly, but from 1, and 4, it is clear that the boundaries and interfaces were becoming a problem, as anticipated by the O.D. team in their enabling strategy (see Figure 4).

The review highlighted a number of areas in which insufficient progress was being made. Some of these are shown in Table 11. These were addressed and action taken to overcome the problems.

By the end of the year the internal organization was beginning to function with

Table 11   Pockets of resistance and barriers to progress

- Mixed commitment to viability of new approach
- Management giving mixed messages
- Far too much on management's plate
- People still trying to do old things/haven't grasped the significance of the changes
- Leadership vacillating between an autocratic and a participative style
- Total Chemical sector needs to be educated on changes which affect not only the central organization but the operating companies
- Black and white thinking in addressing crucial grey areas, especially with regard to operational implications of overall concept

---

sufficient consistency for management to be able to see where further tuning was required to get the balance correct internally. Some activities were seen to be under-resourced.

There were still, however, the major external interfaces to be reviewed. Among these were the key ones with the Chemical Operating Companies around the world, the market-place, and the rest of industry. The complexity of the interfaces is best appreciated diagrammatically, as shown in Figure 5.

Year-end review

In a final review session the interfaces were addressed.

The intent of the review was to focus on the impact on the total Chemicals

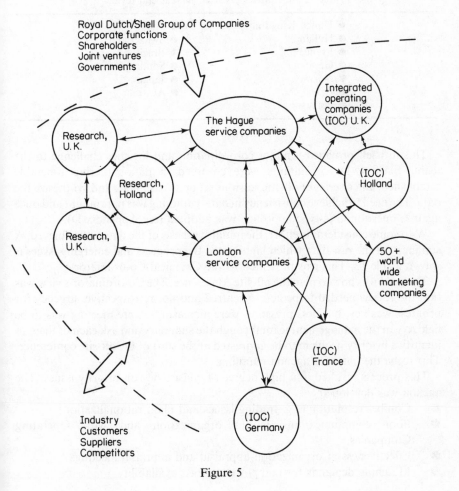

Figure 5

sector—an ambitious and novel challenge. Data was to be gathered from deep in the Service Company organization, from some staff not consulted previously; from a sample of integrated and marketing Operating Companies; and from the R&D laboratories. The scale of the task is illustrated in Table 12.

The O.D. team wished to achieve two things by this review:

(1) a transfer of responsibility to the line to review progress and learn; and

(2) a shift in emphasis from reviewing an organization change to considering the capability of the total sector to plan and adapt to the major business rationalization challenges ahead.

The first point was to be only partially achieved since senior management wished to maintain the services of O.D. in data-gathering and synthesis.

Table 12   Countries involved in year-end review

● United Kingdom	● Spain
● Holland	● Switzerland
● France	● Brazil
● Germany	● South Africa
● Norway	● Japan
● Italy	● Australia
● Portugal	

This in itself provided a major co-ordination and logistics challenge to the team. Extra O.D. consultants were co-opted, a data-gathering timetable established, and a series of off-site sessions set up to assimilate and synthesize the data. The need to achieve consistency in data-gathering was paramount and once again a questionnaire-type approach was adopted (see Appendix D).

With some considerable effort, the initial synthesis of the data was achieved. A summary of the raw data which highlighted the progress and emerging issues is shown Table 13. This was presented to the Chemical Co-ordinator.

The need was now to plan the off-site conference. The Co-ordinator's view was that the review needed to be action centred and not retrospective, urgency for progress was key, business pressures were increasing. A pre-meeting was to be held to run the management team through the summary and ask each of them to identify a priority problem to be addressed at the start of the off-site conference. This to be the basis for agenda planning.

This process resulted in a high degree of consistency on priority issues. The agenda was developed:

● Conflict resolution (e.g. trading issues and plant rationalization).

● Poor communications within organization and with Operating Companies.

● Effectiveness of organization appraisal and appraisal meetings.

● Matching demands for manpower against availability.

● Market quality: is it a long- or short-term issue and who should deal with it, the traders or the strategists?
● Management information mismatch with the roles of the functions.
● Reintegration of divisions (horizontal)—how to get teams working across the sector.
● R&D interface and the balance between innovative research and product development.

The outcome of the review was a series of actions based on a new consensus of what had to be done. This included a new agreement on the way the senior management team should operate and a timetable to ensure that issues were not left by the wayside.

The O.D. team was charged with ensuring that all matters raised by contributers to the review were addressed.

Table 13   Year-end review

Original aims of change	Example of progress	Typical emerging issues
Development of integrated strategies	● Major strategic issues identified ● New strategy development methodology providing common language across businesses	● Strategy implementation presenting a new challenge ● Co-ordinating and integrating meetings needing wider representation
Integrated approach to business appraisal and development	● Positive response from Operating Companies ● Planning cycle meshing better with business processes	● Appraisal function is under-resourced ● Information requirements
Separate central trading identity	● Improved market discipline ● Growing expertise and a focus for a third party supply	● Dichotomy between short- and long-term market objectives ● Higher market visibility required
Strengthening of service and advisory role	● Focus on cost savings and efficiency seen as highly valuable	● An information vacuum developing between manufacturing and marketing oriented functions
Improved mechanisms for conflict resolution	● Time being invested across boundaries ● Staff communication meetings developing well	● Risk-taking still low ● Short-term conflict resolution mechanisms still absent, e.g. product pricing

Feedback procedures to all participants were agreed and follow-up contracts established with some clients as a result of the discussions.

This chapter was written just after this review had been completed. The O.D. team will now go on to consider its longer-term (next three years) position vis-à-vis the major client system in the light of a rich harvest of data and learning.

The spoils of revolution

The future for the petrochemicals business is still uncertain, as is the whole international economy. Those aspects of the Shell Companies' Chemical business were not changed by the revolution.

So what has changed? In essence, a lot.

First, Shell Companies now have a new integrated strategy for their Chemical business.

Second, Shell Companies now have a leaner more efficient Service Company organization.

Third, the organization has under its belt a rich store of change management experience upon which it can draw as it seeks to move forward into a new phase for its business.

And finally, it has the confidence that comes from taking high risk successfully and as such recognizing that different leadership options are available.

These changes are the spoils of revolution, but they were not gained without cost.

So far we have described those aspects of the overall strategy perceived from a leadership standpoint. Some emphasis has been given to the impact on the staff involved. The bias has been towards the leadership challenge—revolution or evolution to achieve business survival? The role of O.D. has been illustrated—but what are the overall lessons?

Memoirs of a war veteran team

Mao Tse-tung's comment on revolutionary processes is perhaps the most appropriate way to introduce this section:

'A revolution is not a dinner party ... it cannot be so refined, so leisurely and gentle ... a revolution is an insurrection, an act of violence.'

The experiences gained from the change programme described in this chapter cause the writers to agree with the late great leader but, unlike him, the writers would be less ready to support continuous revolution. Nevertheless, clearly many of today's businesses will require to leave the textbook for the trenches and O.D. practitioners need to be ready to take their positions in the front line of revolutionary change.

For those who may wish, or be forced, to follow where we have been, and for those who have gone before us, we record our observations in Table 14.

Revolution brings resentment

Revolutionary change can be expected to produce much greater levels of conflict than an evolutionary process. Solutions are seen to be imposed and/or inappropriate. Resistance is high and lengthy periods of denial and resentment occur. The leadership becomes split between the inner cabinet of the revolution and the rear guard. 'Honest brokers', for example, finance management and personnel management quickly become casualties as they attempt to find consensus between the warring groups.

However, in the ranks the range of feelings widens to cover total confusion, disorientation, and withdrawal.

Table 14   Some observations on a revolutionary change process

1. Revolution brings resentment
2. Management energy goes into reducing guilt
3. Different leadership approaches will emerge and can be valid
4. Managers privately seek ways forward
5. Fragmentation occurs
6. Change planning becomes a priority
7. Review is a basis for co-ordination
8. Learning begins to surface after success/progress
9. Revolutions are not all 'bad things'

For O.D. the message is clear. This resentment phase seems to be unavoidable by definition, therefore:

● Confront management with it as a challenge.
● Act as channels for the resentment, spending time with those managers experiencing the greatest difficulty.
● Attempt to enable management to create distance between feelings and tasks so that both may be managed.
● Recognize those in the organization whose resentment is justified and help develop strategies which encourage the issues to be raised, and through time to be resolved.
● Accept that urgent business reappraisal will be more frequently needed; action rather than debate is a way forward.

Management energy goes into reducing guilt

Acceptance of the inevitability of the revolution by the leaders and led in management seems to give way to conflicting responses in which attempts are made to alleviate some of the pain and reduce the number of casualties, whilst at the same time pushing forward with the revolution. The conflict appears to be born out of a need to find common ground in the total leadership team. Having found a common cause—in this instance, top management's responsibility to their staff—much energy can be directed toward this. Members of the management group who are totally opposed to the overall change can be accommodated as long as they are seen to be 'doing the best thing for their people'. Differences at the macro business level are submerged, but failure to adhere at the personnel level (the common good) is not acceptable.

There is a great danger in this phase to the success of the change. Attention is directed away from the major conflicts and the opposition, if it so wishes, has time to regroup.

For O.D. the main thrust must be toward maintaining a balance of focus in the leadership between those issues which unite them and those which divide.

Different leadership approaches will emerge and can be valid

The wide range of management styles and motivations present in most large organizations means that the personal leadership behaviour of key managers varies enormously.

The degree of concern felt for subordinates and the degree of personal risk experienced are two of the main criteria used by managers to assess what actions they should take in terms of their own areas of responsibility. Some will adopt a high task profile, seeking to 'keep the organization busy'; others will take a more philosophical approach and let the organization talk around the situation, allowing a venting of emotion and attempting to provide a supportive, understanding environment. Others will take a highly personalized view of the situation, assessing it in terms of personal opportunity or threat.

The opportunity to reflect back to the various parts of the organization the behaviour being adopted proved useful later when process plans were being developed since managers were more aware of where their organizations were as a result of the leadership style adopted.

Managers privately seek ways forward

Very early on in the change programme the O.D. consultants were approached by some of the senior managers as the implications of the changes began to be assessed. A simplistic view that managers need to fit the same mould in order to achieve consistency is dangerous.

Issues raised included: 'How does my management style fit with a major change?' 'How do I get my new team together to create a change steering group?' 'What do I do about the casualties in my area?' 'How do I handle the disagreement in my organization?' 'What do I do about my own negative views of the proposed changes?' The emphasis on individual leadership capability appears to be key to the re-establishment of credibility and future influence in revolutionary change situations.

For some this phase is open within their management team, for others the process is a one-to-one exploration with the O.D. consultant. It is important to give space to the client to decide which approach to adopt.

This is a critical phase in the client/consultant relationship.

Fragmentation occurs

With parts of the organization supportive of the change and actively seeking ways forward, and others still being led by rear-guard managers, the business quickly enters a dysfunctional phase characterized by a lack of synchronized communication, breakdown of systems, and premature initiatives. Pressure for conformity can arise which can constrain those with concerns from expressing them openly.

In organizations with a functional orientation the finance and personnel functions are usually the first to attract attention due to the extended lead times necessary for systems and staff changes. Marketing and trading activities, as in this case, frequently lead the developments because of their boundaries with the environment and their fast response culture. The justification of protecting the business and getting into action can result in insufficient attention being given to key internal interfaces.

In market-orientated parts of the organization the initiatives tend to be taken by the managers closest to boundaries with the outside world. A differentiation occurs also between the levels of the organization. Middle management tends to be squeezed between the 'young turks' and the leaders, whether reactionary or supportive. Split loyalties can occur in those who need to support the change in order to introduce confidence and certainty in their subordinates, whilst still wishing to question the validity of the changes with their peers and leaders.

This seems to be one of the major disadvantages of the revolutionary approach: there is simply not enough time availble to ensure that all parts move forward in a committed, coherent manner.

Change planning becomes a priority

The fragmentation can be used as an opportunity for the O.D. staff to demonstrate the need for coherence and consistency throughout the period.

The need for a process plan, i.e. a plan which sets out the 'hows' of the change, is often viewed by the organization as unnecessary. The conflict that the fragmentation generates, however, is a sharp reminder of the value of change planning.

The time horizon over which management is willing to plan seems to be foreshortened by the revolution mode. The concept of rapid structural change appears incompatible with change management plans extending much beyond the implementation date. Thus, a two- or three-phase approach may require to be used in change planning. The first phase will focus on the 'parts of the organization which have experienced the major change'. A second phase may be needed to gain commitment for a broader plan embracing 'those parts which the revolution did not reach', while a third phase may have to be proposed before boundaries and interfaces are accepted as being legitimate areas to be included in a change management process.

Review is a basis for co-ordination

In the initial period of the revolution the levels of uncertainty are very high and there is little flexibility in attitude. The leaders are uncertain of the level of support/resistance which will be encountered, and at lower levels the challenge of the prospect of new tasks/responsibilities/relationships can be quite threatening. Hence, the introduction of learning as a technique for managing the change should be delayed until success can be demonstrated in major sections of the organization. In large-scale changes this low learning capacity phase is likely to last for at least six months, and in some areas closely linked to long cycle activities, e.g. planning and finance, the phase may be measured in years rather than months. In a multinational organization the capacity for common learning is further frustrated.

A success-orientated focus by the O.D. staff seems therefore to be called for if the learning capacity of the organization is to be enhanced. Emphasis on spreading understanding both of successes and failures seems to lead to a more cohesive response across large systems.

Revolutions are not all 'bad things'

The ability of this and other major organizations to turn the business around by radical restructuring in short periods of time with O.D. help raises a number of interesting issues, not least of which is the value of breaking the normal patttern of change management. Many of the esteemed principles of traditional, textbook, good management theory have had to be broken in the last two years and new patterns of behaviour have emerged as viable and valuable in the industrial wastelands that used to represent the apex of developed societies. But will the new patterns of behaviour last? Where is the counter-revolution developing? It may be in the unacceptably high levels of the unemployed. It may be in further energy supply shocks. It may be in the growing view that the whole of the twentieth century to date has been one big revolution which is fast running out of purpose. Whatever the future, this one little revolution was not all bad, many individuals and the businesses have survived and come through the experience stronger and with clearer purpose.

Postscript: Revolution as a feature of evolution

A danger of using models and theories as a basis for learning is that most models and theories are not sufficiently comprehensive to embrace the experience or environment of the student. The evolution of theory is in itself an interesting study. Darwin's theory of evolution has undergone many transitions and modifications, one of which postulates the theory of 'punctuated evolution'. In the model the normal evolutionary process is interrupted ('punctuated') by bursts of rapid change and development—a revolution within evolution. Such periods of rapid changes are short lived, in the evolutionary time frame that is, and development quickly returns to the normal slow process.

It would seem possible to extend this model to modern-day organizations and to borrow the term 'punctuated development' as being descriptive of the change process described in this chapter.

From experience it is possible to outline the nature of this phenomenon. Punctuated development is:

(1) A response to an unusual environmental state or opportunity.
(2) Short lived in terms of the history of the organization.
(3) A significant change for the organization.
(4) Accompanied by a high risk of failure.
(5) Experienced as a revolution.

The question is raised as to the applicability of the model to the organization change process. How long can this punctuated phase be maintained? Reference to Figure 6 indicates that the experience gained in this study would suggest that the transition point from revolution back to evolution is somewhere around stage 5: 'Gaining understanding and commitment'—beyond this point real progress cannot be guaranteed under the revolutionary mode.

The 'punctuated development' model fits more consistently with the experience of organization changes described in the literature than an 'evolutionary' model. If this is true then it may be that O.D. as a discipline is about to experience its own punctuation marks!

Epilogue

When in 1981 we decided to change the organization of the Shell Chemical Service Company in London into one which would be more in line with the changed chemical industry environment—especially in the United Kingdom and N.W. Europe—we realized that we would enter a difficult period. The old organization was geared for growth. However, by the late 1970s there were more and more signs that the chemical industry had become more and more mature and was showing little sign of further growth.

For the new organiztion we were looking for a more effective set-up to service our existing operations and one which was able to give a quick response to a

PUNCTUATED DEVELOPMENT		
Change phases	Revolution features	Evolution features
1. Establishing the need	• Conflict and mixed commitment	• Sharing awareness
2. Creating a common vision	• Imposed 'solution'	• Exploring implications
3. Defining aims and principles	• Minimizing casulties among supporters	• Establishing criteria for the change based on personal values
4. Accepting leadership responsibility	• Assessment of personal risk	• Facing up to my responsibilty/ my challenge/ my values
5. Gaining understanding and commitment	• Coerced conformity	• Developing localized initiatives
	Return to evolution ?	
6. Reviewing readiness	• Opportunism	• Preparing coherent process plan
7. Implementing	• Rigid adherence to the programme	• Phasing/ controlling implementation
8. Reviewing performance	• Dealing with the resistance	• Tackling unfinished business
9. Learning and improving	• Indoctrination and suppression	• Valuing and learning from the experience

Figure 6

rapidly changing environment. We set out to obtain a more functional organization which would be able to protect our existing business. Our London operations were seen to serve three roles: that of service to our Operating Companies in both the petrochemicals and speciality chemicals fields; that of our international trading, either intra-group or to third parties on strict commercial terms; and lastly that as the representative of the shareholder in appraising the Operating Companies of their performance in protection of our assets and defence of our business.

In the old matrix organization with business divisions these roles had been somewhat confused and consequently more clarity was sought. In the development of the new organization and in its implementation it became clear that less staff were required. The reduction of staff was dealt with by a voluntary severance scheme, which by its nature took a relatively long time to achieve the desired results.

We therefore had a clear conflict of interest: we wanted to start the new organization as quickly as possible to protect our business, while, on the other hand, we had a long period of surplus staff with no proper jobs.

We therefore decided on extensive O.D. assistance for this transition period.

Looking back at this period of about one year, it can be said that although the strategies/plans on which we started the change had to be modified all along, the process, although considerably time-consuming, was continuous, and led to the stated objective of a new organization, settled in by mid-1982, while protecting our business and with due concern for the fate of the surplus staff. Although finally a 25% reduction of staff was obtained, nearly all of them who needed and wished to have another job were placed, either within the Shell Group of Companies or outside. This enabled us in the end to maintain the morale of the staff, although we went through some deep troughs.

London,   M. J. Waale
U.K.   Chemicals Co-ordinator
May, 1983

Appendix A: Management of staff support

As from the date of the announcement of the changes a Manpower Support Group was established. This consisted of three experienced managers, one senior line manager, and two personnel managers. Its major function was to assist the process of placing as many of the displaced staff as possible in alternative employment, both internally and externally.

Basically, the activities of the Manpower Support Group fell into two major phases of work. Phase A covered the period from announcement of the changes to the establishment of the new organization, a period of five months. Phase B covered the period from establishment through to the end of the 13-month period required by the Company personnel policies to seek redeployment.

Phase A activities

(i) A notification system for vacancies opening up within Shell Companies, both in Shell Centre and with operating companies, was established by the Task Group. This was relatively successful in that the number of vacancies notified up to the end of the five months totalled 111 and it proved possible for the Task

Group to put forward a total of 101 candidates for interview. By the end of phase A, 56 internal transfers had been effected.

(ii) Applications for voluntary severance during phase A were processed by the Task Group. These totalled 40 when the scheme as such ended. Some applicants were also assisted in relation to post-severance employment.

(iii) The Task Group channelled staff interested in leaving the service of Shell Companies to additional services and facilities specially available to staff, e.g. access to the various job training and support networks which exist in the outside world, secretarial, and counselling services. These additional facilities were provided through an 'Opportunity Centre'.

(iv) Overseas Shell Companies with Chemical operations—in particular Canada, South Africa, Australia and New Zealand—were visited and a certain amount of success was achieved in placing a small number of staff in some of these companies.

(v) *First interview.* By the end of phase A each person who had not been placed in the new organization was interviewed by a member of the Task Group in order to establish that the individual:

●   understood the situation;
●   understood the next sequence of events;
●   understood what it was he should be doing;
●   understood what help was available.

It was also planned to give details of a new training programme designed for staff facing redundancy, but in the event the course was not run as such owing to the success of the other measures which left insufficient numbers to warrant a special programme.

Phase B activities

At the close of phase A staff not placed in the new Chemicals organization, and who had not been offered alternative employment within the Shell Companies, were formally informed of the situation. Indication was given that the company would continue its efforts to find a suitable position for each person.

Phase B, therefore, continued the activities of the phase A, although the efforts were to be geared towards helping the reducing number of employees that were facing a possible redundancy situation. In addition, 25% of the employees that had accepted voluntary severance terms decided to seek subsequent employment outside Shell Companies and therefore availed themselves of the resources established to assist existing staff. This phase also included a programme of regular contacts in the form of debriefing and feedback sessions and interviews aimed at ensuring that the employee was fully equipped to deal with his/her developing situation.

(i) *Second interview.* Three months into phase B members of staff still unplaced met their line managers. This interview was designed to:

- check progress on internal vacancies, nominations, and interviews;
- hear from the line manager a realistic assessment of the chances of internal placement;
- receive verbally and in writing from the line manager the notice of redundancy;
- hear from the member of staff of any need or help that might be required;
- check the general state of the member of staff in terms of morale and capability.

(ii) *Third interview.* A third set of interviews was conducted by the Support Group six months into phase B to ascertain:

- the level of success in finding new opportunities;
- the general state of morale and capability;
- what further guidance or help was required;
- hear from the staff of their activities and advise on what else might be done or considered.

(iii) *Fourth interview.* This took place within four weeks of termination of employment. It was conducted by a member of the Task Group and sought to establish that the member of staff:

- had a clear view of what action he/she would take in the future in relation to job search;
- was in possession of all the relevant facts, knowledge, and skill that could be made available to him/her.

(iv) *Fifth interview.* During the last week of employment the member of staff was seen by the line manager and the personnel manager in order that all the necessary formalities were completed.

Appendix B: The steering group

The responsibilities of the Steering Group were, briefly, as follows.

(1) The co-ordination of the implementation of designated processes and procedures previously prepared. These include the principal organizational changes and the new divisional arrangements.

(2) General monitoring of the change process, including identification of areas which are not progressing as planned. Furthermore, analysis of the reasons for any deviations followed by decisions in order to correct or confirm any changes in the processes and procedures.

(3) The approval of the detailed description of the roles and activities of the new divisions in the organization.

(4) The monitoring of financial aspects of the reorganization.

(5) The approval of communications and communication processes to all staff.

(6) The consideration and analysis of the information needs of the new organizations.

(7) The preparation and implementation of specific practices to be adopted in line with the general policies toward staff in terms of voluntary severance, redeployment, redundancy, and the recruitment of the existing staff into the new organization. In particular, the selection of staff 'essential' to the new organization, and overall responsibility for the pool of staff available to it.

(8) The approval of the office facilities and services as required by the new organization.

Appendix C: Mid-year review questionnaire

Questions for service companies

Referring back to the aims of change in the light of experience over the last few months:

1. What examples can you give of *progress*:
    (a) within your own area;
    (b) across the Service Company as a whole; and
    (c) with the Operating Companies?
2. What have been the main *challenges/difficulties* which
    (a) you have encountered
    (b) you perceive
    in progressing towards the achievement of the above aims of change? What steps have you taken or plan to take to overcome these?
3. What have been the *major adjustments* you have had to make personally to match the expectations of the new organization? What further help/training do you judge you and your staff will need to make the necessary adjustments?
4. What, therefore, in your judgement are the key factors *helping* and *hindering the change process*?
5. In the light of your responses to the above, what do you believe should be the *priorities*:
    (a) for yourself
    (b) for your team
    (c) for the leadership group
    to progress the changes within the next six months?
6. Considering the changing business environment and the emerging business objectives, what do you anticipate will need to be done during 1983 in order to create:
    (a) a viable business; and
    (b) an organization approach consistent with that?
7. What is your assessment of the *commitment* to and the *viability* of the new organization structure and philosophy?

3. What *lessons* would you draw from the way the changes have been managed?

Appendix D: Year-end review

Questions for operating companies

1. How do you perceive the way the changes in the Chemicals organization are working?
2. How do you perceive your relationships with different parts of the organization at the Centre? How are they working?
3. In terms of the aims of the new organization, what examples can you give of progress?
4. What examples can you give of conflict?
5. Looking ahead, what potential strengths and/or weaknesses do you see in the organization's ability to cope with future pressures?
6. Are there any aspects which you think have been missed in making these changes?
7. How has the planning/appraisal cycle been this year? Different? Better? Worse?
8. In terms of enhancing the Chemicals organization's capacity to achieve the aims set for the reorganization, what are the priorities for action?

Theme for central offices

The review has as its theme 'capability'. In essence we are seeking to 'assess how well we are doing now as a Chemical sector in enhancing our capability to create and deal with business opportunities today and tomorrow'.

References

Hill, P. (1976) *Towards a New Philosophy of Management* (London).
Mao Tse-tung (1927) 'An investigation of the peasant movement in Hunan', in *Selected Works*, vol. 4, p. 28, Foreign Language Press, Peking, 1972.
Morley, J. (1874) 'On compromise'. Quotation taken from Stevenson, B. E., *Book of Quotations*, 10th edn., Cassell, London, 1974.

People and Organizations Interacting
Edited by A. Brakel
© 1985, John Wiley & Sons Ltd.

Chapter 8

Organization design in Canada: Shell Canada's Sarnia Chemical Plant

Norman Halpern

Background

This case description is related to a Shell Canada chemical plant which came on-stream in early 1979. The facility, built at a cost in excess of $200 million, is designed to produce 70,000 tonnes/yr of polypropylene and 91,000 tonnes/yr of iso-propyl alcohol. It is located in Sarnia—Canada's 'Chemical Valley'—a highly industrialized region, approximately 300 km west of Toronto. The installation is situated adjacent to a Shell oil refinery which has been in operation there since 1952. Propylene feedstock for the chemical plant is obtained from the refinery as well as Petrosar's neighbouring petrochemical complex. The plant employs a total of about 220 persons.

Process operation is continuous—24 hours a day, 7 days a week—requiring a high level of technical skill, with heavy emphasis on quality control. In brief, raw propylene is first passed through a feed preparation unit where purity is improved through fractionation and chemical treatment. The resultant material is directed to both the polypropylene (PP) and iso-propyl alcohol (IPA) units.

At the PP plant, the propylene is combined with a solvent and processed in reactors in the presence of a catalyst (manufactured to rigorous specifications in another section of the plant). Under carefully controlled conditions of

117

temperature and pressure, with the addition of other special chemical agents, the propylene molecules combine to produce a 'polymer' in the form of very fine powder suspended in the reaction mixture. This slurry is then processed to decompose and remove the catalyst, to permit recovery of the polypropylene powder. The remaining materials in the slurry are recycled after extensive purification. The fluffy PP powder is combined with various additives and passed through an extruder, which operates under high temperature and pressure, to produce polypropylene pellets. This product is stored in hoppers, and subsequently either shipped in bulk or packaged in bags or boxes for customer delivery. There are over 20 different grades of polypropylene produced on a single line, in a blocked-out operation, each requiring extremely careful attention to ensure acceptable quality.

In the IPA unit, propylene feedstock is reacted with water over a catalyst, under strict conditions, to form a crude product. This material is then processed in various stages of distillation and dehydration to produce pure alcohol.

The purpose of this chapter is to describe events leading to an organization design based on quality of worklife and socio-technical systems principles for this new Chemical Plant, the design process followed, and results.

In 1973, Shell Canada's Vice-President of Manufacturing commissioned a two-man study team,* to critically examine innovative approaches to organization design. The study consisted of a review of industrial operations where programmes had reportedly been undertaken to improve personnel effectiveness. The investigation revealed that many companies had been successful in improving organizational effectiveness and better meeting workers' needs through a variety of means, namely changing working climate and management style, modifying prevailing work practices, negotiating changes to collective agreements to eliminate restrictive clauses, and redesigning job modules for more effective allocation of duties and responsibilities. A recommendation was made to appoint a senior person with line-management experience to acquire more knowledge and skill in this field, and explore opportunities for implementation of innovative approaches within Shell Canada.

The above report was issued in January 1974. The subject was debated at some length amongst senior managers in Manufacturing and Employee Relations, and eventually received endorsement from all. In September 1974, Halpern was transferred from Winnipeg to Head Office, in Toronto, as Consultant—Organization Effectiveness, reporting to the General Manager, Refining and Chemical Plants, to pursue the activities recommended in this document.

---

*Norman Halpern, Winnipeg Refinery Superintendent, and Warren Jarvis, Employee Relations Supervisor. Events and considerations leading up to this commissioning are described in Appendix A.

Development of design philosophy

In early 1975 a decision had been made to proceed with the installation of a new chemical complex at Sarnia on property adjacent to the refinery. Engineering design was already fairly advanced at this point, and the plant was scheduled to be on-stream in 1978. This provided Shell with the best foreseen opportunity for implementation of an innovative organization—a new facility.

In Spring 1975, Martin Kaplan, Operations Manager at the Oakville Refinery, was appointed Chemical Plant Superintendent. Halpern met with Kaplan on several occasions while he was still at Oakville and reviewed the rationale behind organizational design in general, the desirability of change, and results of novel attempts elsewhere. Kaplan was very receptive to the notion of not simply perpetuating the traditional approach to staffing and agreed to consider alternatives.

One of the messages underlying the findings of the Halpern/Jarvis team was that success rates were low in situations where an external group developed an innovative organization design and then passed it on to an operating group to implement. Shell therefore sought a means for designing this work-place with a maximum involvement of the personnel who would be working there. The obvious problem being faced at that time was that only Kaplan had been appointed thus far, and the plant was not scheduled to come on-stream for another three years. In addition, they would have to deal with a further complication, in that, owing to the fact that Shell had no experience in Canada with the technology associated with these new plants, Kaplan and most of the 'staff' members of the organization would have to spend a considerable portion of their time in the United Kingdom and Holland for design and training purposes.

The approach taken in June 1975 was to initially establish a Task Force comprised of individuals who had some interest in the outcome of the Chemical plant design and could make a contribution, even though they would not ultimately be an integral part of the new organization.* As personnel were appointed to the Chemical Plant staff they were added as members. During the first few meetings the Task Force addressed itself to such questions as: Why do we want to change anything at all? What is wrong with the way in which we conduct ourselves today? If we could, what would we wish to change to?

This led to the generation of a list of concerns related to prevailing organizational practices which the Task Force considered to be undesirable from

---

*With General Manager sanction, a group was formed consisting of Halpern, Kaplan (Chemical Plant Superintendent), Bob Brawn (Sarnia Refinery Superintendent), Jim Hadler (Sarnia Refinery Employee Relations Manager), and Stu Rees (Head Office Industrial Relations Manager). John Fisher, Refinery Manager, joined several months later, after being transferred into Sarnia from a similar position in Vancouver to replace the retiring incumbent. Lou Davis, Chairman of the Centre for Quality of Working Life at UCLA, was engaged as a consultant.

the standpoint of productivity and employees' perceived needs. Items cited fell into the following general categories:

● inadequacies with communications systems and information flow;
● under-utilization of employees;
● excessive control;
● potential for improved capability to respond more expeditiously to problems;
● dissatisfaction with shift work;
● high attrition;
● boredom;
● limited opportunities for growth for non-technical employees;
● changes in abilities, attitudes, and expectations of the work-force not considered;
● artificial status differentials;
● lack of employee commitment.

After considerable time was spent debating the reasons behind perpetuation of practices related to the above issues, a Philosophy Statement Related to Work Design was drafted (see Appendix B). This Statement was to provide the framework for organizational and technical design decisions associated with the new Chemical Plant. It generally states a commitment to the concept of joint optimization of social and technical systems, and expresses a belief that workers are responsible, trustworthy, capable of self-regulation, and interested in opportunities for decision-making and growth. Other design objectives set out were related to reducing 'shift' work, modifying pay systems, eliminating artificial jurisdictional boundaries, improving communication systems, and altering problem-solving practices.

Implementation of design philosophy

Securing senior management sanction

The Task Force members realized that if they were to continue with the socio-technical systems design in accordance with the Philosophy Statement, they would obviously be faced with a heavy commitment in time, energy, and money, and would be considering some fairly radical, possibly risky, alternatives. They therefore thought it prudent to approach senior management at this stage to explain the situation and solicit their endorsement. A half-day meeting was called in October 1975,* which focused on presentation of the Philosophy Statement to clarify the Task Force's perception of implications of working within the framework of this document. The purpose of the session was to obtain

---

*Attended by the Vice Presidents of Manufacturing, Chemicals, and Administration (Finance and Employee Relations), and all general managers reporting to them.

endorsement of the Statement, along with approval for commitment of resources to conduct a socio-technical systems design.*

To underline ownership of this proposal and commence movement away from the image of it being 'Halpern's' or 'Head Office's' project, the presentation, on behalf of the Task Force, was led by Kaplan. His approach consisted of reviewing the Philosophy Statement, while referring to a parallel list of specific prevailing policies and practices which the Task Force viewed as contravening the Statement—outlining, for instance, changes that might be introduced to comply. This procedure served to clarify the interpretation of the Task Force so as to ensure fairly reasonable understanding by senior management of what it was they were being requested to sanction.

In addition, obstacles to attaining and sustaining an innovative organization at this site were tabled and reviewed. Key ones identified were proximity of the new plant to the existing refinery, pressures from neighbouring external plants for Shell employees to conform, the need to staff extensively with personnel experienced in traditional work practices, the presence of a union in the neighbouring refinery, the need for all levels of management to accommodate to the new philosophy, and the fact that they were attempting to introduce a novel style of management while dealing with a technology which was totally new to Shell Canada.

After several hours of discussion, unanimous approval was granted by senior management for all aspects, and a mandate to proceed was granted to the Task Force.†

Involvement of the union

The Task Force was conscious of the presence of the Oil, Chemical, and Atomic Workers Union (OCAW) in the neighbouring refinery, and was aware of the likelihood that the certification might extend to employees within the new chemical plant. The nagging questions were related to:

● the role that the union might play in the design of this facility;
● their response if approached and invited to participate;
● the company reaction if the union opposed the design philosophy and objectives.

It had never been a goal of this endeavour to seek a union-free plant. The prime objective was to ensure success of the new plant design and a key concern was that the union would not fully support this effort. However, a forceful argument

*It was envisaged that the Task Force would meet formally for a three-day period once a month, and the cost was estimated to be $75,000, covering consultation fees and travel expenses. The latter was fairly high in this case because of the need for key personnel, assigned to the new plant, to spend substantial time in Europe.

†In addition, a Senior Management Steering Committee, consisting of four general managers (Refining, Engineering, Employee Relations, and Chemicals) was appointed, to monitor, guide, and sanction the Task Force activities, and generally serve as a sounding board as the design progressed.

was presented by some to the effect that the OCAW leadership was indeed interested in pursuing actions related to the improvement of quality of working life, and that there was a very strong likelihood that they would sincerely wish to participate in this exercise. The decision was therefore made to seek their co-operation.

An initial meeting was convened with Neil Reimer, the National Director of OCAW, to review proceedings to date.* Reimer expressed an interest to pursue the matter further, stating that an improvement in the quality of working life had long been high on his priority list. Two more meetings were subsequently held with additional members of the national executive, the Ontario Regional Co-ordinator, and the Sarnia Refinery local executive. Having heard the Company's side, the union representatives at the last meeting retired for a short private discussion, and then returned to advise that they had an interest in collaborating with the Company on this study, but would do so only on the condition that they would participate as 'full partners and maintain a high profile'. This was certainly totally acceptable to the Company and the local president was nominated to join the Task Force.

The traditional organization

To satisfy a corporate need for budgeting and manpower planning, it was necessary to estimate staffing requirements for the new plant almost immediately after Kaplan's appointment in 1975. This was accomplished by examining other similar operations and by developing an organization modelled after existing typical polypropylene (PP)—isopropyl alcohol (IPA) installations. The design thus arrived at is presented in Figure 1.

A traditional arrangement would consist of four 'process operating' departments or sections (IPA, PP reaction, PP extrusion, and PP warehousing), a scheduling section, a maintenance department, and a laboratory for quality control testing—each working through a hierarchy of several levels of supervision and management, as shown. Two sets of shift supervisors for each shift, reporting to three-day supervisors under two process managers, would be included in the operations department; quality control testing would be the responsibility of a group of technicians under the direction of a laboratory supervisor assisted by a lab technician and chemist; production scheduling would be handled by an independent group; and equipment repair responsibility would be assigned to the existing maintenance manager in the refinery, who would be supported by a supervisor, planner, two foremen, and a contingent of craftsmen.

Engineering design was proceeding accordingly. Two separate control centres—one for IPA and another for PP—were being provided, the laboratory was to be located within the refinery about a mile away from the chemical plant

*Shell's representatives were John Fisher, Sarnia Refinery Manager, and Stu Rees, Head Office Manager—Industrial Relations.

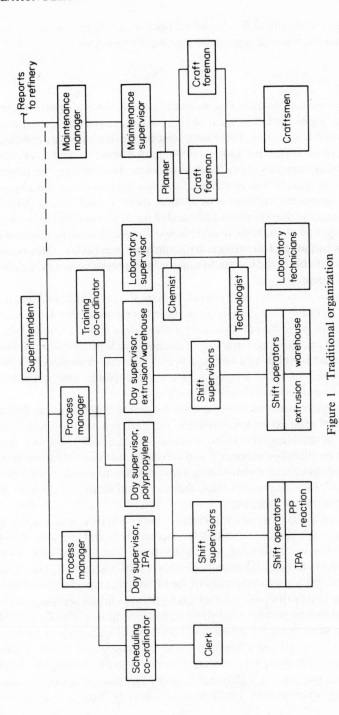

Figure 1 Traditional organization

site, and general facilities for employees (lockers, lunch rooms, offices, etc.) were planned on the basis of segregated groups of employees.

The alternative design

When examined against the Philosophy Statement, several contraventions were immediately apparent. The most obvious was in relation to departmental and jurisdictional boundaries. These were seen to be established in accordance with the criteria identified by Miller (1959) as the most common in traditional organizations: territory, time, and technology. In debating the rationale for boundary location, it was concluded, in consideration of the links between the various components of the system, that there should be no jurisdictional divisions at all within the entire chemical plant. It was decided to work towards the development of a scheme to maximize self-regulation at the operator level by providing individuals or groups with the necessary skills, information, and authorities to function in this manner. The concept of a multi-skilled shift operating team emerged.

Discussion then followed, over a period of many months, regarding the optimum mix of skills within the team. Questions posed were: How much could one expect an individual to learn over a reasonable period of time? What was a reasonable period of time? In trying to develop a jack-of-all trades, at what point does one start to suffer as a consequence of 'dilution of knowledge'? Of all the skills required to most efficiently operate the plant, how should they be distributed amongst individuals or groups?

Two key objectives were tabled during this period of deliberation: first, that the skills profiles be based on 'need-to-know' rather than a 'nice-to-know' basis, with the goal of enabling people to respond expeditiously to most frequently occurring problems or variances; and secondly, that consideration be given to making shift workers competent at handling tasks normally dealt with during the 'day' period, so as to possibly allow them to spend more time on days and thus improve their work schedule.

Following an analysis of experiences at other PP/IPA plants with regard to such items as problems frequently encountered and reasons for loss in productivity, it was concluded that it would be highly desirable for every member of each team to be fully capable of operating all sections of the plant. Because of the tight integration of all the units of the PP plant, and the low surge time in the system, the ability to understand effects of changes in one section upon another was considered to be vital, and there was much value in having the flexibility within the work-force for operators from various units to assist one another during upset conditions. While one could reasonably look upon IPA as being separate from PP, there was reluctance to establish an independent work-force for that unit on somewhat different grounds. Polypropylene operation is rather demanding, whereas IPA production is relatively trouble-free. Having two

RGANIZATION DESIGN IN CANADA

roups of operators on the same site, working out of the same control centre,
ith such wide difference in demands upon them, was considered to be totally
nacceptable. A general chemical plant operator, without specific designated
ffiliation to either PP or IPA, was judged to be most appropriate.

The Task Force determined that a complement of 20 persons per shift would
e required to operate the total facilities (this provided for allowance to train and
over for vacations and sickness). Attention was then directed to specification of
ther skills desirable for this team to satisfy the objectives of greater self-
egulation, improved response time to problems, and opportunities for day
ssignments to meet the objective of reduced shift work. Detailed examination of
ther similar operations with a view to identifying operational needs led to the
specialty skills' profile within the team, as shown in Table 1.

Table 1   Specialty skills profile within each shift team

Speciality skill	No. of team members
Instrumentation	2
Electrical	2
Pipefitting	2–3
Millwrighting	2–3
Analyser	2
Laboratory	4
Scheduling/warehousing/dispatching	5
	—
	20

The depth of knowledge and the elements included in each of the areas shown
in Table 1 were to be defined on the basis of support necessary to the operation.
Hence, there was no intention to develop the electrical specialist into a
journeyman electrician, but rather to have him acquire the necessary skills to deal
with frequently occurring electrical problems which called for expeditious
attention. More sophisticated, less frequent events would be handled by a
journeyman electrician.

To supplement these shift teams, the need was identified for a 'craft team',
composed of 14 journeyman craftsmen working days only, Monday to Friday. It
would be the role of this group to train the shift team members in their specialty
craft and effect repairs requiring a higher level of skill. It was recognized that
supplementary contract maintenance workers would be required until such time
as shift team members acquired significant craft skills.

Working $37\frac{1}{2}$ hours a week requires $4\frac{1}{2}$ teams to cover the 24-hour period on a
rotating shift schedule. After a lengthy assessment of opportunities for shift
operators to utilize their specialty talents on days, it was decided to form six shift
teams. This would allow $1\frac{1}{2}$ teams (on average) to be on days, Monday to Friday,

at all times. During this period they would work in their specialty area, joining with the craft team or functioning as schedulers, warehousemen, and quality control testers. The determining factor as to the number of shift teams actually formed, and the distribution of specialty skills, was the availability of opportunities to productively deploy the workers during their swing onto days. It was believed that the 'day' period would also provide an ideal time for some of the training to be conducted.

The work schedule currently in effect is shown in Figure 2. The following features are noteworthy:

- combination of 12- and 18-hour shifts;
- time spent on 'days' is two-thirds total time versus only one-third on a traditional 8-hour, three-shift pattern;
- considerable days off coinciding with weekends;
- a large number of days off in general, including the two 9-day blocks during every 18-week cycle;
- shift integrity, i.e. same groups of people work together at all times.

Referring back to the traditional organization (Figure 1), managerial and supervisory positions were next examined against the inherent objectives of the

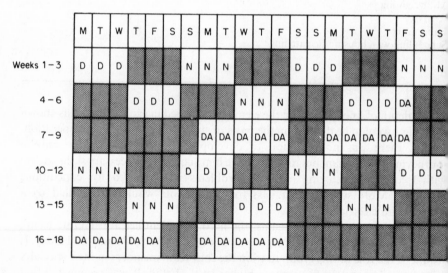

	M	T	W	T	F	S	S	M	T	W	T	F	S	S	M	T	W	T	F	S	S
Weeks 1–3	D	D	D			N	N	N				D	D	D				N	N	N	
4–6				D	D	D			N	N	N				D	D	D	DA			
7–9								DA	DA	DA	DA	DA			DA	DA	DA	DA	DA		
10–12	N	N	N			D	D	D				N	N	N				D	D	D	
13–15				N	N	N			D	D	D				N	N	N				
16–18	DA	DA	DA	DA	DA			DA	DA	DA	DA	DA									

D — 12-hr shift, 7 a.m. to 7 p.m.

N — 12-hr shift, 7 p.m. to 7 a.m.

DA — Day assignment: 8 hr shift, 8 a.m. to 4:30 p.m. ($\frac{1}{2}$-hr lunch).

▨ — Day off.

Figure 2   Chemical plant shift schedule

Philosophy Statement. What were the roles of such personnel in an environment where the emphasis was on a higher level of self-regulation?

An analysis was made of the activities consuming the time of the first line shift supervisors in the existing plant. While the Task Force was hard pressed to articulate why all of these functions could not be totally assumed by an autonomous work-group, it was felt that such a move was too drastic at this time. Considering that they were dealing with a rather complex and very sophisticated manufacturing process which was new to Shell Canada, and having had no experience to date with such an organization, it was believed prudent to put in place some form of 'supervision'. The Task Force decided to provide a single 'team co-ordinator' for each shift team, who would act as a resource person and facilitator to assist the team to function as autonomously as possible. It was generally acknowledged that these individuals were key to the success of the proposed organization, and that much effort would be required in their selection and training.

Attention then moved to the next level of supervision—the day supervisor. This role was reviewed in the light of the prime objective of developing a work team at the operating level which was highly confident and competent to deal with constantly varying conditions encountered 24 hours a day, 7 days a week. This led to the conclusion that the team and its co-ordinator must be allowed to mature to a state of independence. There was concern that, with the day supervisor in the line as indicated in Figure 1, there would be a tendency for him to usurp some of the powers of the team, thereby weakening it. It was concluded that the 'day supervisor' could best serve the organization in a staff position, acting as a technical adviser, providing continuity for day-to-day operation, and assisting with the co-ordination of activities related to scheduling of maintenance and long-range planning. (He was subsequently retitled Operations Co-ordinator.)

The shift team co-ordinators would, therefore, report directly to the two process managers. In reviewing the latters' responsibilities, little justification was found for two such positions. Furthermore, the distinct split between process and maintenance was regarded to be inconsistent with the general objective of eliminating traditional, artificial jurisdictional boundaries. Such an arrangement would tend to establish a potential 'win–lose' atmosphere, with the maintenance manager striving to minimize equipment repair costs while the process manager's interest would be in maintaining production. It was therefore decided to merge the two positions and have both—as operating managers—jointly responsible for the overall well-being of the plant.

As far as the superintendent position was concerned, there was a need seen for such a role, particularly during the complex period of design, construction, commissioning, debugging, and lining out to a steady-state condition. It was felt the position could become redundant once a mature stage of operation had been attained.

A requirement was identified for additional technical and operating staff t
assist during the commissioning and start-up phases of the project. Trainin
programmes had to be developed, operating manuals written, and instruction
provided to new employees. One option considered was to augment the initia
staff complement with persons who would be gradually weaned from th
organization after two to four years, as their knowledge and expertise wa
absorbed by others. The Task Force felt that such an approach, however, woul
lead to these 'temporary' advisers becoming permanent fixtures. An alternativ

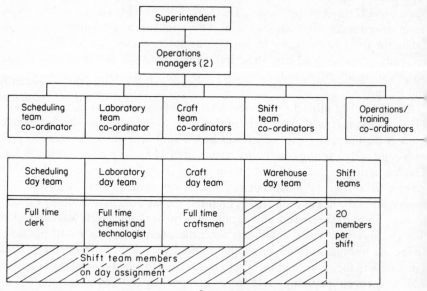

Figure 3   Chemical plant organization

course of action was therefore elected, wherein experienced expatriate assistanc
from Europe was brought in on a two to three year assignment basis. Thi
eliminated the need for costly training, and provided a group of individuals witl
a high degree of motivation to pass on their expertise so as to be able to returr
home within a reasonable period of time. (Subsequent experience revealed th
need for longer than anticipated co-ordinator support, and temporary assistan
co-ordinators were appointed following departure of the expatriates.)

The resultant alternative organization is depicted in Figure 3 (see Figure 1 fo
comparison). Note that it is an arrangement whereby multi-skilled shift team
members rotate through cycles of day assignments, working as members of a
'day' team alongside permanent day workers—as schedulers, laboratory
technicians, warehousemen, or craftsmen. The entire organization is regarded as
a single department composed of various sub-teams.

The remuneration programme

The relevant section of the Philosophy Statement states: 'compensation should be on the basis of knowledge and applicable skills, rather than the task actually being performed'. Historically, organizations in the petrochemical industry had been designed on the concept of job classifications, i.e. there were specific positions each defined by tasks to be performed and a corresponding rate of pay. Each position was filled at all times, and in the event of absenteeism an employee at a lower classification would be temporarily upgraded to fill the senior vacant position. Promotion from one classification to the next occurred only when someone left the system, and seniority was the key consideration. The shortcomings of this system were that employees often had to wait long periods of time before getting a permanent increase in pay, even though they were very capable of handling the more senior jobs (and in fact usually did for extended periods of time as vacation and sickness reliefs), and that frequently imcompetent individuals were temporarily upgraded because of the requirement to fill every slot.

Over recent years, a 'progression' programme has evolved within Shell whereby, up to a certain point, employees are paid in accordance with their demonstrated skill and ability, regardless of what they were called upon to do. There still remains, however, provision for promotion by vacancy at senior levels.

In the Chemical Plant, to comply with the intent of the Philosophy Statement, a scheme was developed to provide opportunity for everyone to progress to the top level, contingent upon acquiring a multiplicity of skills. As outlined above, each shift team member was expected to become competent to operate every section of the plant, in addition to acquiring skills in a specialty area (see Table 1). For the purposes of training and compensation, the 'operations' portion of the complex was divided into ten job knowledge clusters (JKCs), and each of the specialty areas (i.e. instrumentation, electrical, pipefitting, etc.) broken down into forty modules (refer to Figure 4). Upon entry (at $1124 per month based on rates in effect at the time of signing of the first collective agreement in 1978) an employee would commence basic training, which encompasses a spectrum of items at an elementary level. After demonstrating, through testing, that this portion has been satisfactorily mastered, an increase in pay would be granted. To earn the next rise, an employee must demonstrate competence in one JKC and four modules of his/her specialty skill. This progression continues, in such combination, for nine more stages until the top wage is reached. It was estimated that, on average, the top rung would be attained within about seven years.

The decision was made to adopt a monthly pay system for the entire workforce, similar to that normally reserved for staff personnel, as a further step to ameliorate the traditional 'we–they' atmosphere.

Modifications to the technical system

While the social system was being designed in accordance with the Philosophy Statement, the technical system was constantly surveyed to assess its compatibility. Unfortunately, there were no representatives from the engineering design project group on the Task Force, but Kaplan and others subsequently appointed to the Chemical Plant were kept up to date on technical decisions being made.

SALARY†—$/MONTH	PROCESS OPERATIONS	SPECIALTY SKILL
	TOTAL	TOTAL
1698	10 JKC'S*	40 MODULES
1643	1 JKC	4 MODULES
1588	1 JKC	4 MODULES
1536	1 JKC	4 MODULES
1483	1 JKC	4 MODULES
1429	1 JKC	4 MODULES
1376	1 JKC	4 MODULES
1322	1 JKC	4 MODULES
1269	1 JKC	4 MODULES
1215	1 JKC	4 MODULES
1162	1 JKC	4 MODULES
ENTRY-1124	BASIC TRAINING	

* JKC—Job Knowledge Cluster
† Basis 1978 Wages

Figure 4   Progression programme

The need for several major changes became obvious as the organization design evolved. The proposed two control centres—one for each of PP and IPA—were merged into a single facility. (The engineering designers had assumed that separate work-forces would operate these units.) The laboratory was relocated within the control centre building, since quality control testing was to be an integral part of the process operator's job. (From a capital cost standpoint it was somewhat less expensive to renovate an existing building on the refinery site, about a mile away, and have testing conducted there by a separate specialist group.) Administrative and operating accommodations were located as close to each other as possible, and office facilities rearranged to permit close interaction between operating and maintenance personnel. The necessity for extremely costly blast-proofing prohibited putting all personnel housing under one roof. A single parking lot for everyone was provided inside the fence with no reserved spaces. (The original design called for two lots—one outside the plant gate for hourly-paid workers, and a second inside for select staff personnel. When examined against the notions of minimizing artificial status differentials and assumptions of trust and responsibility, such an approach could not be supported.) A single lunchroom was included, and offices sized and furnished on the basis of need rather than status.

In reviewing the activities required of the multi-skilled teams in the manufacturing process, one function was judged to be intolerably mundane, considering the expected skill level of this work-force. This was the task of manually placing bags, to be filled with polypropylene, onto a bagging machine. Even though the workers would probably adjust to the ordeal through sharing of this chore, the most desirable solution was deemed to be elimination of the need for this assignment. The engineering designers were approached with this issue and, after much investigation and discussion with bagging machine manufacturers, they emerged with an automated bag-placing system.

The implications of the proposed social system probably had the largest impact on the design of the communications and information network. The importance attached to this linkage is clearly reflected by the numerous references to this aspect in the Philosophy Statement. Those for whom these issues had the most significance were the designers and programmers of the computer system. A decision had been made shortly after formation of the Task Force to include a process computer in this plant, thereby offering an opportunity to make available information, at various levels in the organization, in forms and frequencies which would otherwise have been impossible. Because of the recognized importance of data collection and dissemination in this environment, the computer designers became members of the Task Force upon their appointment.

The computer was capable of accommodating considerable closed-loop control. The extent to which this was initially done, however, was kept to a minimum, largely because polypropylene manufacture is still in many respects an art, and many of the operations associated with it cannot be represented by the precise mathematical correlations required for closed-loop control. Therefore, this system was being designed as a source of information to assist operating personnel in making effective decisions.

With the Philosophy Statement objectives in mind, emphasis was on providing 'meaningful' information at the shop-floor level. In response to the request for 'meaningfulness', feedback was provided, where appropriate, in economic terms. Therefore, rather than operating from a stance of 'our target temperature on the reactor outlet is 250°C, please try to maintain it', the operator is now advised 'our target temperature is 250°C; we are now actually at 225°C; the incentive to attain target is an improvement in yield outturn to the extent of $550/day'. No other instructions are necessary. It is quite well understood that the objectives, within constraints of safety and protection of the environment, are to maximize profits or minimize costs. As the operator makes moves to adjust the deviant variable, he/she is provided with feedback every few seconds as to the impact of his/her efforts *in meaningful terms*. If there are several conditions requiring correction, he/she now has the information to decide where efforts should be focused. Traditionally, the rationale behind target-setting resides in an engineering or planning office, and instructions are issued accordingly for operating personnel to follow faithfully. The outcomes are meaningful only to those who understand the significance of achieving the objective.

The collective agreement

Several courses were explored in search of a means to satisfy union representation of the employees at the Chemical Plant, consistent with the objectives of the Philosophy Statement. Attempts were made to alter the existing refinery collective agreement by noting clauses which would not apply to the new site or by including an addendum with modified provisions. These approaches were found to be unsatisfactory. It was eventually decided to treat the new facility as a separate unit with its own bargaining committee and agreement. The prevailing contract was then set aside, and negotiations commenced from a 'carte blanche' status.

Both parties agreed that the make-up of the collective agreement should reflect the general aims of the Philosophy Statement and the resultant organizational design. The assumptions of trust, maturity, responsibility, and capacity for self-regulation and problem-solving would have to be extended to encompass the employee's life in the area of labour relations. It was considered unacceptable to create a work-place based on minimal prescription on matters related to plant operations, and yet have a collective agreement composed of tight rules and regulations decided by an external management–union body. The direction taken, therefore, was to develop a contract which specified the absolute minimum, to provide only a framework and set of guidelines for employees to work within. Responsibility for filling in any necessary details would be left with the work-force.

The complete text of the original agreement, signed in 1978 and re-negotiated three times virtually unchanged, is presented in Appendix C. It is worthy of note that the contents of this contract are contained on eight pages, as compared with seventy-five for the traditional one covering employees at the adjoining refinery, and there is neither a management's right clause nor a specified grievance procedure. The intent is expressed in the Foreword which confirms that the purpose of the agreement is to provide an 'enabling framework' to ensure a productive operation with meaningful work for employees.

Support systems

During the research conducted by the two-man Task Force, described above, it was revealed that many organizations had experienced failure because they developed and implemented an innovative design, staffed it, and walked away from it with the expectation that it would function as intended.

However, one cannot simply engage any group of people, thrust the copy of the Philosophy Statement in their hands, declare 'You are now a responsible, trustworthy, self-regulating team—go to it', and expect a miraculous departure in behaviour from tradition. Many people would disagree with the assumptions made in designing the new organization, and would therefore have no interest in working in such an environment. Others, for whom these concepts have appeal, might be eager to join; however, in spite of all their good intentions and efforts, there is a strong probability that they would lack the necessary skills to function effectively in this mileu. This is particularly true if they have already worked in a traditional system, have been conditioned to behave in a particular fashion appropriate for that organization, and have developed attitudes and habits which would be in conflict with the new philosophy. Roles in plants designed to utilize extensive participation, problem-solving, and decision-making by all levels of personnel, often in groups, are decidedly different from those in traditional plants characterized by centralized control and highly specialized, often narrow, jobs. Many who are successful in traditionally structured organizations will not necessarily shine in the newly styled ones.

Essential components for successful implementation and sustenance of a novel organizational design, therefore, include: effective employee recruitment, role clarification, relevant social skills training, and development of mechanisms for self-management.

Employee recruitment programme

Team co-ordinators. As described above (p. 127), a decision was made by the Sarnia design Task Force to include a co-ordinator within each of the work teams. While this individual's role was rather fuzzy at the time, it was envisaged that the co-ordinator would not simply be a replica of the typical shift supervisor, but rather would be a 'facilitator' and 'resource' person for the team.

The usual selection would have been to approach the various operating locations across Canada, indicating opportunities available at Sarnia, and requesting nominations of candidates for consideration. There was much concern, however, regarding criteria against which others would assess suitability for these positions. Customarily, seniority and operating competency were significant factors. Would these still be key in the minds of those not having participated in the Task Force over the lengthy period to date? If so, then many interested, potentially good individuals might be overlooked. It was acknowledged that there was a need to be particularly selective in the case of the team co-ordinator, since this person would be the link between organized labour and management, and during the majority of the time would be effectively the site manager. Consequently, the Task Force recommended open advertising within the Company, allowing application from all. This somewhat radical step was discussed with management at the locations which might be affected, and an advertisement describing the position was subsequently publicized.

Approximately 75 responses were received. The initial coarse screening was done by the superintendent and an employee relations supervisor who reduced the number of candidates to about 35. This latter group was then interviewed by an operating manager and an operations co-ordinator, who, while appraising the overall person, concentrated on technical competency. This was followed by a two-hour in-depth interview by an external consultant for assessment of 'social skills' and personal characteristics. Interviewers then convened for a day, at which time ratings were compared and debated, and a final selection made.

Team members. There were 108 shift team member positions to be filled. Because past high attrition rates had left most of Shell's other operating locations with a relatively inexperienced complement, there was little opportunity to transfer Shell operating people into the new site. Therefore, except for a handful, the total work-force would have to be recruited externally. Recruitment would be handled by the team co-ordinators, with staff assistance from the Employee Relations Function.

On the basis of experiences reported by others in this area it was estimated that in excess of 2000 applicants could be expected. (In fact there were 2600.) Apart from the scheduling logistics, there was concern regarding the capability of inexperienced recruiters to assess the suitability of applicants, consistency in evaluations, and mechanisms to effectively inform the applicants of the organizational concepts proposed for this plant so that they could make an intelligent choice as whether they wished to work in this place.

To assist in this regard, workshops on Recruitment and Selection were conducted. These were designed to: (1) identify desirable characteristics for persons working in this environment; (2) provide interviewers with skills to make such an assessment; and (3) develop a suitable system for conveying information to applicants regarding the intentions for this work site. (In consideration of the large numbers of applicants expected, this latter objective was fulfilled through establishment of information centres and development of a video tape.)

Implications of the philosophy statement

Although organizational design work was progressing well, it was evident that there were many interpretations of the various clauses of the Philosophy Statement, and the need was felt to attempt to reach a common understanding. Therefore, in October 1977, when all management and staff personnel had been appointed, a five-day residential workshop was convened. The prime purposes for this session were to clarify the implications of operating within the Philosophy, identify appropriate behaviours, and negotiate roles.

Self-management skills training

Even if clear agreement had been reached regarding behavioural norms for this novel organization and recruiters had been successful in selecting personnel with the requisite personal characteristics appropriate for this plant, there would be a need for people to develop skills to function effectively in this environment. To address this requirement a 32-hour training programme was developed. Without detailing the content of the course, aspects covered were:

- Self-assessment, individual differences.
- Group dynamics, task-maintenance concepts, observation skills, feedback, members' roles.
- Group problem-solving, group decision-making, concept of leadership.
- Competition versus collaboration.
- Communications.
- Concepts of motivation and developmental discipline.

Team formation

Shift teams had as yet not been formed by the time self-management skills training was completed. This task was intentionally deferred as long as possible to allow members to get to know one another, since it was planned to use a process that allowed choice regarding specialty skill and the team to which a member would be assigned on a permanent basis. A committee, consisting of six nominated team members and three co-ordinators, was established to organize this exercise and make the final decisions. Elements which had to be taken into account when considering team composition were distribution of skills, balance of experience/inexperience, age distribution, and membership compatibility. Each member was requested to complete a form denoting first, second, and third choices of specialty skills he/she would like to acquire and choices of peers he/she would like to be with on the same team. All of this information was processed by the team formation committee and, happily, just about all of the members' choices were accommodated.

Development of norms

By design, a minimum in the way of rules and regulations had been prescribed in advance for this plant, with the objective that members of the organization would be responsible for developing the 'norms'. Shortly after team formation, a 28-hour structured exercise was undertaken for this purpose. Members were requested to identify areas requiring norms setting, and articulate appropriate norms. Lists were generated by each team, discussed amongst all teams, and compromises negotiated where necessary.

The following is a sample of statements agreed upon:
- members will recognize responsibility to their relief (punctuality, information, housekeeping, safety);
- teams will ensure equal opportunity for advancement;
- team decisions will be supported, even if a member is not in total agreement;
- personal problems will be kept confidential within teams, as long as they do not affect other teams;
- individuals are expected to attempt to reach the highest level of training within their capabilities;
- overtime meals will be supplied, if needed;
- teams will be instrumental in choosing new members;
- teams will perform the technical competence check-out of individuals and will be involved in developmental training;
- regular team meetings will be held;
- there is an expectation of individual sacrifice for the team benefit.

Team norm review board

A Team Norm Review Board (TNRB) was established, consisting of the following membership: one representative from each team; one team co-ordinator; one operations manager; the union vice president; and a representative from Employee Relations; a total of eleven persons. The charge to the TNRB was to edit norms, interpret and disseminate norms throughout the plant, monitor team norms for appropriate consistency, suggest modifications to norms, support the teams in their attempt to uphold norms, receive recommendations from teams regarding norms and suggested changes, encourage utilization of developmental discipline, and deal with recommendations and requests from teams and members regarding problems and disciplinary issues. This board operates by 'consensus to support', with each member having veto power.

Each team also identified the need for several functional roles to be filled within each team by various members on a rotating basis. These typically include a chairperson, secretary/recorder, work and duty scheduler, training scheduler, vacation scheduler, social director, treasurer, safety representative, TNRB representative, overtime distribution scheduler, and union steward.

It was agreed that all teams (including management and staff) would meet regularly to review and assess how things were progressing *vis-à-vis* expectations, air problems, agree on necessary action, and set plans for the future. Minutes would be recorded for all sessions for distribution to everyone in the plant. Issues which could not be resolved at the team level would be referred to either the TNRB, management, or the union–management committee.

Continuous re-design

One of the principles of socio-technical systems design is the 'principle of incompletion' (Cherns, 1976). The notion expressed is that the design is never complete. One is continuously learning and modifying accordingly. It is therefore essential to institute a system for handling proposals for re-design.

The mechanisms at Sarnia are via the TNRB or specially appointed *ad hoc* task forces. Considerable modifications from the original design have already been implemented. These include modifications to work schedules, mechanisms for distributing overtime, changes to progression/pay systems, alterations to staffing complement, establishment of minimum performance standards, re-design of quality control procedures, re-design of staffing in warehouses, alterations to training procedures, and changes to methods for supervisory selection.

Outcomes and what has been learned

There is a need to understand that the hoped-for organizational design performance will not be achieved on the first day—an evolutionary process leading to a distant objective is involved. In order to reach that objective there is a need to operationally define it—'how will we know when we have achieved it?'—and to develop some mechanism for continuous assessment as to 'where we are'.

Ideally, criteria and methodology for assessment should have been established and implemented immediately. However, because of the preoccupation with start-up issues and difficulties encountered in operationally defining the Philosophy Statement, this issue was perpetually deferred. It was not until early 1980 that a formalized approach was commenced. It was agreed to pursue evaluation at three levels: the individual, the team, and the entire organization.

A Task Force was initially established to develop mechanisms for individual assessment, with the resultant outcome of a Performance and Development Review (P & DR) system. This includes identification of agreed criteria and operational definitions (in categories of 'needs improvement, satisfactory, exceptional'). Assessment is based on self, peer, and supervisory evaluation. The purpose is 'developmental'—there is no link to remuneration—and the team assumes responsibility to work with the individual member to fulfil agreed action plans.

A second committee was subsequently formed in mid-1981 for evaluation at the team and organizational level. The stated purposes were:

- To provide information externally as to how we are doing, e.g. to the corporate office, the national union executive, external Shell, news media, other quality of working life groups, etc.
- To assess strengths and weaknesses within the organization.
- Since this organization is considered to be a 'learning one', we need information for continuous re-design, i.e. need to know where changes, if any, are required.

- Need to be able to answer the questions: Are we successful? Is the design working? What is the payout/return? What would we do differently?
- Need data for design of future plants and organizations.
- Need data to allow teams to measure performance.

As of 1983, work has consisted of identification of data and information required. The next step is to establish means for collecting and interpreting this data.

There is reluctance at this early stage to make definitive claims regarding results. However, some beneficial outcomes are apparent:

- Shift team members have developed a high level of operating competency. Evidence indicates that when equipment mechanical problems are under control, plant operation is exceptionally efficient.
- Benefits of 'multi-skilling' are obvious. Quality control (handled entirely by operating personnel) is excellent, and contributions of shift team members to equipment maintenance and repair is becoming very significant.
- There is widespread participation in all matters. *Ad hoc* task force output is extensive and of high quality. Examples of issues dealt with were cited in the previous section on continuous re-design.
- There is acceptance of the notion that this is a 'learning' organization. Members are coping well with the idea that they are in a never-ending process of re-design.
- While there was considerable scepticism at the beginning related to assumptions and objectives outlined in the Philosophy Statement, the level of support and commitment is now high.
- Problem-solving is now occurring in a fairly efficient manner. This has been as a result of substantial follow-up training in this regard.
- Union–management relations are excellent. The thin collective agreement has been renewed, virtually unchanged, for a third time. In 1983, the plant superintendent has been formally involved in only three 'grievances' (versus 66, plus a number of arbitration cases in the neighbouring, traditional plant over the same period of time).

The following is a list of what has been learned from the Sarnia project.

- A participative design, including as many as possible who will ultimately work in the environment in question, is essential. The problems encountered during the early stages of operation, owing to a lack of experience with a novel 'social' system, are of such a magnitude that, without very strong commitment to the objectives, one might readily succumb to the pressures to return to traditionalism. (Undesirable alternatives to the participative model include design by a very few from the organization or, worse, design by external experts).
- There is a need to get early commitment to the design objectives from senior management. This facilitates obtaining their approval for departures from the norm on critical issues (e.g. wage systems, nature of collective

agreement). Also, it ensures their support during the bumpy, early learning period.

- During the process of design, conditions must be established to encourage creative thinking. Lessons have been that one must allow participants to suggest outrageous ideas and objectives without requiring them to outline in detail all the elements of actual application. Identification of obstacles and development of strategies to overcome obstacles should be dealt with separately from 'idea generation', with support from the entire design team.

- It is necessary, in examining the rationale for change, to view it from the standpoint of all key parties involved. A useful exercise is to explore, from management, employee, and union perspectives, the question: 'What's in it for me?'

- Different interpersonal and social skills are required to function effectively in a 'participative' environment *vis-à-vis* an authoritarian one. Such skills are not easily acquired, especially for persons with a traditional background. Training in this regard is complex, and classroom instruction by itself, prior to commencing work, is inadequate. There is a need to develop a system for continuous on-the-job training, tied to actual experiences encountered. To achieve this, it was found necessary to add a 'facilitator/trainer' to the Sarnia organization to be available to work with the various groups and individuals as the needs become evident. Of significance in this regard are issues related to appropriate leadership style, problem-solving, decision-making, conflict resolution, role clarification, and conduct of meetings.

- There is a tendency for varied and unrealistic expectations to emerge— primarily related to the time required to meet stated objectives. Not having achieved 'instant Utopia' leads to considerable frustration. There is a need to deal with 'realism' and somehow get the understanding across that people are involved in an evolving, growing, developmental situation— that espoused objectives are long-term targets and, indeed, some may never be realized to everyone's satisfaction.

- In line with the previous item, it is essential that managers and supervisors be conscious of the need to practise 'situational' leadership—i.e. to be sufficiently flexible in their style to be able to move from an authoritarian to a participative mode as appropriate for the occasion. While there is an expectation and thrust to push down responsibilities and keep decision-making at the lowest possible level, there is the matter of competence which must be considered. During the early stages, the majority of skills and knowledge resides with a few people and, in order to ensure that organizational objectives are being achieved, those with the competence must be quite directive. The trick is to manage in such a fashion that necessary skills are transferred and the reins loosened at optimum rates.

This issue has been one of the greatest sources of frustration at Sarnia, and similar views have been expressed by other companies. In an organization based on 'minimum critical specification' and minimum prescription, there is a need to devote considerable time to activities designed to clarify roles. Such exercises are necessary at all levels, and should be extended to persons outside the immediate organization with whom there is regular interface, e.g., Head Office, engineering support groups, union officials, etc.

- While there is considerable emphasis on modifying and improving management and supervisory 'social' skills, it has been found that, for these people to be effective and respected, it is essential that they be technically competent. As a priority, efforts must be made to ensure a high level of technical development for management personnel.
- It is desirable to establish criteria for evaluation purposes as part of the initial design, along with data-gathering mechanisms.
- Work in participative systems is not for everyone. Misfits can be very unhappy and disruptive. There is a need to find an effective way to communicate to perspective employees what is expected of them, and to improve skills in assessment of job applicants. In addition, an effective mechanism is required to identify and deal with those who turn out to be unsuitable.
- In this organization, there has been a tendency to focus job re-design at the 'process operator' position without equivalent attention being paid to the craft team and staff support groups. This is an area which needs addressing.
- Since one is dealing with unknown systems, it is impossible to predict and provide for all events at the design stage. Those involved must have the ability to live with uncertainty, and be prepared to deal with unexpected issues as they arise.

Diffusion

Inspired by the outcomes at the Sarnia Chemical Plant, Shell Canada has followed similar approaches in several other sites. Socio-technical systems designs have been implemented for a gas plant, an *in situ* oil sands pilot unit, a fibreglass tank manufacturing facility, a lube and grease plant, a coal mine, a word processing department, and a research laboratory. Designs are currently under way for a new oil refinery and styrene-monomer chemical plant. In the more recent efforts, advantage is being taken of learnings from previous designs, and particular attention is being given to:

- appropriate management style and extent of self-regulation at start-up versus maturity;
- clarifying expectations—especially with regard to how quickly stated objectives can be achieved;

- availability of resources to aid in the implementation and provide necessary training;
- design of multi-skills training programmes and wage progression systems—again recognizing the need to differentiate between start-up and steady state.

In recognition of the prevailing high resistance to change in existing organizations, most of the effort is now being directed to situations involving new facilities. These obviously provide greatest opportunity. With regard to the former, the strategy consists of:

- providing information to key parties regarding results in socio-technical sites;
- offering suggestions regarding possible opportunities;
- awaiting signals of interest, opportunities/needs, and 'state of readiness'.

This activity is being supported in the company by a network of organization effectiveness consultants, in key locations across Canada, and an educational programme designed to improve practitioner competence and increase awareness throughout the organization.

Appendix A: Some early developments

In 1972 Shell Canada's Vice President of Manufacturing commissioned a Senior Management Task Force* 'to seek out and develop opportunities to improve utilization of people at all levels in manufacturing'. This was done in anticipation of expansion and a consequent need to release from the existing organization a considerable number of technical personnel to design, construct, and operate proposed new facilities. Accordingly, The Task Force concentrated on the 'professional staff' portion of the organization and was, indeed, successful in identifying many opportunities to improve the Company's *modus operandi*, thereby springing a significant complement for other functions.

While no specific changes were suggested with regard to the hourly worker level, the Task Force final report contained the following:

> In exploring the areas for improvement in utilization of manpower, it was assessed that the greatest potential existed amongst the hourly paid workers. Although Manufacturing has achieved much gain in productivity/man improvements through mechanization (hardware technology and consolidation), we feel that there has been relatively little increase in utilization of the worker himself. Basically, he is required to do little more or differently than 20 years ago, yet today he is better educated, more highly skilled, more job secure and more affluent. The continuing improvements of the hourly paid worker's position *vis-à-vis* his minimal increase in utilization is not seen within Shell as being much different than elsewhere in the oil industry as a whole. However, this group represents some 2/3 of all employees in

*F. Wood, Refinery Manager; N. Halpern and R. Picard, Refinery Superintendents; R. Back, Manager, Engineering; and D. Taylor, Manager, Marketing.

Shell Canada's Manufacturing function, and for this reason alone, it is difficult to accept that the increasing cost spiral of this group can be tolerated without a real offset in personal contribution.

Although improvements will be difficult to realize from the existing work places, once the 'know-how' is acquired its application and the benefits will be available at the outset to new installations. When we consider the magnitude of currently envisaged projects, there is now a need and incentive for Manufacturing to start on a program that will utilize this latent potential to the fullest extent possible.

We see, within the hourly ranks, increasing numbers of highly experienced and knowledgeable individuals who are capable of more significant contributions. In our opinion, however, they are to a large extent alienated in the work place and thus not motivated to the task of achieving a 'best' operation. The reasons are many and have often been cited—but we would like to review briefly what *we think* are the most significant.

1. *Lack of Involvement*—The hourly workers do not feel a part of the organization to the extent that staff people do, and we believe they see themselves as persons uninvolved in decision making and required to do merely what they are told to do. This situation is aggravated by a social 'we–they' division which exists, admittedly perpetuated largely through the establishment of labour unions, but also due in considerable measure to a management that has made relatively little effort to involve the hourly worker in other than his prime area of responsibility.

2. *Lack of Sense of Achievement*—The hourly worker—and this applies to a much greater degree to the continuous process worker rather than the day man—cannot relate his own personal efforts to achievement of overall objectives and results. The system is not intended or designed to tell him how he is doing and thus we believe this man is deprived of a vital motivating force.

3. *Limited Career Opportunities*—It is a fact that hourly personnel generally face limited upward mobility, with the foreman level or equivalent as the top of his career. Although not a formal policy in this regard, levels beyond are generally conceived as being closed to employees who are not university graduates.

4. *Shift Work*—We believe many operators generally do not like shift work and are dissatisfied/demotivated by the few opportunities to get into a day job.

5. *Weak First-Line Supervision*—First-line supervision associated with the hourly forces is considered in total to be relatively weak both by Management and the hourly worker. Although often considered a separate problem, it cannot be isolated from the significant impact it has on utilization and motivation of hourly personnel.

It is against these prevailing conditions that productivity improvement will need to be realized. Obviously, the traditional 'engineered' solutions, or ones in which employees are advised on how to overcome what we perceive as their problems, will not yield the desired results. We believe, to be effective, any actions taken must have their origin in the employees they affect and, therefore, derived from an approach which involves the joint participation of both employee and management. The task will be extremely difficult and will take several years at best to achieve when it is recognized that:

1. There is no blanket approach.

2. Not all hourly-paid employees will want to be more motivated, have a greater sense of achievement, more personal growth, etc. The best we can do is

probably satisfy those who want more out of their job and the future, and isolate and use the remainder to the best of our ability.

3. There are some very basic and fundamental attitude problems which must be overcome on the part of the hourly-paid who are bound to be suspicious, distrustful, and possibly fear that any role played in an improvement program is tantamount to doing themselves out of a job.

4. There are some ideals and forces in the work place that will make it increasingly more difficult to reconcile Corporate goals with that of the hourly-paid worker. Today, the worker still wants more money, but also more time off and time away from the work place.

5. There could be adverse reactions from staff, particularly at the lower levels, who in part believe that too much attention is already focused on the hourly personnel.

Our recommended action to more fully utilize the potential of the hourly personnel, and to do so with their full participation, must be viewed against the above considerations and with full recognition that:

● We will need plenty of expert assistance from both inside and outside Shell Canada,

● We will need very open and receptive attitudes to innovation and change,

● We will need to spend considerable money,

● We may fail, make things worse, or create a mess; and on the other hand, we may be extremely successful.

It is recommended that Manufacturing, with Corporate Relations support, initiate immediately a concerted effort to more fully utilize the potential of hourly-paid refinery personnel with a view to:

1. Enhancing the work life and reducing overall costs of this group within existing refineries.

2. Gaining experience necessary to develop the concepts under which tasks presently performed by this group will be accomplished in new future operations.

The recommendation is aimed at the hourly-paid worker's potential for greater personal contribution. Fundamentally involved are human attitudes and motivation which must be changed in order to reach the stated goals, and which, in our opinion, can be changed only through a significant and meaningful contribution from the hourly-paid workers themselves. Thus, the approach recommended recognizes the expectation of the employees in this regard and the need to utilize knowledge developed by the behavioural sciences.

The approach is envisaged as a three phase project, each one of which at completion will impact on the feasibility, complexity and cost of the next phase.

Phase I   Thoroughly review and evaluate, with in-company and outside assistance, past efforts/applications involving innovative organizational methods within the continuous processing industry in North America and Europe, and assess the probable success and risks of a comparable type undertaking within Manufacturing.

Phase II   With assistance of outside expertise in behavioural sciences, develop a base program and technique for a trial application in Manufacturing with goals and targets to be achieved along with estimate of costs and time involved.

Phase III In conjunction with the hourly-paid personnel evolve the specific program and implement it at a small refinery.

To ensure the highest degree of success, the project must have senior management direction and involvement from Manufacturing and other functions involved, backed up by a commitment of resources (manpower and funds) with full recognition that it will be a difficult undertaking, costly, time consuming, and without guarantee of success.

Appendix B: Sarnia Refinery and Chemical Plants—philosophy related to work design

The primary objective of Shell Canada Limited at the Sarnia Refinery and Chemical Plant is to obtain an optimum return on investment in capital and human resources, operating in a safe environment as a responsible member of the community, while being responsive to its employees' needs. It is believed that this objective can best be achieved by establishing and sustaining an organization and management system consistent with the following philosophy.

Social and technical interactions

The Company recognizes that, in order to achieve its primary objective, it is necessary to give appropriate consideration to the design and management of both the social and technical aspects associated with its operation. The former is related to employees and encompasses such areas as organizational structure, levels of responsibility and authority, supervisory roles, communication networks, interpersonal relationships, reward systems, etc., while the latter deals with the physical equipment—its capacity, layout, degree of automation, etc. Although our operations involve a high degree of sophisticated technology, which can be exploited to improve efficiency, it is only through the committed actions of our people that the full benefits can be realized. The social and technical systems are interrelated and must be jointly taken into account to achieve overall optimization.

Key considerations for the social system

Communications. Our operation is a tightly integrated system, functioning on a 24-hour, 7-days-a-week basis, with associated support activities carried out on a weekday schedule. Involved are people at various levels and widely dispersed in locations both inside and outside the plant. The nature of our industry is such that delay in recognizing errors or need for operational changes, and taking corrective action, is likely to result in substantial costs. Considerable consideration must therefore be given to the design and maintenance of a communication network that avoids lapses of attention and errors in observing, diagnosing, and communicating or acting upon information. Accordingly, information should be directed to the individual capable of acting most promptly and for that individual to have the authority to take action and to be internally motivated to do so.

Individual commitment. An essential ingredient for the success of our operation is a high level of individual employee commitment. Such commitment, however, can only be expected to develop if, in addition to the provision of satisfactory working conditions and terms of employment related to remuneration and benefits, other needs such as the following are met.

(1) The need for the content of the work to be reasonably demanding of the individual in terms other than those of sheer endurance, and for it to provide some variety.

(2) The need for an individual to know what his job is, how he is performing in it, and how it relates to the objectives of the Company.

(3) The need to be able to learn on the job and go on learning.

(4) The need for some area of decision-making where the individual can exercise his discretion.

(5) The need for the individual to know that he can rely on others in times of need and that his contribution is recognized.

(6) The need to feel that the job leads to some sort of desirable future.

The relative significance of these needs vary from individual to individual and it is not possible to provide for the fulfilment of particular needs. Allowance must therefore be made to accommodate individual differences.

Implementation and maintenance of the philosophy

In developing a social system within our plant, the following are regarded as key criteria to be incorporated.

(1) Policies and practices should reflect the belief that:

- our employees are responsible and trustworthy;
- individuals are capable of making proper decisions related to their sphere of responsibility, given the necessary information and training;
- groups of individuals can work together effectively as members of a team with minimal supervision, collaborating on such matters as problem-solving (operational and personal) training, 'hands-on' operations, maintenance, etc.

(2) Employees should be permitted to grow, advance, and contribute to their fullest potential and capability.

(3) Compensation should be on the basis of knowledge and applicable skills, rather than the task actually being performed.

(4) Communications should be open and meaningful. Direct communication across departmental boundaries between specific individuals concerned, without passing through intermediaries, is most effective.

(5) Information flow should be for the purpose of ensuring that the most expeditious action is taken on the basis of that information, and should,

therefore, be directed to those in a position to most quickly act upon it. Dissemination of such information to others should be only for purposes of appropriate audit and not for the purposes of decision-making and exercise of control.

(6) 'Whole jobs' should be designed, so that individuals are involved from start (premises, conception, economics, etc.) to end (evaluation of results).

(7) Systems should be designed to provide direct, immediate feedback to the individual of the results of his actions in meaningful terms, to the fullest extent possible.

(8) Work should be designed to permit the workers a maximum amount of self-control and discretion. They should be given authority commensurate with position, and held personally accountable.

(9) A system should be developed which permits any employee to undertake any task required for the efficient operation of this plant, provided he has the skills to do the work effectively and safely. Artificial, traditional departmental or functional demarcation barriers should be eliminated and work allocated on the basis of achieving most effective overall results. The training and remuneration programme must be designed accordingly.

(10) Jobs should be designed and work schedules developed to minimize time spent on 'shift'.

(11) A system and climate must be established for early identification of problem areas with problem-solving occurring in a collaborative fashion.

(12) It is necessary to have a climate which encourages initiative, experimentation, and generation of new ideas. Error situations should be reviewed from a 'what can we learn' standpoint and not from a punitive one.

(13) Status differentials should be minimized.

It is recognized that bringing about change in an ongoing operation is an extremely difficult task which must be approached realistically and patiently, because we are dealing with deep-rooted attitudes and practices. The most promising opportunities lie in 'grass-roots' circumstances. Building a new facility adjacent to an existing one does not necessarily require that the practices of the older operation be extended to the new installation. Indeed, the new installation provides an opportunity to introduce changes to the older organization.

There are many factors which place restraints on the extent to which the above criteria can be embodied in our management systems. Our task will be to properly examine all our practices and determine strategies for overcoming these obstacles. Recognizing that there are risks involved, senior management endorses the principles and objectives outlined in this document, and supports and encourages their implementation.

Appendix C

Text of the agreement signed on 20 January 1978.

Foreword

The purpose of the agreement which follows is to establish an enabling framework within which an organizational system can be developed and sustained that will ensure an efficient and competitive world-scale Chemical Plant operation and provide meaningful work and job satisfaction for employees. Recognizing that there are risks involved and that there are many factors which can place restraints on the extent to which changes can occur, both management and the union support and encourage policies and practices that will reflect their commitment to the following principles and values:

- employees are responsible and trustworthy, capable of working together effectively and making proper decisions related to their spheres of responsibilities and work arrangement—if given the necessary authority, information, and training;
- employees should be permitted to contribute and grow to their fullest capability and potential without constraints of artificial barriers, with compensation based on their demonstrated knowledge and skills rather than on tasks being performed at any specific time;
- to achieve the most effective overall results, it is deemed necessary that a climate exists which will encourage initiative, experimentation, and generation of new ideas, supported by an open and meaningful two-way communication system.

Recognition

The Company recognizes the Oil, Chemical and Atomic Workers International Union Local 9-848 as the sole bargaining agency for all multi-skilled operators (hereinafter referred to as shift team members) and journeymen (hereinafter referred to as craft team members) of the Shell Sarnia Chemical Plant at Corunna, Ontario.

Plant committee

The Company acknowledges the right of the union to appoint or otherwise select a plant committee. This committee, on behalf of its membership, will be responsible for the negotiating of revisions to the collective agreement where applicable or any other matter which may be mutually agreed between the parties. The Company agrees to recognize one steward from each shift team and in addition one steward from the craft team.

Grievances

There shall be developed and maintained a system to ensure the prompt and equitable resolution of problems at the Chemical Plant. In any event, to augment this system the appropriate provisions of the Ontario Labour Relations Act are available to the parties.

Hours of work and rates of pay

All employees covered by this agreement will follow appropriate work schedules that provide for an average basic workweek of $37\frac{1}{3}$ hours.

Where circumstances require shifts or schedules other than those in common use, discussion between management and the union prior to implementation will occur.

Where a schedule change occurs as per the above whereby the starting or stopping time of an employee is altered by four hours or more, or his/her days off are changed, the employee will be paid, in addition to his/her regular salary, a premium payment of three-quarters time on the first day of his/her new schedule, and his/her days off will become those shown on the new schedule. If an employee works more than 42 regular days over a cycle of 63 days as a result of a change of schedule, the additional hours will be paid at time and three-quarters. If a change of schedule occurs on a statutory holiday, the premium rate for the change of schedule will be paid on the first day worked on the new schedule, immediately following the statutory holiday.

All overtime hours will be paid at time and three-quarters.

A minimum payment for call-out work will be equivalent to four hours regular pay, except where, with previous notice, an employee starts to work two hours or less before commencement of his/her regular working day.

In addition to the regular monthly salaries outlined in Schedule 'A' below, there shall be paid a 'shift bonus' of 5% of the employee's equivalent hourly rate for each hour worked between 3.30 p.m. and 11.30 p.m., and 6% of the employee's equivalent hourly rate for each hour worked between 11.30 p.m. and 7.30 a.m. Team members working days who are placed on a schedule that begins before 6.00 a.m. or ends after 6.00 p.m. will receive 5% of their equivalent hourly rate for each hour worked between 4.30 p.m. and midnight, and 6% of their equivalent hourly rate for each hour worked between midnight and 8.00 a.m.

Deduction of union dues

The Company will deduct from all employees covered by this agreement an amount equal to the regular monthly dues of the union and remit the amount deducted, together with an itemized list, to the Secretary–Treasurer of the union. Two changes in the deduction of dues in any calendar year, as notified by the Secretary–Treasurer of the union, will be permitted.

Seniority

Seniority shall refer to continuous service at Shell's Sarnia Chemical Plant, and for the purpose of establishing seniority of employees at Shell's Sarnia Chemical Plant, the first day of operation shall be deemed to be 1 March 1978.

In the event of a layoff, reverse-order seniority will be followed, provided that remaining employees are capable of fulfilling all job requirements. Re-call, within a period of one calendar year from date of layoff, shall be in accordance with plant seniority, subject always to the same provisions as outlined above.

Vacations

Every employee covered by this agreement will have the following vacation entitlement:

Completion of one full year's service	two weeks' vacation with pay
Completion of three consecutive years' service	three weeks' vacation with pay
Completion of ten consecutive years' service	four weeks' vacation with pay
Completion of twenty consecutive years' service	five weeks' vacation with pay

Statutory holidays

Days designated as statutory holidays are as follows: New Year's Day, Good Friday, Victoria Day, Canada Day, Civic Holiday, Labour Day, Thanksgiving, Remembrance Day, Christmas Day, and Boxing Day.

Statutory holiday pay and pay for work performed on a statutory holiday are distinct and separate. Team members required to work their regular shift and/or overtime on a statutory holiday will be paid at time and three-quarters their regular salary rate, in addition to receiving 8 hours statutory holiday pay.

Safety and health

The Company agrees that the union, in consultation with team representatives, may appoint two representatives on the Safety Committee and that these representatives shall be notified in advance of meetings of this committee which have been called for purposes of safety or to investigate accidents involved in injury to employees.

Termination

This agreement shall remain in force for a period from the 1st day of February 1978, up to and including the 31st day of January 1979, and shall continue in force from year to year thereafter unless in any year not more than 120 days, and not less than 30 days, before the date of its termination, either party shall furnish the other with notice of termination of, or proposed revision of, this agreement.

Schedule 'A': basic monthly salaries

Team members (shift)	Basic monthly salaries	Hourly rate equivalents
Phase 12	$1,698	$10.47
Phase 11	1,643	10.13
Phase 10	1,588	9.79
Phase 9	1,536	9.47
Phase 8	1,483	9.14
Phase 7	1,429	8.81
Phase 6	1,376	8.48
Phase 5	1,322	8.15
Phase 4	1,269	7.82
Phase 3	1,215	7.49
Phase 2	1,162	7.16
Phase 1	1,124	6.93
Team members (craft)		
Journeymen	$1,551	$ 9.56

Epilogue

The experience at the Sarnia Chemical Plant has demonstrated that, indeed, we have choices regarding work design, organizational structures, and deployment of both technical and human resources. The evidence reveals the vital need to critically examine prevailing values and assumptions about people when developing a work environment, to ensure that these are consciously taken into account during the process of organizational design. The systems at Sarnia are based on beliefs that employees are responsible, trustworthy, capable of self-regulation, and sincerely desirous of contributing as fully as possible to ensure high organization effectiveness, and we have not been disappointed. The challenge for management is to provide the necessary conditions and remove obstacles to allow employees to contribute in accordance with their fullest capability.

Formal evaluation, to assess achievement at Sarnia, is currently underway. This exercise was intentionally deferred to permit some growth and development to take place. Perhaps the most important lesson learnt in this endeavour was related to managing unrealistic expectations as to how quickly the alternative objectives could be realized. We are dealing with attempts to alter attitudes, behaviours, and practices developed over a long period of time—and this does not occur overnight. Without patience, commitment, and a true belief that 'we are right and we will get there', chances of surviving the initial hectic learning–unlearning period are slim. Much credit is due to all employees at Sarnia for having had the fortitude to carry on during the early years when it surely must have seemed that this was all an unachievable pipe dream.

This experience also serves to demonstrate that union and management can, indeed, work collaboratively to the benefit of all. The Energy and Chemical Workers were involved during the early design stages, and their relationship with company management continues to be an example of ideal labour relations. While both parties obviously still have differing, conflicting demands and views, the norm for resolution is through problem-solving rather than negotiation. The original eight-page collective agreement has now been renewed for a fourth term.

Shell Canada's satisfaction and confidence in the approach followed at Sarnia are evidenced by the fact that socio-technical systems designs of a similar nature have been undertaken for all new installations since. These encompass a variety of applications, including a gas processing plant, an *in situ* oil sands pilot project, a fibreglass tank manufacturing facility, a coal mine, a lube and grease plant, a refinery and chemical plant. Our next challenge is to successfully apply these principles to existing, older organizations.

Toronto   W. M. Catterson
Canada   Sr. Vice President
May, 1983   Oil Products
                                             Shell Canada.

References

Cherns, A. (1976) The principles of socio-technical design, *Human Relations*, **29** (8), 783.
Miller, E. J. (1959) Technology, territory and time: The internal differentiation of complex production systems, *Human Relations*, **1959**, 243–272.

ople and Organizations Interacting
lited by A. Brakel
1985, John Wiley & Sons Ltd.

Chapter 9

Development in A/S Norske Shell's Organization

Lars V. Gjemdal

Introduction

A/S Norske Shell is a fully integrated oil company, which means that it is involved in the exploration, production, refining, and marketing of oil products. The company has operated in Norway since 1912 as a marketing company. The Refinery was started in 1967 and the Exploration and Production Department has been active on the Norwegian Shelf since 1965.

The company is one of the three major international oil companies in Norway. When the O.D. activity started in 1970, it had about 1000 employees and a share of approximately 23% of the inland market.

Only drivers and depot operators were unionized (the Transport Workers' Union). The relationship with the trade unions is very good.

The company has its main office in Oslo and 35 work locations spread around the whole country.

Before we go in detail about the O.D. activity, it is necessary to take a brief look at the environment in which the company operates, since we must look at the organization as an open system which is affected by environmental forces.

Norway covers a large geographical area, approximately 325,000 km², and has a population of about 4 millions. Industry was late in developing, and the

country largely avoided the industrial revolution and the associated problems
With some simplification, it may be stated that it was industry that had to adjus
to local conditions.

At the same time, it has been a society without the large social class difference
which can be found in some other countries. In this connection, it may b
mentioned that when the country got its Constitution in 1814, the nobility wa
abolished at the same time.

From 1936 to 1981, Norway had Labour governments with few interruptions
while it got a Conservative minority government in 1981. There is littl
disagreement about the political aims; disagreement is concerned with the means

The employment sector is well organized with both responsible trade union
and an employers' organization. There is good contact between the parties, an
they have jointly established a 'Collaborative Council'. The parties in th
employment sector use two years' collective bargaining agreements as a basis
and when the agreement period is running, the parties are obliged to respect th
agreement. Strikes are illegal. This has the effect that the number of strikes i
relatively modest.

Unemployment has been limited, and has fluctuated between 1 and 1.5% unti
1981/82 when the percentage crept up to about 2%.

Enterprises in Norway are small by international comparison (see Table 1)
Industrial democracy is a well-known concept which started in Norway in th
1960s when Professor Einar Thorsrud from The Work Research Institute i
Oslo, in co-operation with the Tavistock Institute of Human Relations, London
started the first experiments with partly self-autonomous groups in Norwegia
industry. Later, in 1977, Norway got a new Working Environment Act, wher
§12 in particular is of importance:

§12
Planning the work

1.   General requirements
      Technology, organisation of the work, working hours and wage systems shall
      be set up so that the employees are not exposed to undesirable physical or

Table 1

Employees	Number of companies	Per cent	Number of employees	Per cent
less than 5	5.829	42.0	13.841	3.6
5–9	2.681	19.3	18.850	4.9
10–19	2.136	15.4	30.228	7.8
20–49	1.726	12.4	55.585	14.4
50–99	760	5.5	55.403	14.3
100–199	313	2.2	59.882	15.5
200 and above	428	3.1	155.447	39.6

mental strain and so that their possibilities of displaying caution and observing safety measures are not impaired.

Conditions shall be arranged so that employees are afforded reasonable opportunity for professional personal development through their work.

2. Arrangement of work

    The individual employee's opportunity for self-determination and professional responsibility shall be taken into consideration when planning and arranging the work.

    Efforts shall be made to avoid undiversified, repetitive work and work that is governed by machine or conveyor belt in such a manner that the employees themselves are prevented from varying the speed of the work.

    Otherwise efforts shall be made to arrange the work so as to provide possibilities for variation and for contact with others, for connection between individual job assignments, and for employees to keep themselves informed about production requirements and results.

3. Control and planning systems

    The employees and their elected union representatives shall be kept informed about the systems employed for planning and effecting the work, and about planned changes in such systems. They shall be given the training necessary to enable them to learn these systems, and they shall take part in planning them.

We may therefore conclude that the company has operated in an environment which is characterized by political stability, responsible trade unions and employers confederations, little unemployment, a large degree of equality, and acceptance of the welfare state.

The term 'organizational development'

In general, it may be said that whereas *organizational planning* is concerned with the structuring of tasks, jobs, and reporting lines, organizational development is 'all planned activities for the purpose of improving the possibilities of an organization to attain its objectives through more effective use of the total resources, including the human resources'. O.D. is thus a process for systematic changes of the total organization through a developed programme and not a short-term change through training alone and limited to parts of the organization. An important point is that these activities shall be systematic and under continuous control with regard to costs and the time used.

The question of planning for the best possible development of an organization—and whether time and money will be spent on this—must of course be seen in light of the fact that there is at all times *some* development of the organization taking place. Failing such a plan, this development will take place on an *ad hoc* basis without any special aim, and probably in different directions within different departments. The environment to which this development leads will thus be a *fait accompli* at any time and may have an inhibiting effect on the wish to carry through plans which, at the time they are relevant, will not be 'accepted' within the environment made up by the company.

A plan for organizational development, which also has the purpose of improving the possibilities of the organization to attain its objectives, may contain a number of components which will usually differ from one company to another. The purpose is to find out which parts of the organization may benefit from improvements in working methods, communication, and possibly work distribution. Before we stipulate any objective for an organizational development, a 'diagnosis' will be required, and this must be developed with assistance from and acceptance by the sections where the changes are considered to be desirable.

Even though the individual parts of an organizational development will vary from situation to situation, we will find the same main components. If, for our purpose, we define an organization as a rational co-ordination of the activities of a certain number of persons to attain a definite purpose or an objective with the help of a division between work and function and through a hierarchical system for authority and responsibility, we will see that as long as the purpose of the co-ordination is *the activities* and not the people, the role concept becomes very important. An organization may thus also be understood as a pattern of roles and a recipe for the co-ordination of these. The preparation of this is what we call 'organizational planning'. Organizational structures, technology, etc. will only work, however, to the extent that individuals and working groups fill their working roles in a satisfactory manner. A ready-made recipe for the co-ordination of the roles does not by itself guarantee an efficient organization.

What we are looking for is through more effective use of the employees to increase the organization's efficiency applying methods which do not seem to be sufficiently maintained through traditional organizational planning. A point of departure may be to list some of the problems which limit the efficiency of the supervisors and/or their departments, and to look at these in conjunction with practical measures for solving the problems. In this instance, it must be taken into account that the management of a company is under continuous development, a development which is largely subjective and characterized by *ad hoc* solutions. Such a development may be in an acceptable direction, but may also be undesirable. A typical example of the latter is that 'fiefdom' phenomena and fractionalism may occur quite extensively in spite of wishes from the management of the company in the opposite direction.

Why did the company initiate O.D.?

There were several reasons why in 1969 evaluation was initiated of measures which could both improve the working environment and make the organization more efficient and better able to face changes.

An important element was increased knowledge of the results from behavioural science; another was changes in values and attitudes by the young; a hird was some doubt whether the existing functional organizational structure was the best.

As a part of the preparations, Professor S. M. Kile from the Norwegian University of Business Administration carried out a study among some supervisors in the company. The result of this showed that there was a large degree of uncertainty and fear present in the organization, and that there was a lack of security and openness which was considered necessary to create an efficient organization and a good working environment.

The company's management decided in the course of 1969 that an O.D. process should be initiated. The objective should be to increase the efficiency of the organization and to improve the working environment of the employees. Increased efficiency was defined as more flexibility and better ability to adapt to changes, and to achieve economies. An improved working environment was defined as more participation and more meaningful jobs.

How did we start?

When the decision about O.D. had been reached, the term O.D. was relatively unknown in Norway, and most of the people probably associated O.D. with Blake and Mounton's grid.

The decision to initiate O.D. was taken by management, as mentioned above, but also among the middle management there was a clear recognition that something should be done. One of the reasons for this was that there had been some lecture/discussion evenings with middle management. For these events, the company invited lecturers from work research institutes, universities, etc. to talk about behavioural science, organizational theory, etc.

A question which came up was how we should get started. Should we:

- purchase an O.D. package or create our own?
- make use of internal or external consultants?
- start at the top, in the middle, or at the base of the organization?
- start with a pilot group or start broadly?

It became clear, after most top managers had completed 'The Managerial Grid', that there was a desire to develop the company's own O.D. process. The background for this was a clear recognition that this had to be a process that started within the company and which the employees could take part in. Furthermore, it was considered as a prerequisite that the process was based on a diagnosis, put forward by the employees themselves.

Following this decision, it was relatively easy to agree on using in-house consultants. It was assumed that by selecting good and well-accepted employees as consultants, their acceptance in the organization would balance the lack of professional qualifications (see page 161 below about in-house consultants).

Top management decided not to take part in the O.D. process from the start but gave support to the activities in the form of time, money, and human resources.

It was considered important that the first O.D. groups were successful and gave results, so that this would constitute a positive spreading effect. It was therefore decided that a pilot group should start in the spring of 1970, and that this should be broadened with three or four new groups in the course of the autumn 1970.

When we talk about O.D. groups in this instance, it is the supervisor and those reporting to him that make up an O.D. group. The groups may vary from six to twelve persons. Each supervisor thus took part in two groups: his own with the people working for him, and his supervisor's group together with his colleagues. In some groups, there could be more than two levels.

The pilot group was selected from the level below the top management with a Class-of-Market Manager and those reporting to him. This department was selected since all were interested in starting an O.D. process.

Later, groups were started when required by the departments. From the company's point of view, no pressure was put on anybody to start; however, it cannot be disregarded that in some instances there were cases of pressure from the department itself to get everyone to participate. There were a couple of instances of employees close to pensionable age who did not take part, something that did not seem to have any negative effect on the process.

Experimentation

The intention to start with a pilot group, and then gradually increase the extent of the process, was that it was difficult to see in advance what the correct line of attack should be. We had studied the O.D. process in other companies, but were aware that conditions vary from organization to organization, so that it would not be possible to make direct use of the experience of others. We had therefore to be willing to experiment, and to accept the fact that mistakes would be made. By using the trial-and-error method with the pilot groups, who had good motivation for starting an O.D. process, and who accepted that it could take a little time before we found the best form, we became more sure of success when we started up on a broader basis. Nor could time schedules be fixed until we had gained experience of how the pilot groups would develop. When the process was first planned it was seen as a three-year programme for middle management. However, it soon became clear that the process would have to cover the total organization, and that it was an ongoing process with no time limit.

This willingness to experiment in the initial phase also became very important later in the process, because it formed the basis for developing a good learning environment, and for finding unconventional solutions to problems (see Results, page 164 below).

The very process

The O.D. process consisted of several phases (Figure 1). The input phase consisted of six meetings, of approximately two to three hours each, arranged during working hours. The purpose of this phase was to give participants some knowledge about motivation theory, behavioural science research, group work, and organizational theory. In this phase, the consultant functions as a teacher. He presents and lectures about the subject-matter, and initiates the discussion. The input phase is important in order to create confidence both within the group and between the group and the consultant. The discussions in this phase are relatively neutral, and efforts are made to avoid raising controversial questions in the department.

The input phase could be arranged as a two-day seminar, but in order to initiate a process we decided to arrange the meetings three to four weeks apart. This offered opportunities to read recommended subjects between the meetings, for reflection, and for discussion between colleagues.

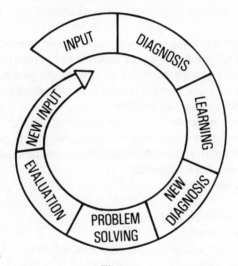

Figure 1

The next phase, the diagnostic phase, is critical—this is where the foundations are laid for success or failure. Depending on the maturity of the group, the consultant has a range of tools to initiate the diagnosis—interviews, questionnaires, brainstorming, etc. When the process was initiated, interviews were often used. The interviewer could be either the consultant himself, or one of the participants. The group decided for itself which tool they would use, and who should be the interviewer, if applicable.

In the course of the later years, it has become more usual to make use of

brainstorming. The experiences from the diagnostic phase is that even if th
ambition and need for an in-depth diagnosis is present, the first effort t
formulate a diagnosis will usually be somewhat superficial.

The reason for this is frequently a fear of criticizing. Criticism is looked at a
something negative. It is therefore a task for the consultant to make th
participants look at criticism as something positive, which may help them t
improve both efficiency and the environment.

Since some groups find it difficult to progress from this stage, a learning phas
has been incorporated. The purpose of this phase is to give the groups a
opportunity to consider in detail material which they consider important for
better diagnosis. The groups are free to choose, but so far most groups hav
selected the so-called group process seminar, supervised by Professor S. M. Kile
This seminar, which lasts for three days, has the following objectives:

● To provide increased knowledge and ability in cooperation.
● To increase the individual participant's knowledge about himself and hi
  own feelings.
● To enhance his appreciation of the reactions and feelings of othe
  individuals.
● To learn to communicate better with other people, to express oneself better
  and to interpret the meanings of others more correctly.
● To learn about groups by living in a working group and to study it
  development here and now, at location, and to see what inhibits and wha
  promotes a positive group process.

This seminar has turned out to be very important for future O.D.

The problems solution phase follows when the group has agreed on th
diagnosis. An action plan is formulated which may contain the following point
after the problem has been identified:

● criteria for a good solution;
● procedures;
● relevant factors to be evaluated;
● alternative solutions;
● advantages/disadvantages in the choice of solution;
● decisions.

Examples of change/problem areas have been:

● The relationship between the headquarters/district offices, including whc
  shall take part in deciding on the policy, and priorities between work tasks
  at the headquarters and in the districts.
● Poor communication; information does not reach those who need it in the
  decision-making process.
● The process for setting objectives.
● The organizational structure: 'is our department organized so that it may
  effectively solve the tasks put on it?'.
● Co-operation between salesmen/engineers/drivers.

The results attained in the first group were so positive that the desired spreading effect of the O.D. process was quickly arrived at.

Evaluation of the O.D. process will be dealt with in a later section.

The O.D. consultants

As previously mentioned, it was decided that in-house consultants should be used, but it was clear at the same time that their professional level would be lower than in the case of full-time external consultants. In order to mitigate this effect, a manual for O.D. consultants was prepared. Regular meetings were also arranged with the consultants to exchange experience. Also, external lecturers were invited to these meetings.

The O.D. consultants' objectives were: 'to help the company's O.D. groups in their work to attain the aims of the O.D. activities by contributing material for reading, proposing alternative working meetings, assisting in formulating problems, and solving problems. Furthermore, they should generally be at the disposal of the group in all questions relating to O.D. Their ultimate objective is to make the groups able to conduct the O.D. work independently, integrated with their usual tasks.'

Which criteria should then be stipulated for an O.D. consultant? The ideal requirements were considered to be:

- Fast-moving brain, i.e. the ability to quickly catch up on different aspects of a process.
- Maturity and experience in dealing with/handling people.
- Not extreme in behaviour, i.e. neither 100% authoritarian nor 100% democratic.
- Must not be dependent upon a high degree of structure.
- Flexible/adaptable.
- Analytical abilities; must be able to diagnose.
- Sound judgement; must be able to evaluate the effect of changes.
- 'Political acumen'.
- Involvement.

To start with, only personnel staff were O.D. consultants. As the activity increased, the lack of consultants was a bottleneck in the process, and it became necessary to educate more consultants. Consultants were then selected both from personnel and from line departments. In order that consultants should get enough time for the O.D. work, it was agreed that the work as an O.D. consultant should be included in the work programme and that sufficient time should be set aside for the work as a consultant.

One of the problems for the O.D. consultants was to what extent they should become involved in the process; how much should they provoke? It is difficult to give a general answer to this question since it depends, among other things, on the group itself and the experience and knowledge of the consultant. We found that most groups expected that the consultant should drive a relative hard bargain to clarify the underlying factors of a problem. The groups knew full well that problems existed, but they did not always succeed in bringing them into the open, without help.

As it appears from the objective, the consultant's final aim was 'to enable the group to conduct O.D. work itself, integrated with their usual work'. In the beginning, this was understood to the effect that when a group was well underway, it was left to its own devices. This turned out to be untenable; after a while the O.D. activities would fade away. It was therefore concluded that the O.D. consultant should meet with his groups a few times every year. The purpose was to look at the decision-making process and to contribute with more updated input.

It became clear that the consultant had three functions in relation to his O.D. group. The first was that of *teacher*. This function is prevalent in the input phase when he should transfer knowledge about behavioural science, as well as at the beginning of the diagnostic phase when he must teach the group to make use of feedback and instruments to get the diagnosis started. In this part of the process the group depends on the consultant; if he is not present, the whole meeting will fall into shambles. As the group gets started on the diagnostic phase, the group assumes more of the responsibility for the process and the consultant then becomes *the coach* who helps the groups to defeat their own weakness and to develop the knowledge and abilities to attack the problems which they are faced with, for instance MBO, job development, job analysis, conflict-solving, and problem-solving.

As the groups become more able to control their problems, the consultant's role is changed yet again, and he now becomes *an adviser*, whom the group approaches as necessary. At the same time, however, the consultant also has a responsibility to keep contact with the group a couple of times each year.

Short description of the O.D. process from 1970 to 1982

The elements of the O.D. process when it was started in 1970 are shown in Figure 1. It was originally envisaged that the O.D. process should be part of the three-year management development plan of the company.

It quite quickly became clear, however, that O.D. was more than management training, and that it was a process that had to encompass all groups of employees.

The model (Figure 1) which was used as a start, and which comprised a fair amount of reading of behavioural science material, turned out to be less well suited for employees at a lower level. They wanted to start from a 'here and now' situation. On this basis, a new model was prepared (Figure 2). In this instance it was decided to start with the work situation of the individual, and the expectations he had of the job. Afterwards, other circumstances affecting the job are looked at, such as the relationship with the boss, colleagues, customers,

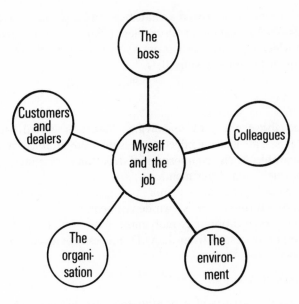

Figure 2

dealers, etc. The diagnosis is usually performed in connection with each individual subject. Since there is little theoretical input in this model, subject brochures were prepared about feedback communication, work in groups, etc. which could be used as required.

At one of the larger depots there is a group consisting of supervisors at different levels, as well as shop stewards from trade unions. To start with, the shop stewards were somewhat doubtful in relation to the O.D. work, in that they did not clearly see the borderline between subjects raised in the O.D. work and things that they would raise with the management in a formal manner in their capacity as shop stewards. However, the group turned out to function well, and later, several other groups were established inside the depot.

As mentioned above, management decided not to take part in the O.D. process from the start. However, as the process progressed, and middle management could see that they had partly changed their management style to a more participative style, they asked questions about the management style of top management. They felt that this was still authoritarian, and that management also had to take part in a fair part of the O.D. process if the O.D. process were to really be penetrative. Management then decided to take part.

In 1976, approximately 600 of the 800 employees of the company at the time were involved in O.D. activities. All levels and all parts of the organization took part.

In 1979, management approved a 'Statement on Organization Development' (see Appendix A). A statement on 'Principles on Participation' had already been approved, in which O.D. was seen as one way of achieving a more efficient and rewarding organization (Appendix B).

Results

As mentioned above, the problem-solving phase was started with relatively simple problems. This had the effect that results were attained at three levels.

(1) Simple problems, e.g. composition of department meetings, information, objectives for one's own department.

(2) Interpersonnel problems, e.g. more participative management style, more delegation, restructuring of one's own department.

(3) The total organization, e.g. reorganization.

A few examples of results from the O.D. process are given below.

Retail management group

The retail market consisted of a headquarters organization with a Class-of-Market Manager, who had a planner, an aftermarket supervisor, and engineers, etc. reporting to him. Furthermore, there was a district organization consisting of seven retail districts. The policy of the market was determined by the headquarters organization and then notified to the districts. During the O.D. process it appeared that the district managers found this to be less than satisfactory. They felt that they were the ones with most contact with the customers, and that they should therefore have an influence on the development of guidelines and policies for the retail market. This was discussed, and it was agreed to establish a Retail Management Group consisting of the Class-of-Market Manager and the seven district managers. This group meets once a month to discuss and decide on guidelines and policies.

Partly autonomous group

(i) Three regional sales representatives within the industrial market in three neighbouring districts found that they could better utilize the resources if they worked as a partly autonomous group, reporting directly to the Class-of-Market Manager at the Head Office rather than to one district manager each. This was accepted. It was further accepted that the group, after its performance had been evaluated, should itself be able to distribute the individual wage rises. There were some conflicting opinions on this, namely that they would either split the amount equally or that they would even out the differences already existing. Nothing of the kind happened; to the contrary, the differences in wages increased.

In another partly autonomous group, where there were greater differences both in ages and job groups than in the one just mentioned, they declined to divide the wage increases themselves.

(ii) When the Manager of Internal Audit resigned, the employees proposed that they should function as a partly autonomous group. The problem here was that Internal Audit reported directly to the Audit Committee, and the question was who should represent Internal Audit in relation to the Committee? A solution to this was found in that the person responsible for each individual case would present at to the Audit Committee.

Election of manager

The Manager of the Computer Department was transferred to another job, and the employees in the department were of the opinion that the new manager should be found from among the employees of the department. The management accepted this. Among the employees there were several who felt qualified to take over as manager. A meeting was then arranged to stipulate the criteria which the new manager should meet. An open discussion followed about to what extent the individual candidates satisfied the criteria. In the end there were two candidates left between whom there was no way of distinguishing. The management was therefore asked to appoint one of these as a new manager. This was done.

Rebuilding a gasoline station

A district had to rebuild a gasoline station. The planning of this started in the traditional manner. The planner and engineer within the retail market performed the planning and presented to the district manager a proposed solution, which the latter accepted.

Within this district, which had approximately 25 employees, there had for a long time been an O.D. process in development, and the feeling was that O.D. had become part of daily life. Thus, a monthly meeting attended by all employees, where matters of importance for the district are discussed, had been arranged. At such a meeting, an orientation was given about the rebuilding of this gasoline station. It turned out that the drivers had strong views on how the new station ought to be, and they brought into this new elements such as the number of filling places. With one rather than three filling places, they could shorten the stay at the station and thus attain a more efficient distribution. The planner, supported by the district manager, argued for their own point of view, and tried to demonstrate the weak points in the arguments of the drivers. The O.D. consultant took part in the meeting where this was discussed, and felt that the points raised by the drivers had not been evaluated when the solution had been selected, and that upholding the authority of the positions was about to prevail out of reason. The consultant discussed the matter with the district manager, and it was agreed that the matter should be raised again at a new meeting where the district manager would be totally unbound in the question of which solution should be selected. The result of this meeting was that the views of the drivers was heeded, and the station was built with one filling place.

The reaction of the drivers to the handling of this matter was very positive. 'Now we feel like Shell employees with fully equal rights.' The planner and the engineer also realized that the drivers as 'users' of the station should have been involved in the planning process. What seemed for a while to become a matter of prestige was therefore solved through an open discussion to the satisfaction of everyone, and became part in forming a basis for increased efficiency and better co-operation between the employees.

The 1973 oil crisis

In connection with the oil crisis, the general manager at that time stated that the organization could not have reacted so quickly and efficiently to the changes which ensued because of the oil crisis had the O.D. process not been a factor. A new pattern of distribution/allocation of oil products put an extra strain on staff. The company experienced an unexpected ability to improvise and willingness to work long hours. These factors were much appreciated by government departments with whom the company had to co-operate.

Reorganization

Since 1963/64 Norske Shell has been organized mainly along functional lines, within the sales function according to the 'class-of-market' principles. The organization was based on four main principles:
(1) specialization of sales efforts (through class of market);
(2) the skills/abilities will be best utilized through specialization;
(3) centralized management control should be exercised through policies and guidance, and not through centralized decision-making processes;
(4) stringent and objective budgeting to check what happened against what had been envisaged.

With time it turned out that the organization had certain weaknesses, such as difficulties with co-ordination/integration of matters involving several categories of work, excess specialization, as well as too strong centralization for decisions.

Analyses performed indicated that there were trends in the direction of specialization and, to some extent, a strong trend to create special sectors. It was not only the management which saw the weaknesses in the existing organization; these problems were also raised in the O.D., groups where employees also pointed to the need for effectiveness.

In 1973 it was therefore decided to re-evaluate the said principles.

The factors which were considered to be the most important reasons for the need for a new evaluation of the organization were as follows:

External:
- increased emphasis on the company's social responsibility;
- participation;
- increased pace in the process of change in general;
- increased competition, small margins, increased costs;
- changes in attitudes (in relation to salary, authority, work);
- increased expectations of job satisfaction.

Internal:
- changed personnel policies;
- changes in attitudes;
- increased dependence between the individual units in the company;
- change of generations;
- poor financial results.

The following was used as a basis for re-evaluation. 'The explosive development within administration sciences and behavioural science will continue and the consequences for industry and commerce will be considerable. New administrative techniques and new ways to organize the work must be evaluated in relation to new knowledge about people, groups, and teams. A higher education level and increased demands on job content will also affect the organization and the ability of managers to use the resources represented by the employees.' New organizational principles were adopted after extensive consideration at all levels of management (Appendix C).

The organization was looked at as a concept comprising four elements:

(1) the employees;
(2) our technology;
(3) our activities;
(4) the structure within which we work (the organization).

The whole middle management echelon was involved during 1974 in discussions of principles and structures, which were given full support and acceptance. Important questions were:
- functions and tasks of headquarters and districts, as well as the relationship between them;
- training and information;
- uneasiness/uncertainty in the face of changes.

The first phase was the reorganization of the company's sales districts and distribution areas. Earlier, there were different geographical borders between the sales districts of the individual markets, and between these and the distribution areas. The co-ordination between sales and distribution took place at Head Office.

Integrated areas were now established with a management team consisting of representatives for sales and distribution. In larger areas, the office function could be represented too. The main change in the new organization is that Head Office is no longer the first step where the co-ordination between markets and functions takes place.

In phase 2, the structure of Head Office was evaluated. Again, there was a wish to involve as many as possible in the evolution process. For this reason it was decided to 'contract out' a number of tasks and problems to sub-groups whose members were, above all, employees who were competent in relation to the tasks, but also outsiders who could bring in other points of view. The result was that Sales and Distribution were merged into one function, Marketing. At the same time a new function was established, Supply and Trading. Furthermore, the number of markets was reduced.

In phase 3, a further study was performed which mainly affected Head Office—namely how integrated tasks should be handled. In this phase, integration was only looked at on an interfunctional basis. Integration aims to link something together as a whole. Through integration, efforts are made to create the best possible decisions and actions through taking into consideration all factors of importance for the case involved. In Norske Shell, integration means:

● a way of organizing;
● a way of working;
● an attitude.

As examples of integrated tasks (where integrated groups have been established), the following may be mentioned:

● working environment and safety group;
● computer-user group;
● MTM committee;
● training group;
● planning committee;
● public affairs group.

In the phases which the organization has gone through, it has moved from a relatively well-defined and specialized organizational pattern towards a more flexible and integrated pattern. It is important to point out that the principles are more important that the structure decided on. Different ways of structuring may nevertheless satisfy the principles (see Appendix C).

Evaluation

It is difficult to evaluate an O.D. process since it contains so many qualitative elements. In the case of Norske Shell, other than the survey performed by Professor Kile and mentioned above, no comprehensive analysis had been made of the organization before the O.D. activities were started.

In the first couple of years, the Personnel Department had to perform a cost–benefit analysis of the O.D. activities, which was presented to the management. On the basis of this analysis, and in view of the experiences from their own function, the management concluded that the O.D. activities contributed to a more efficient organization and a better working environment, and that the gain far outweighed the costs.

In spite of this, a need was felt for a more thorough evaluation. The possibilities for such an evaluation were present when three students from the Norwegian University of Business Administration put forward a request whether they could perform an evaluation of the O.D. activities within Norske Shell as part of their final examination. This was accepted, and the survey took place at the turn of the year 1975/76, i.e. five years after the O.D. activities had started.

The students were given *carte blanche* to interview employees, to visit the districts, and to study our O.D. material. This open attitude surprised the students somewhat. They seemed to have expected a quite different attitude from a large, multinational oil company.

In the first instance, the students interviewed some employees to get an understanding for the organization and the O.D. process. Afterwards, they developed a questionnaire which was submitted to 142 employees, all of whom had completed the group process seminar; the percentage of answers was 97.2%, which of course was a positive incentive for the students in their further work.

The survey comprised:
● the O.D. consultants;
● the group process seminar;
● the diagnosis phase;
● inter-human relations;
● co-operation and efficiency;
● the O.D. activities at present.
It would go too far to refer to all the results from this survey, but the following is quoted from the conclusion:

> It is quite clear that Organisation Development has been of great importance to Company development and that the Company has become less authoritarian and bureaucratic; in other words, the Company has become easier to live in. It is our impression that the majority of personnel get much greater satisfaction from their assignments, that there is greater flexibility and the ability and will to cooperate are much more pronounced than they were before. Efficiency in the various sections has improved because personnel are more flexible, and think more as a group than they did previously. We would also mention that time is saved and headaches avoided because people know more about each other, and more direct relationships are encouraged, for better or worse.

Looking back—what would we have done differently

When we look back at the start-up in 1970, is there then something which we would have done differently had we in 1970 had the experience which we have now?

Yes, there is no doubt that:

(1) We would have educated more consultants prior to start-up. The spreading effect turned out to be greater and materialized at an earlier point than

we had envisaged. The reason for this was that the groups that started the work quickly reached results, and that knowledge about this was spread through the organization. The lack of consultants was therefore very significant through the initial period.

(2) The input phase should have been mandatory for the whole organization. It was a principle that it should be a voluntary matter whether an employee would take part in the O.D. process. However, some felt uncertain about what O.D. really was. If we had kept the input phase separate from the actual O.D. process, and rather considered this as an introduction to O.D. before it was decided that O.D. should be started, we would probably have gained greater acceptance to start with.

(3) Some managers did not feel commitment towards the O.D. process. Greater effort should have been exerted in order to get them to accept the company's objectives in this area.

(4) In the beginning, when we had few consultants, we started with the management of the departments. This, frequently, turned out to have a negative effect on the rest of the department. They got uneasy and asked questions about what the management was discussing now which they were not let in on. As soon as we had enough consultants, we let the whole department initiate the O.D. process at the same time, and we rapidly got a far more positive attitude. The most important in this connection was the interplay which occurred with time between the different O.D. groups of the department.

(5) In the first period, we were of the opinion that when the groups had become mature enough, O.D. would become part of the day-to-day activities, and the groups would no longer require the help of a consultant. This turned out to be wrong. The groups made it for a while, but after a while many slid back into the old ways of functioning. When this problem was analysed, it was decided that each group should maintain contact with a consultant, also after one had progressed so far that O.D. had become part of the daily life. The consultant should no longer take part in regular meetings, but he should be on call when problems occurred. If the consultant did not hear from the group in the course of a six-month period, he should himself establish contact, with a view to take part in one of the monthly meetings, to see how, for example, the decision-making process was functioning.

(6) Even if the top management was involved and gave its support to the process, it was itself no part of it from the beginning. This was not of any consequence at the start, but was of greater importance after $1\frac{1}{2}$–2 years. At that time, middle management started to see that they had changed their management style to some extent, and that there had become a more participative management style downwards in the organization. However, they did not feel that it functioned this way upwards in the organization. In connection with the evaluation which took place in 1975/76, it was stated '... there was considerable uncertainty about Management's attitude to the whole project, but this situation

improved as soon as Management began to participate more actively'. This uncertainty was also felt by those who were responsible for the O.D. process. Management recognized the importance of its role in the process, and in spite of conflicting opinions amongst members in management it started the O.D. process within its own group and further problems were avoided.

Pitfalls

These are some pitfalls which should be avoided.

(1) Focusing too much on individuals and too little on the tasks to be solved. An organization is established to perform certain tasks to attain its supreme objectives. In an O.D. process, where human beings are central, this may easily have the effect that everything is focused on interhuman relations alone, without seeing this in relation to the tasks which are to be solved. If this is done, the O.D. activity will soon be discredited since it does not contribute to increasing the efficiency of the organization.

(2) That the consultant fails to clarify who his client is. If the consultant identifies himself with one part of the group, he may quickly lose credibility among the others. It is therefore important that there is a quick clarification of who is his client/client system.

(3) That in-house consultants refrain from intervening. An internal consultant is not an experienced psychologist and he may therefore be unsure as to what extent he should intervene. We have seen examples of groups that have come to a halt both because of too little intervention and too much intervention. It is important that this becomes a main part of the training of consultants. At the same time, there should be contact with experienced professionals from outside of the organization who may assist the consultants.

(4) In groups where there was little involvement to start with, the consultant may be tempted to take charge of the process. However, this is the safest method to kill the initiative in the group. Even if it goes slowly, the consultant must show patience and let the group itself take responsibility for what happens.

(5) That O.D. is looked at as something which has nothing to do with the day-to-day work. O.D. meetings are held to discuss interesting things about human behaviour and organizations, but this is not projected into the working situation. This again is a secure way to destroy the process. O.D. is looked at as meetings which do not contribute to solve any of the problems of the organization. It is therefore important that the diagnosis and problem-solving phase are initiated as soon as possible, and that problems are discussed which really create improvements in the organization.

Management information system on employees' attitudes

In order that the management are able to take the right decisions, they are continually informed about the company's operations through a set of

'Management Information Reports' (MIR). Through a long period, these reports have dealt with conditions relating to sales, profitability, economy, etc. With regard to human resources, there has been little information. This in spite of the fact that these resources, according to the objectives of the company, are '. . . the most important creative factor which shall secure the company's growth and progress'.

The development of a system for polling opinions was therefore entered on the activity list of the Personnel Department in 1976. The MIR which was then developed tells what the employees feel about some important factors in connection with the work situation.

This report, which was designated MIR 13, was developed in close collaboration with the employees. In order that it should be of value, it is necessary that the percentage of answers is high: a high answer percentage again depends on employees finding the questions to be relevant.

From the start, efforts were made to create a system which:

(a) uses a commonly understandable language on a comparable basis to express levels in employees' perception/attitudes towards the company's human resources management;

(b) measures a set of human factors of importance for the achievement of business activities;

(c) works on a regular basis sufficiently frequently to illustrate trends and important changes over time;

(d) provides a basis for objective-setting which allows assessment of a manager's effectiveness in managing and developing human resources;

(e) secures the anonymity of individuals;

(f) to be presented in similar form as other MIRs in use;

(g) encourages line managers and their subordinates to explore the results with a view to action planning.

After an internal working group, having consulted the employees and the management as mentioned above, had arrived at the questions which they felt should be included in a system for Norske Shell, Ashridge Management College* was asked to undertake a final design of the system. They had then already developed a computer system for processing the data which could be used by Norske Shell.

A questionnaire was prepared with 26 fixed questions and a character scale from 1 to 6. Beyond this, each poll would be an opportunity to supplement up to six additional questions. The 26 questions were grouped in eight areas:

(a) salaries;

(b) personal development;

(c) working conditions;

*Berkhamsted, Hertforshire, U.K.

(d) communication;
(e) participation;
(f) job satisfaction;
(g) efficiency;
(h) environment.

Polls are taken twice a year. On each occasion a random sample of employees is asked to fill in the questionnaire (Appendix D). For the whole company a sample of 15% would have been sufficient. However, as we want the feedback to be sent to each work-place, and the work-places are rather small, we need a greater sample to get statistically valid information. Consequently, on each occasion, 33% were asked at work locations with less than 50 employees, and 25% where there are more than 50 employees.

The results appear on computer printouts where average scores and standard variations for each question and for each function/work location are compared with numbers for the company as a whole.

Each individual department will thus get its own results and may compare these with the company as a whole. We are not interested in comparison between the departments. What is of importance is the trend over time, and how the individual department uses its own results. It is only after three or four polls that we can say that we have reliable trends (Appendices E and F).

MIR 13 turned out to be quite selective in its reaction to special circumstances, all the way down to the individual department/area. There have been effects over time as well as within several departments which have had obvious reactions and where the results have improved again after implementation of the necessary measures.

Conclusion

By way of conclusion, there are many reasons to point to the enormous learning process which takes place in connection with an O.D. process over a longer period of time. The importance of learning behavioural science, organization and organization theory, group processing, decision-making processes, areas within the organization other than one's own, the total objectives of the company, etc., together with a clear philosophy of participation, has the effect that the staff will be given a far higher level of appreciation of the company and its problems and of the wishes and needs of colleagues.

Appendix A: Statement on organization development

Retrospect

The company's O.D. programme, which was introduced in 1970, is based on results from research within the social sciences. The activities have so far been centred around the internal problems of the various departments, and to a limited degree on interfunctional matters (with some exceptions).

Briefly the objectives were to:

(a) clarify circumstances which are a hindrance to efficiency;
(b) increase information to managers on leadership principles, etc.;
(c) encourage improvement efforts;
(d) develop a satisfactory organization climate.

O.D. has contributed to an organization which is characterized to a greater extent than before by:

- increased efficiency;
- fewer departmental barriers;
- improved co-operation;
- more openness;
- increased job satisfaction;
- improved job competence.

These are all improvements recorded in an investigation made prior to introducing O.D.

New organization forms and new tasks make it important to continue the company's O.D. process. Therefore it may be practical to re-value the objectives in view of the development which has taken place since 1970.

Definition of O.D.

O.D. is 'any planned activity which intends to improve the ability of an organization to reach its target by making use of the total resources more effectively, particularly those of human nature.'

O.D. is a process for systematic change of the total organization through a development programme and not a short-term change by training only and limited to parts of the organization. An important point is that these activities should be systematic and under control with regard to costs and time.

Future objectives for O.D.

The O.D. objectives are to contribute to the achievement of the company's overall objectives by promoting:

- *an effective organization*, and
- *a working environment* which corresponds to the general development of the Norwegian society.

Further details concerning the objectives

An effective organization is:
- profitable;

result-oriented;
● maintaining an effective goal-setting procedure;
optimally staffed.

working enivronment is also:
giving the employee opportunities, within the framework of the company's objectives, to use their abilities and talents;
characterized by job security and job satisfaction.

The principles of organization, leadership, and participation specify what is ecessary for the company to develop in the desired direction.
O.D. will contribute to the realization of these principles.

The strategy

The following items are emphasized:

(a) To make O.D. an integrated part of the company's daily operations/activities.

(b) To develop efficient team work, also cross-functionally.

(c) To maintain and develop openness and informal relations among colleagues at all levels.

(d) To assist our managers in achieving their objectives by practising the principles of participation and a high degree of delegation.

(e) To contribute to identifying training needs to enable everyone to function as well as possible in team relations.

(f) To follow up the attitude survey (MIR 13) as an important instrument in O.D. work.

Approved by Management January 1979.

Appendix B: A/S Norske Shell's principles on participation

To ensure that the company develops in the desired direction it is necessary that:

(1) The principles of management by objectives are applied throughout the company. We hope to achieve this through specialized training and the continued development of systems already in existence, such as our staff report system.

(2) We continue our efforts to make the organization more efficient and more rewarding for those who work in it. This is to be achieved through our management training and our O.D. work. In so doing we hope to introduce a more consultative/participatory climate in the organization.

(3) We develop a more flexible organizational structure with less emphasis on formal distinctions/demarcations between divisions and functions and more emphasis on the competence of the individual.

(4) Our line managers carry out these principles in their work.

(5) The company's personnel policy at any time is in harmony with ou objectives.

The most important factor in producing the desired effect as set out in thi statement is for people to see concrete evidence that this is meant in earnest. I practice this is tantamount to saying that the Company must put a lot of wor into implementing point 4.

Appendix C: A/S Norske Shell's principles on organization

The environment and the company

The objectives, structures, and way of operating must meet the present and futur demands of society and the markets, i.e. the organization must be able to chang as changes in these demands occur.

Objectives and results

All activities shall be objective- and result-oriented both qualitatively an quantitatively.

Management

The management style and the work methods will be group-oriented, with a hig degree of autonomy—for the individual as well as for working teams.

Decision-making

Decisions shall be made as close to the source of information as possible, with high degree of delegation as a means of training and motivation.

Controls

Control functions, i.e. performance versus targets, should as far as possible b based on self-control. Company controls such as legal, safety, and audit ar centralized, as well as the design and maintenance of systems in finance an personnel.

The needs of the individuals

The tasks, i.e. the jobs, should be structured in order to achieve the objectives and at the same time satisfy human needs.

Appendix D: Questionnaire

1–26: Standard questions
27–29: Special questions
(for survey 2/1979)

	Entirely disagree 1	Tend to disagree 2	More disagree than agree 3	More agree than disagree 4	Tend to agree 5	Agree entirely 6
01 My salary development in Norske Shell is satisfactory	01–02					
02 There are good opportunities to get further education/training if I need it	03–04					
03 The company demonstrates social responsibility towards its employees	05–06					
04 My job gives me great satisfaction	07–08					
05 I get the information and guidelines I need to do my work properly	09–10					
06 I feel that my future in the company is secure	11–12					
07 I get opportunities to become involved in company problems and tasks outside my normal work	13–14					
08 My day-to-day work bores me	15–16					
09 I receive recognition for my work	17–18					
10 The company puts heavy emphasis on industrial safety	19–20					
11 In my part of the company we are always striving to improve work methods and routines	21–22					
12 Co-operation is good between the company's various departments	23–24					
13 The last staff appraisal interview has proved of benefit to my work	25–26					
14 The various units of the company are hampered in their work due to insufficient information	27–28					
15 The company has a good reputation	29–30					

APPENDIX D: Questionnaire

1–26: Standard questions
27–29: Special questions (for survey 2/1979)

	Entirely disagree 1	Tend to disagree 2	More disagree than agree 3	More agree than disagree 4	Tend to agree 5	Agree entirely 6	
16	I feel that employees have increasing influence on company decisions						31–32
17	I am sure Shell will continue to be one of the leading oil companies in Norway						33–34
18	My salary gives a fair impression of my work for the company						35–36
19	I feel I have a say in decisions affecting my own work						37–38
20	I feel I can raise any question in the staff appraisal interview						39–40
21	The company does a great deal to improve the physical work environment						41–42
22	My superiors do not show any genuine interest in my point of view						43–44
23	I consider that promotion in the company is made on a fair basis						45–46
24	I am encouraged to take on responsibility in my work						47–48
25	Personal relationships are bad in my section						49–50
26	I feel it is my duty to work towards achieving the objectives of my section						51–52
27	I consider that sufficient time was allocated for the staff appraisal interview in 1979						53–54
28	Priorities in relation to my work assignments/objectives, laid down in connection with the staff appraisal interview, have been discussed carefully and agreement has been reached on them						55–56
29	Priorities in relation to work assignments, recorded during the staff appraisal interview, are followed up regularly with my chief						57–58

Appendix E: A/S Norske Shell—opinion poll

Period: May 1981
No. of answers: 10

Department/group consists of:
Place of work:

Question	No.	Main Areas		Group/ Departm. Response	Company Total Response
My salary development in Norske Shell is satisfactory	1		Average	4.2	4.1
			S.D.	1.4	1.4
My salary gives a fair impression of my work for the company	18	Salary	Average	3.5	3.9
			S.D.	1.9	1.4
There are good opportunities to get further education/training if I need it	2		Average	5.1	4.7
			S.D.	0.7	1.7
The last staff appraisal interview has proved of benefit to my work	13	Personal development	Average	4.1	3.7
			S.D.	1.1	1.5
I consider that promotion in the company is made on a fair basis	23		Average	3.9	4.1
			S.D.	1.6	1.3
The company demonstrates social responsibility towards its employees	3		Average	5.3	5.2
			S.D.	0.8	1.0
I feel that my future in the company is secure	6		Average	3.5	4.7
			S.D.	1.6	1.4
The company puts heavy emphasis on industrial safety	10	Work condition	Average	5.2	5.1
			S.D.	0.7	1.0
The company does a great deal to improve the physical work environment	21		Average	5.0	4.8
			S.D.	0.6	1.2
I get the information and guidelines I need to do my work properly	5		Average	4.0	4.5
			S.D.	0.8	1.0
The various units of the company are hampered in their work due to insufficient information	14		Average	3.6	3.1
			S.D.	0.8	1.3
I feel I can raise any question in the staff appraisal interview	20	Communication	Average	5.1	5.1
			S.D.	1.4	1.3
Personal relationships are bad in my section	25		Average	2.1	1.8
			S.D.	0.8	1.2
Co-operation is good between the company's various departments	12		Average	3.4	4.0
			S.D.	1.6	1.4
I get opportunities to become involved in company problems and tasks outside my normal work	7		Average	3.0	3.5
			S.D.	1.5	1.5
I feel that employees have increasing influence on company decisions	16	Participation	Average	3.5	3.8
			S.D.	1.3	1.4

APPENDIX E: A/S Norske Shell—Opinion Poll

Period: May 1981   Department/group consists of:
No. of answers: 10   Place of work:

Question	No.	Main Areas		Group/ Departm. Response	Company Total Response
I feel I have a say in decisions affecting my own work	19		Average	4.6	4.4
			S.D.	1.2	1.4
My job gives me great satisfaction	4		Average	4.6	4.6
			S.D.	0.7	1.2
My day-to-day work bores me	8		Average	2.0	2.0
			S.D.	0.9	1.3
I receive recognition for my work	9	Job satis- faction	Average	3.9	4.3
			S.D.	1.5	1.4
My superiors do not show any genuine interest in my point of view	22		Average	3.1	2.8
			S.D.	1.4	1.5
I am encouraged to take on responsibility in my work	24		Average	4.8	4.6
			S.D.	1.2	1.4
In my part of the company we are always striving to improve work methods and routines	11		Average	4.9	4.8
			S.D.	1.1	1.1
I feel it is my duty to work towards achieving the objectives of my section	26	Effici- ency	Average	5.8	5.6
			S.D.	0.4	1.0
I am sure Shell will continue to be one of the leading oil companies in Norway	17		Average	4.5	5.1
			S.D.	1.0	1.0
The company has a good reputation	15	Environ- ments	Average	5.0	4.9
			S.D.	0.6	1.1

S.D. = Standard deviation.

Epilogue

O.D. in the 1970s

In the 1970s, O.D. work was aimed at participation, group work and group processes, leadership styles, and objectives.

About 800 of the company's employees were involved in, and obtained strong impressions from, the O.D. process. This applied to all levels, from management to drivers and operators, and was spread over all functions.

Based on the O.D. objectives, the process became a massive activity which

Appendix F: MIR 13

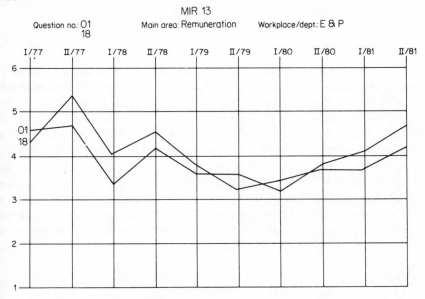

MIR 13

Question no.: O1
18

Main area: Remuneration   Workplace/dept.: E & P

both influenced and created a good learning environment, and which had a decisive influence on management, organization, personnel policy, efficiency, and the daily life of A/S Norske Shell.

O.D. in the 1980s—second generation O.D.

The O.D. objectives, i.e. a more efficient organization and a better working environment, will always take first place in an organization's operations, but it is obvious that the problems which must be solved in the 1980s are different from those faced in the 1970s.

It is assumed that requirements in the 1980s will be related to the rate of change, productivity, efficiency, organization, future planning, lifestyle, use of resources, equality, and automation. Furthermore, conditions within the company will be influenced by the fact that we are an integrated company with three principal functions, E & P, the Refinery, and Marketing, which have definite characteristics as regards assignments, staffing, and working conditions, but at the same time all three have to work as a single unit.

As a result of this, we must find out what is common and accept that which is different. The O.D. process carried out in the 1970s had more or less the same structure for all O.D. groups.

This will not be possible in relation to the second generation O.D., for which we shall have to accept different forms of attack, and various techniques based on the individual requirements of the departments.

Starting the second generation O.D.

If an O.D. process is to be successful, it is essential that it is based on a diagnosis made by individual departments. The traditional way to start is to examine the current situation, then the desired situation, and then plan how progress is to be made from the current to the desired situation. Here there should also be flexibility. On the basis of the overhead value analyses (OVA), the management information system on employees' attitudes (MISEA) and previous O.D. activities, some departments will probably find it more productive to start by asking the question: 'What is the desired situation?' What must be avoided is to look upon O.D. as just theory, and something that occurs in addition to the daily work of the company. The process must therefore be based on the overall objectives of the company and its functions, and on how individual departments can contribute to achieving these objectives as efficiently as possible.

Experience gained with our own internal consultants in the sphere of change has proved very good. Training of such consultants has therefore been started, and 13 candidates have already completed the first phase of the training process. We assume that we shall need 15 O.D. consultants, each of whom will use about 15 days annually to assist departments in the O.D. process.

In order to adapt O.D. activities to the requirements of individual departments, 'training packages' will be prepared. Examples of such packages are as follows:

- Effective meetings.
- Time planning/personal efficiency.
- Communication.
- Creativity.
- Presentation techniques.
- Life planning.
- Objectives procedure/MBO.
- Group processes.

The O.D. consultants will be able to master some of the above-mentioned sectors themselves, but in certain cases they will have to draw on the expertise of others.

Management commitment

It is necessary that the process has a planning and follow-up procedure. This will be on two levels.

Management. Extensive research and experience indicates that the best results have been obtained where management are actively involved in O.D. work.

'hus, by drawing up objectives and guidelines, management can inspire those ⱱho carry out the work of O.D. from day to day. The Personnel Department will rrange the more systematic and long-term planning and will also annually ubmit feedback to management regarding the previous year's activities.

he ERFA Group (experience group). In connection with the first generation).D., it proved to be useful to establish an ERFA Group for O.D. consultants. 'his group should meet a least twice a year to discuss problems/exchange ⱱperiences regarding the O.D. process, suggest changes to and perhaps prepare ⱱew training packages, and furthermore, bring the consultants' knowledge up to ate.

'he above contains a number of conditions for further developing the rganization in order to cope with the uncertainties of our world; the emphasis ⱱill remain on *flexibility* and on *learning*.

Paul Waaktaar
Personnel Director
A/S Norske Shell

)ecember, 1983

People and Organizations Interacting
Edited by A. Brakel
© 1985, John Wiley & Sons Ltd.

Chapter 10

Working Life in Japan

*Osamu Hattori**

Introduction

It is generally pointed out that the Japanese people are characteristically
obedient and work well in the group to which they belong. As Tetsuro Watsuji, a
Japanese philosopher, said, 'Japanese sacrifice their ego for family or group
familiarity relationships'; Ruth Benedict, an American sociologist, in her
Chrysanthemum and Sword (1946), after an extensive and lengthy investigation
commented similarly that, 'Japanese children learn to abandon individuals'.
Satisfaction is obtained by making sacrifices for the sake of the group to which
one belongs. The reward given for appropriate behaviour is that of being agreed
with and accepted by other people and one learns that to be scorned is to be
punished; thus is developed the 'culture of shame'.

After the Second World War a democratic way of thinking was introduced to
Japan from European countries, urbanization increased, and *esprit de corps* was
weakened; and at the same time values diversified. It is often said that these
external influences and internal changes helped to change Japan's culture, but a
recent investigation reveals that the mentality of 'groupism' has not changed.
According to an investigation conducted in 1979 by Nihon Hoso Kyokai
(NHK)—the Japan Broadcasting Corporation—Japanese children's attitudes

---

* With the assistance of C. K. Gunner (Shell Japan).

are characterized by (a) homogeneity, (b) a slow growth of independence, and (c) a passive posture with little self-assertion.*

A survey by the Prime Minister's Office conducted in 1980 came to similar findings, endorsing NHK's survey.† In spite of these conclusions, we can point out one recent difference. In pre-war days traditional collectivism was considered to be a value which superordinated the individual, and collectivism, i.e. obeying passively at the sacrifice of ego, had in itself an ethical significance. But following the Second World War, there is no such significance to be found, rather it is simply a *harmonious* attitude towards the group which is revered. Professor Masumi Tsuda, a Japanese sociologist, opines that in Japan the ideal form of relationship between the individual and the group is one of harmony and identification, not conflict, and that the work place is the obvious place for individuals to be 'absorbed' but at the same time allowed to develop.

There are few data which have been collected internationally to demonstrate how Japanese differ from people of other countries, or to what extent the Japanese value collectivism, but an attitude survey conducted by the Prime Minister's Office in 1979 covering employees in the United Kingdom, the United States and Japan is significant (Figures 1 and 2). According to the survey, the USA and UK had many similarities but data in relation to Japan shows a different approach in terms of attitudes to the work-group, to work itself, and to life in general. As regards the importance of the superior–subordinate relationship, or the relationship with peers, workers in the three countries gave a common response (A and B of Figure 1), however Japanese workers showed a greater preference for close association between superiors and peers, even outside office hours, and preferred to spend time improving those associations away from the workplace (C and D of Figure 1). In a comparison between work life and social life, the emphasis placed on work by the Japanese was remarkably strong when compared with that of the United Kingdom or the United States (A of Figure 2).

It is noteworthy that the difference in scores between adults and youth was comparatively greater in the case of Japan, which may signify that Japanese young people are not provided with work in the organization which is of sufficient importance to give them a sense of self-worth. At the same time this may show there has been a change of attitude by youth towards work which can be illustrated by another survey conducted by the Prime Minister's Office.‡ ('The current youth compared with those ten years ago, 1981' shown in Table 1.)

* Published by Nihon Hoso Kyokai in 1980 under the title *Nihon no Kodomotachi* (*Japan's Children*).

† The survey by the Prime Minister's Office was published in 1980 under the title *Nihon no Kodomo to Hahaoya* (*Japan's Children and Mothers*). A reference to Prof. Masumi Tsuda's remark may be found in *Nihon Keiei no Yogo* (*Support for Japan's Business*) published by Toyo Keizai Shimpo in 1976.

‡ The survey by the Prime Minister's Office was published under the title *Soshiki de Hataraku Seishonen no Ishiki Chosa* (*Opinion Survey on Youth Working in Organisations*) in 1978.

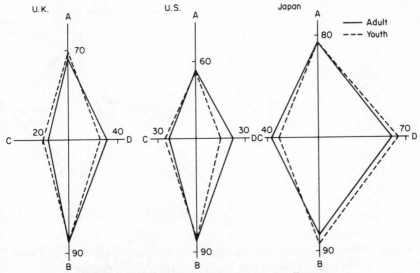

Figure 1   Relations with superiors and colleagues

A: Relations with superiors and subordinates are like those with seniors and juniors in school days, and for that reason are valuable.

B: In relations with colleagues one's fate is to some extent shared and colleagues are likened to brothers, and for that reason are valuable.

C: Free hours outside work are spent with colleagues from work unless arrangements have been made with the family.

D: Relations with superiors and colleagues at the work place are extended to associations outside the work place.

Since this sort of comparison has not been made historically, it is impossible to show how the attitudes of the Japanese have changed from the past, but it can safely be said differences reflect the changed cultural background and management style in industry, and these are considered to be factors which have certainly affected the development of organizations in Japan.

More directly, the factors which are inherent in Japanese management and which affect the progress of organizational development activities in Japan can be summarized as below:

Life-long employment

Since the 1950s, employment up to retiring age has been the general practice in Japanese industry. The retirement age in the 1950s was about 55 years and as such did not differ markedly from the then life expectancy of 60 years. Longevity has advanced remarkably since then to 74 for men and 80 for women, and the retirement age has tended to be postponed to around 60. Employers make every effort to ensure that employment can continue up to the employee's retirement age, even in the face of severe difficulties, by taking action to increase

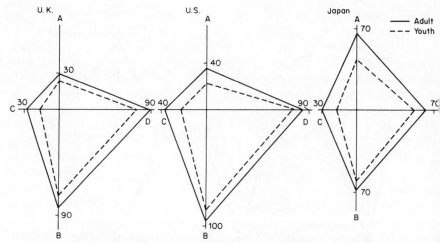

Figure 2   Worth, concern, and expectations on company, work-place, and work

    A: Comparing 'work' with 'others', worth is found through work.
    B: Worth of life is found in the current job.
    C: Away from the office, work does not leave the mind.
    D: Expectations of working for the company are satisfied.

productivity, and through diversification, the scrapping of surplus facilities, etc.
At the same time, employees give of their time and effort unsparingly
spontaneously co-operating and sacrificing their demands for more pay or better
working conditions for the general corporate good. There is a trust and reliance
between employers and employees whereby employers ensure employment, and
employees respond with their full co-operation. The merit of the life-long
employment system lies not only in a sense of security and of belonging on the
part of employees, but also in that the system encourages employers to try and
develop employees through the workplace and employees to positively make
efforts to develop themselves.

Table 1   Current youth compared with those of ten years ago. Frequency of multiple
answers to the question 'what do you consider worthwhile in your life?'

	1970 (%)	1980 (%)
Committing myself to work	30	17
Committing myself to sports or hobby	44	54
Committing myself to social services	9	7
Committing myself to study	9	8
Being with friends or colleagues	39	59
Being with my family	21	17
Being alone without being bothered by others	18	8
Others	9	3

Neither universities nor high schools in Japan are considered capable of meeting the educational requirements of enterprises; rather they are places where the more general arts and sciences are taught. Specific skills and capabilities required by enterprises must be gained therefore after joining a company. It is generally accepted practice for an employee to develop himself through accepting educational investment made by companies; self-development also involves the individual's effort and the widening of his experiences through the job rotation scheme generally used by companies. This scheme involves the assignment of an individual to a number of different types of work, often at varying locations and sometimes as often as every four or five years. Indeed, it is rather rare for employees in medium and large-sized companies to be assigned to one specific job for many years, except in the case of manual workers and operators. And even in the case of workers and operators, it is required that they broaden their skills in order to adapt themselves to technological development or diversification of the business. It is thus not usual in Japan to say; 'he is a system designer' or, 'she is a personnel specialist', but rather 'he works for so-and-so company'. For an employee to be assigned to a job which is new to him is not an unhappy incident, for that is considered to be a good opportunity to broaden one's experience and to develop oneself. In fact, in the first year after a job transfer, the results of the work appraisal of the transferee will, in general, fall, as does the amount of merit pay increase, but this does not last for long, and ultimately the transferee is left with the benefit of his broadened experience. To maintain the practice of life-long employment means, on the part of companies, to secure employment in spite of changes in the business environment, changes in the business itself, technological innovation, etc. Employers therefore expect employees to be able to cope with change, and that employees, as a matter of course, will try to acquire new skills, and adapt themselves to new technology in accordance with the changing environment.

In-house unions

It is not true that the unions in Japan have always co-operated with employers regarding productivity improvement. Especially in the 1940s, significant difficulties in industrial relations were seen irrespective of the size of the enterprises. Around 1947 a series of long rounds of strikes were staged by coal unions, power industry unions, etc. Although there were a few companies which introduced participative management in pre-war days, and which passed through the days of turmoil without any serious dispute, the majority of companies experienced numerous labour disputes and were forced to improve their industrial relations for fear that sterile disputes would be repeated. In fact, both management and the unions learned much from that period. Labour unions in Japan are mostly 'in-house' unions, with a few exceptions which exist on a nation wide basis. Unions have learned to take the stance of viewing the development of the companies and the well-being of union members from a medium and long term viewpoint, i.e. unions basically choose to moderate their demands, in order to ensure that large pay increases will not lead to impoverishment of the company. The unions prefer to first take a cooperative attitude for the development of the companies and, after that, try to get 'their share'. Accordingly, the union executives in Japan are required to have deep insight into the national economy, the current business situation, as well as future prospects. These insights are considered imperative qualifications with which union executives are equipped to develop discussions with management on an equal footing. In fact, some 70% of large companies in Japan have on their board of directors members who have had experience as union executives and about 20% of all directors have had experience as union executives.

Pay for capability

Thirdly, the remuneration system in Japan, i.e. pay for capability, is considered to be associated with the development of 'Quality Circles' and organizational development activities. Different from the system of 'pay for the job' which is common to European countries, pay for capability is the concept where one is remunerated in accordance with one's capability irrespective of the job one is assigned. Accordingly, if one demonstrates capability to assume a higher job, one is ranked higher and paid accordingly. This has the inherent demerit of increasing personnel costs but gives employees under the scheme encouragement to develop themselves continuously. Thus, where the job content is simplified for efficiency by automation or mechanization, the job may be evaluated as less taxing than before, but the incumbent of the job may remain in the same salary group or may even be ranked higher as a result of his efforts to improve efficiency. Even when a job opportunity ceases to exist due to the introduction of office automation or other such measures, the company secures alternative employment for its employees who, in turn, are expected to try to adapt themselves to their new jobs by developing and expanding their capabilities.

If the system of pay for the job and no security of employment were to be adopted, any movement towards mechanization or simplification would likely encounter resistance on the part of employees. The comparatively smooth introduction of robots in Japan, for example, is attributable to the underpinning of the Japanese remuneration scheme, life-long employment, and the cooperative attitude of the unions. And likewise, employees' positive attitudes towards productivity improvement through the formation of Quality Circles or 'family training', is closely associated with Japan's management style. (Though it will be discussed in some detail later, 'family training' is an activity of organizational development carried out through the participation of superiors and subordinates at the workplace in which they combine to identify and overcome problems.)

As a characteristic of Japan's organization, seniority rule (pay and promotion for age) is typically cited, but, nowadays, this is not a dominating rule at all. The rule seems to have given way in the face of technical innovation, progress of automation, rapid aging of the population and other such developments.

Background to introducing organizational development into Shell Japan

Shell started its business in Japan over 80 years ago in 1900 under the name 'Rising Sun K.K.', dealing in the trade of candles and kerosine. In 1949 it changed its name to Shell Sekiyu K.K., (Shell Oil) when the company resumed its business after temporary suspension during the Second World War.

Currently, Shell Japan conducts its business in the fields of oil, petrochemicals, business related to service stations, natural gas, coal, and metals, has some 2200 employees, and covers all parts of Japan.

The market in Japan is extremely competitive and Shell Japan is ranked, in terms of the domestic market for oil, fifth, with annual proceeds of £4000 M.

The Royal Dutch Shell Group, to which Shell Japan belongs, requires that each operating company operates its business autonomously, with necessary coordination from the Group's central advisers. Thus, though Shell Japan is a foreign capitalized company, its personnel administration is principally carried out based upon Japanese culture, with some adoption of western management techniques when they are found useful.

In looking at reasons for introducing 'organization development' activities into Shell Japan, consideration of the formal training courses previously conducted is useful. Before 1970, about 100 training courses with nearly 40 different purposes were conducted annually, involving more than 1000 staff members. Emphasis was placed on know-how and skills required for carrying out the job properly and efficiently. The training courses were run based upon the training needs identified through personnel appraisal conducted by superiors, and each participant, prior to attending the course was informed of the aim of the course, the expectation of his superiors as regards the course, etc. However, the results were often disappointing. The fact was that what had been learned through the training courses was only to a very limited extent transplanted to the actual business scene. One of the reasons behind this might have been due to poor follow-up following the formal training course, but in most cases, the desired behaviour learned through the course was simply not applied in the 'back-home' situation due to insufficient readiness of the work group (i.e. a group of people who generally work together or alongside one another) to accept that behaviour. For example, various measures for improvement of work procedures were taught in the Methods Planning Course, but it was rare for the measures to be applied to actual work so as to help improve efficiency. Most attendants put the files which contained what they had learned into their desks and forgot them. In view of this sort of waste of time and money, efforts were made to ensure that follow-up activities were carried out with the cooperation of line management, but this was not successful either. It became crystal clear that what is learned in an isolated situation is not applicable to the actual scene unless the climate of the workplace itself is guided to accept the change.

Another problem lay in the fact that the formal training was in most cases carried out with members from horizontal levels of the organizational hierarchy, i.e. Managers' Training, Supervisors' Training or New Entrants' Course. When discussions took place between groups of homogeneous members in terms of the organizational level on problem identification or how to cope with an identified problem area, the discussions were apt to be carried out in an undisciplined manner, shifting the responsibility for problems to other layers of the organization without examining what they themselves could do to solve the problems. Citing a couple of examples, subordinate groups claimed that jobs could efficiently be carried out if their supervisors sought better coordination with other related parties, and supervisors grumbled about the lack of explicit policy from managers. When the discussion is carried out in a situation isolated from the workplace, problem identification tends to be centered around the others' responsibility. This of course will never lead to the genuine problem solving. On the contrary, it sows the seeds of new problems. It was keenly felt that the parties concerned with problems should get together and discuss ways of identifying their problems and clarify what each individual should do to overcome them.

In seeking the solution to these kinds of difficulties in running the formal training courses, the Managerial Grid method developed by Professors R. R. Blake and J. S. Mouton was introduced to Japan. The method consists of six phases aiming at the embodiment of a superior organizational climate, and it was decided, after careful examination by management members as to the significance of the method, to introduce the method to Shell Japan.

The six phases comprise the following:
  (i) a Managerial Grid Seminar,
 (ii) Team Building,
(iii) Inter-group Development,
 (iv) Design of an ideal Corporate Model,
  (v) Implementing Development, and,
 (vi) Consolidation.

The first phase, the Grid Seminar, offered us a completely new type of training, more advanced than the conventional managerial training, with learning experiences giving attendants insight into their own management styles. As well, the seminar was designed for attendants to learn the importance of candour in communicating with others and of building effective team work. Participants stressed, as a result of the seminar, that they placed high value on the importance of candid communication and of active listening. After nearly two dozen Grid seminars were held involving almost all managers and supervisors in Shell Japan, it was decided that a Team Building Exercise, (phase two of the Grid method) should take place with a management team from the Marketing function. The team consisted of the Marketing manager, managers of supporting divisions in Head Office and ten Branch managers. The phase two exercise aims at clarifying the crucial barriers to excellence and formulating targets for the team and for each individual. The team building exercise, however, was not favourably accepted by participants, due to an overly structured programme, leaving little room for participants to deviate or dwell on matters of interest to them, and because of psychological resistance to detailed discussion of each other's management style felt by those closely related in the execution of daily business. This Team Building Exercise was not repeated after the first trial because of unfavourable reaction from managers and supervisors and it was decided to look for an alternative method (which is discussed later) in place of the Grid method.

The importance of having a management philosophy was one thing which emerged from the Grid seminars. At the final session of the Grid seminars, members were assigned a theme to discuss regarding barriers to optimal organization. One of the matters frequently pointed out at the sessions held was the problem of a lack of company philosophy or sense of direction which all staff members should bear in mind.

At the follow-up meeting after the seminar, where top management members and seminar participants discussed the barriers mentioned, the necessity for a management philosophy was discussed, and the aims of a management philosophy were examined. In 1975, a draft statement of management philosophy was prepared by the Personnel Department and after one year's discussion involving managers, supervisors, and those in work groups, the philosophy was completed. It is noteworthy that this management philosophy was not compiled by top management members or by a few staff members but was completed with the participation of middle management as well as members down the line. Paragraph 4 of the philosophy reads:

'The maintenance of our corporate security and the performance of our responsibilities to society requires the active participation and dedication of all members of the Company. It is management's conviction that this requires the creation of a climate within the Company in which everybody has the opportunity, incentive and willingness to give of his best and to participate fully in the establishment of policies and in the realisation of the Companies' objectives and duties.'

This formed the basic framework for organizational development activities in Shell Japan thereafter.

The second effect of the Grid seminars was to intensify the consciousness on the part of participants regarding problems latent in the organization, and heighten expectations of change. At the same time, participants came to appreciate the value of candid communication in achieving effective team work and this appreciation played an important role in subsequent organizational development activity.

When seeking an activity to help solve the latent problems in the organization it was noted that industrial relations in our companies were not stable, e.g. the number of strikes in the period 1973–1975 was high compared with earlier years. One reason for this was considered to lie in the inadequate relationship between superiors and subordinates. More participative management and building of a sound organization climate were considered vital. Simply making structural changes was not considered likely to be effective.

Organizational development activity in Shell Japan

As mentioned in the preceding section, organizational development in Shell Japan was launched after consideration of past training courses and unstable industrial relations, on a trial and error basis. A summary of the organizational development experience and its related activities are as below:

(a) *Data collection and feedback in the form of an attitude survey.* Attitude surveys were conducted at intervals of two or three years to find out the views of employees towards the Company, management, supervisors, work group, work itself, personnel policy (such as compensation), job placement, training, etc. and consisted of about 70 questions. The result of the survey was fed back to each work group showing both the data for the whole company and isolating that of the specific work group.

(b) *Family training.* The details of 'family training' are described later, but suffice it to say here that over twenty workplaces (i.e. departments, branch offices etc.) have undergone 'family training', involving some 1600 employees or over two thirds of the total number employed.

(c) *Manpower blueprint exercise.* In 1979 and 1982, a 'manpower blueprint exercise' was carried out aimed at finding the most efficient form of organizational structure and manpower distribution across the organization, involving both managers and work groups down the line of the organization.
   The exercise relates to, for example, the number of layers in the organization, job enlargement and job enrichment, and pooled jobs, in which each member of a work group carries out more than one task in order to increase skills and increase job satisfaction.

(d) *Labour and management conference.* Union executives and a top management team is convened to discuss management policy, business plans, and business results. The aim is to enhance mutual trust and understanding by exchanging views and to increase efficiency by encouraging participation and commitment.

(e) *Labour and management council.* Union executives from the union's Central Executive Office, and the local union chapter, and management members at the workplace convene to discuss working conditions, and measures to increase efficiency of productivity, and to communicate important matters related to the work group, with the aim of achieving greater satisfaction for and enthusiasm from, both sides, labour and management.

(f) *Sensitivity workshop.* This workshop was originally designed for sales supervisors and salesmen to establish sound and strong team work in each branch office with the assistance of an external organizational development consultant, but later the workshop was extended to members other than Marketing functions.

(g) *Appraisal training for supervisory staff.* Training is held once every year for all supervisory staff for proper implementation of staff appraisal, putting emphasis on management by objectives, interviewing, etc.

The basic thought behind our organization development activity is that organization development is the process where work group members themselves can learn and develop the capability to identify what is required of the work group under given circumstances, what the problems are which hinder the fulfilment of the requirements and how to solve these problems. Thus, our organization development activity has primarily put emphasis on improvement of the organizational climate, viz. improvement of communications and relationships and resolution of conflicts, paying attention, at the same time, to any structural development that may be necessary.

To attain this, what is most important is the will and commitment of the work group to improve, and thus the Personnel staff who help promote organization development activity must concentrate their efforts on making certain that line managers and others fully understand the meaning of the activity, but they must do so without any kind of coercing.

This kind of organization development activity cannot satisfactorily be developed without understanding and enthusiasm on the part of the union, and a joint committee called the Organization Development Steering Committee comprising representatives from the Company and the union was formed in 1979 by recommendation of the Central Labour and Management Council's Special Committee for Training in order to seek the right course of action to be taken for the promotion of organizational activity, to exchange views and experiences regarding its implementation and to review the results of that activity.

The targets of organizational activities can be summarized as follows:

(a) To cause the work group as a whole and individual members of the group to commit themselves to working with initiative and autonomy.

(b) To ensure the organizational set-ups and work procedures are suitable for achieving the targets of the work group.

(c) To ensure that communication is not biased either vertically or horizontally and that expression of emotion is acceptable to everyone.

(d) To ensure that the overall objectives of the work group and those of its constituent members are integrated.

(e) To ensure that the work group and its members recognize that the raison d'etre of the work group will be lost unless it relates closely to the external environment and adapts itself to external requirements.

(f) To ensure that conflicts in the work group are explicitly discussed and solved.

(g) To maintain the work group practice that each member gives feedback to others and they learn through that feedback.

(h) To ascertain that the work group has a climate to encourage and accept, even with risks, the trial adoption of any measure if considered appropriate, for achieving the targets.

(i) To ensure that the decision is made at the place where relevant information is obtainable, i.e. that delegation and decentralization are properly carried out.

The usual process of implementing organization development activity, especially that referred to as 'family training', is as follows:

Phase I. Preparation

Step 1. Discovery of problems. This is the stage where members of a work group recognize the existence of problems in a vague way. The line manager of the work group and/or Personnel staff members are responsible for taking steps to identify th problems and to record the process of identification of problems through discussion with the members.

Step 2. Decision by line manager. This is the stage where the line manager concerned decides if any measure for change should be introduced. Staff members in Personnel have to discuss with the line manager what he thinks of the problems and how he wants to cope with them.

Step 3. Organization of a steering group. With the agreement and support of the line manager, a steering group is formed, the members of which are highly conscious of problems and are active in coping with them. At the same time, the necessity to involve external resources, viz. a professional organization development consultant outside the company, Personnel staff or member of the Organization Development Steering Committee, is examined by the line manager or by the steering group. In some cases, the first reaction of line managers is that the work group should carry out 'family training' by itself since its members do not want to expose themselves to criticism from outsiders, but this signifies an implicit refusal to openly discuss problems and the lack of will to tackle them, so that it is up to the Organization Development Steering Committee to try to make the line manager understand the importance of using outside resources and to get his agreement.

Step 4. Preparation for 'family training'. With the agreement of the line manager, preparation for family training is progressed mainly by the steering group. In most cases, the steering group gets together several times after working hours or at lunch time to discuss the problems they will have and what type of intervention is most appropriate. During this process, it is expected that the problem consciousness and insight into problem solving can be deepened among the members of the steering group. To take as an example a supporting function in Head Office, preparatory meetings were held more than ten times to identify the problems and their cause and effect relationships, and this greatly helped the smooth running of the family training which followed. It is important that the records of the examination conducted by the steering group be kept for use in any following activities.

It is wise to find out, at this stage, who among the work group are likely to be strong supporters and who dissenters, and to take 'appropriate action', prior to holding the plenary meeting, in order to ensure its effective implementation. ('Appropriate action' in this context simply means that efforts are made to convince dissenters of the usefulness of the proceedings.)

Phase II. Diagnosis

Step 5. Diagnosis. The process of diagnoses of the work group covers all the members of the group and makes clear to them the need for organization development activities. A survey is conducted either through interviews carried out by organization development specialists or through questionnaires or by examination of the result of the attitude survey. The questionnaire which is generally used for this purpose is set out in Table 2, but depending on the need of the work group, the items in the questionnaire may be modified.

The results of the survey should, of course, be recorded.

Step 6. Problem identification. All the members of the work group get together after office hours, say starting from Friday evening and going through to the following Saturday afternoon, to be briefed on the concept of organization development activity, to learn its objectives and targets, to grasp problems latent in the work group and to find out how to cope with them. The one-and-a-half day session is effectively a 'kick off' of the 'family training' involving the participation if possible of all the members of the work group. Attendance at this meeting is not compulsory but by dint of effort of the steering group, the attendance ratio of the

Table 2   Questionnaire on climate of work group survey for subordinate group*

1. Is your work group full of vitality?	7 6 5 4 3 2 1
	Absolutely Yes Absolutely No
2. Does your work group have an atmosphere conducive to candidly expressing your views?	7 6 5 4 3 2 1
	Absolutely Yes Absolutely No
3. Does your work group have an atmosphere conducive to positively tackling difficult tasks?	7 6 5 4 3 2 1
	Absolutely Yes Absolutely No
4. Does your work group have a creative atmosphere which accepts new ideas to improve work efficiency?	7 6 5 4 3 2 1
	Absolutely Yes Absolutely No
5. Does your work group have an atmosphere conducive to making efforts for increased knowledge and skills related to the job?	7 6 5 4 3 2 1
	Absolutely Yes Absolutely No
6. Doesn't your work group have an atmosphere conducive to shifting responsibility onto others?	7 6 5 4 3 2 1
	Absolutely Yes Absolutely No
7. Does your work group make efforts to examine the results of work and to reflect upon it in terms of the next job?	7 6 5 4 3 2 1
	Absolutely Yes Absolutely No
8. Is your supervisor given accurate information?	7 6 5 4 3 2 1
	Absolutely Yes Absolutely No
9. Does your work group conflict with other groups?	7 6 5 4 3 2 1
	Absolutely Yes Absolutely No
10. Are your colleagues cooperative with you when you need help in performing your job?	7 6 5 4 3 2 1
	Absolutely Yes Absolutely No
11. Does your work group have a good relationship with others in term of communication?	7 6 5 4 3 2 1
	Absolutely Yes Absolutely No
12. Does your work group understand well the objectives or targets of the organization?	7 6 5 4 3 2 1
	Absolutely Yes Absolutely No

13. Does your work group have an atmosphere conducive to positively cooperating with other groups?	7 6 5 4 3 2 1
	Absolutely Yes · Absolutely No
14. Do you think efforts for improvement are properly rewarded?	7 6 5 4 3 2 1
	Absolutely Yes · Absolutely No

* There was a similar questionnaire given to the supervisors' group.

work group is usually fairly high. Before the end of the meeting, the details of follow-up activities are discussed and clearly defined by all the participants in an effort to ensure their successful implementation. Since this kick-off meeting is considered a very important step in ensuring the success of the following activities and for gaining a thorough understanding of the problems, an external organization development consultant is usually invited to steer the meeting. The details of the meeting will be illustrated in the next section. The results of the discussions which take place in this meeting are summarized and recorded for the use in follow-up activities.

Phase III. Formulation of action plans

Step 7. Setting the targets. This step can be carried out either in the course of the previous kick-off meeting or separately after a discussion meeting of the work group. When this step is carried out after the kick-off meeting, it is usual to divide members of the work group into small groups of say five or six members since it is difficult for *all* the members of a work group to get together frequently to discuss the targets. The result of discussion conducted by each 'small group' is discussed and summarized by representatives from each such group.

Step 8. Action plan. This step can also be included in the kick-off meeting or can be taken separately. The action plan is usually set up taking into account important targets and core problems which the work group has, taking into consideration their priority, the possibility of their being implemented, the degree of urgency, etc.

When the discussion for formulating the action plan is held after the kick-off meeting, it is carried out by the 'small groups' mentioned above. The action plan includes a concrete plan for each one in the work group, a due date for completion, the timing of reviews, who is responsible for which action and review, etc.

Phase IV. Implementation and critiques

Step 9. Implementation. This is the step where each one in the work group makes efforts to implement and stabilize the proposed action in accordance with daily routines. After the boost of the kick-off meeting, this is the most critical as well as difficult time for ensuring the success of the organizational development activities, and the existence of persevering individuals who follow up the action plan is vitally important. The morale of the members is heightened when a core problem shows signs of being solved or even when a trivial item is resolved. In this sense, it is important for something (albeit minor) to be successfully resolved at this stage to consolidate the basis for further progress.

Step 10. Critiques. In the several months following the formulation of the action plan, a review of the process of the 'family training' is undertaken through such means as questionnaires, interviews or meetings by representatives of small groups to identify what has been achieved, what has not and the reasons behind that. Through this process, new problem areas can be found and another cycle of activity starting from Phase I is again pursued. Data collection by questionnaire is in some cases misleading since the members whose problem consciousness or expectation is at a higher level tend to evaluate the current position less favourably so that, after the family training, the average survey score may in fact register a fall. More direct and accurate evaluation can be obtained from discussion with members of the work group.

The procedures mentioned above are the usual method of conducting 'family training', but in parallel with this, a 'labour management council' is also convened, which is comprised of management members and union executives from each workplace. Family training is carried out in close liaison with this council at the workplace. The council, which differs from the family training groups in that the latter are carried out with the participation of *all* members, is conducted by representatives of each party and though having the same purpose as family training (such as productivity improvement, effective team building, etc.), functions as the official machine to confirm the decisions made through family training, and promotes the latter's activities and reviews its progress.

Family training

Here, an example is given of how family training is conducted, based upon the case of a small marketing branch office.

The branch is one of a number of small marketing branches with about forty members, headed by a Branch Manager, and under him, there are five sections; Sales No. 1 Section, Sales No. 2 Section, Regional Operation Section, Finance Section and Personnel and Services Section. As the branch itself is small, a sort of cohesion existed among members but at the same time, the atmosphere was such that employees were too reserved to speak frankly to the manager and there was excessive obedience to superiors; this was felt by some of the members to be a problem. According to the attitude survey, there was a considerable gap between superiors and subordinates in terms of communication in the workplace.

Against this background, the local chapter of the union expressed the wish to conduct family training and at a discussion meeting between the manager and section heads, the necessity of family training was discussed.

The Branch Manager agreed to start family training and asked Personnel staff in the Head Office to assist him. Since the particular Branch is located far from the Head Office, no detailed preparatory decision was possible between the Branch Manager and Personnel staff in advance except as regards the necessity of inviting an external organization development consultant, as was requested by the manager. In the Branch Office, the purpose of the meeting was conveyed to all the employees present and all except two, who were unable to attend, expressed their willingness to attend the meeting. At the same time, a small group consisting of representatives of section heads, union executives, and others was formed to investigate core problems in pursuing effective work in the office. The meetings were held several times and a draft programme which showed problem areas was completed prior to the kick-off meeting.

The meeting was held starting on Friday evening, continuing through Saturday afternoon, and an outside consultant and a Personnel staff member visited the office on the Friday morning to discuss with a representative of the small groups the definition of the problems and to discuss with the manager the programme of the meeting, which was as follows:

Friday	19:00–19:15	Opening talk by Manager.
	19:15–21:00	'Ice breaking session', communication game by a consultant.
	21:00– (Open ended)	Discussion of problems. All participants were divided into small groups to discuss problems identified by the preparatory exercise and to add to or change them in accordance with their own views.
Saturday	9:00–10:00	Presentation of the problems by representatives of small groups.
	10:00–11:00	Theory input by a consultant on the direction and targets of organization development.
	11:00–14:00	Discussion by small groups: How to overcome the problems and to achieve the ideal situation.
	14:00–14:30	Presentation of the previous discussion.
	14:30–15:00	Study of the individual action plans by each member.
	15:00–16:00	Declaration of each individual's action plan.
	16:00–16:30	Discussion on the follow-up activities and closing.

In this case the sharing of the problems and discussion of action plans were carried out at one meeting since the size of the work group was small. After the 'kick-off' meeting, the salient points of the meeting were conveyed to those who had been absent and four small groups were formed covering all the members in the office arranged in a 'diagonal' organization pattern, e.g. one group was formed by the Section Head of No. 1 Sales Section, an assistant in Operations, a salesman in No. 2 Sales Section, two clerks in Personnel and Finance and the Manager's secretary. Each small group was assigned one item of the Action Plan to further discuss, arrive at a method of achieving the target and in relation to which to review progress. Each group met once a week at lunch time to discuss those matters. The representatives of the small group met approximately once a month to exchange views and to report progress.

The problems identified by the kick-off meeting were mostly associated with socio-technical aspects as shown below:

Organizational climate

(a) Low degree of consciousness of problems, i.e. little concern for excellency.

(b) Low degree of concern for customer orientation, i.e. poor consideration for visitors to the office.

(c) Little flow of communication from bottom to top.

(d) Reservation against candour.

(e) No rewards or punishment.

(f) No responsible work for women and at the same time poor discipline of women.

(g) Sycophantic attitude towards superiors.

Institutional matters

(a) Lack of conviction on the side of appraisees for personnel appraisal exercises due to shortage of feedback from superiors.

(b) No on-the-job training by superiors.

Relationships

(a) Little mutual trust created from candid communication.

(b) Little understanding of others' work, i.e. low concern for others.

(c) Little *esprit de corps* among colleagues.

(d) Irresponsible criticism of superiors by subordinates.

Policy or vision

(a) Vague and ambiguous policy.

(b) Excessive volatility of policy in the face of change in environment.

Given these problems, immediate targets which the members had to attain were:

(a) to achieve candid and frank communication; to speak with courage and listen with patience.

(b) to behave with a customer-oriented mind; to decide what can be done for customers and act accordingly without delay.

(c) to pay concern to others in the office and give frank advice to those who it is felt are in need of improvement.

(d) to engage in spirited morning greetings and a disciplinary morning gathering.*

Three months after the kick-off meeting, a review of the progress of the targets was conducted by the labour and management council at the workplace. Items (b) and (d) above were confirmed as having been implemented, but regarding (a) and (c), individual efforts were insufficient. It was confirmed that each member should try to do his or her best, making use of the discussion between superior and subordinate at the time of staff appraisal.

Six months after the kick-off meeting, a small group proposed that the groups, being organized on diagonal organizational section basis (explained above) should be re-grouped into actual work-group sections so that authentic relationships could be built up between superiors and subordinates of the same team. This proposal, however, was turned down as the organization was not at the time sufficiently mature as to allow unreserved communication between superiors and subordinates.

After more than one year since the kick-off meeting, a few members are reported to have developed the trait of speaking with candour habitually but others have fallen back to their previous behaviour, the enthusiasm kindled at the meeting dying away gradually.

It can be said, however, that all the members of the branch learned the importance of candid communication through the kick-off meeting and succeeding follow-up activity, and where they were confronted with problems, they at least try to face the problems and to discuss matters as frankly as possible.

In connection with the foregoing experience there are a number of points which may be made.

(a) Even after several preparatory discussions, the view may be put by attendants that an outpoken expression of problems will be detrimental to harmonious team work. It is not easy to recognize that only candid communication leads to authentic and genuine human relations. This is not fully understood until a successful case is experienced.

* The morning gathering is a few minutes meeting at the start of the day's work where the work group confirms the day's schedule and targets to be achieved, and commits itself to disciplined behaviour.

(b) There are many instances where the targets agreed upon by members cover only the peripheral and mechanical aspects, not related to core problems. For example, the promotion of cheerful greetings in the morning to accentuate the start of work, holding of regulatory meetings, etc. That is to say, the agreed action plan may tend to centre around the items which are comparatively easily attainable. It is desirable to start by implementing easier targets first to hasten further development, but if people are satisfied with the completion of easier targets without addressing the core issues, that will discourage members from becoming further committed to organizational development.

The point is to direct members' efforts towards tackling the core problems after thorough preparation and strengthening of the autonomous power of members.

(c) Activities like family training tend to come to standstill without persistent promoters. What can generally be said is that problem identification can be done smoothly with the help of proper intervention but problem solving becomes a much more difficult task and as the enthusiasm of the meeting disappears, action tends to dissipate in the hustle and bustle of daily business. Line managers and supporters of development activities should be fully convinced of the worth of the activities and promote them persistently.

(d) There are three types of members encountered in the process of developing organization development activity. One is the member who positively uncovers the veil of latent problems and who tackles the problems. The second one is the member who covers up the problems and thinks that a solution in his hands is impossible. The third is situated between these two. Some measures should be taken prior to the meeting for those who are considered to be in the second category, giving them opportunity to air their views individually and informing them of the meaning of the activity. Otherwise a great deal of time will be wasted at the meeting where members of the work group get together.

(e) Enabling evaluation of the results of efforts in some tangible way will certainly improve the motivation of the members, but we have not so far found any clear and appropriate criteria for this purpose. The reduction of manpower required for a certain task, the cost or the degree of stability of industrial relations can be useful indicators, but the degree of external influence is great in the oil industry and further study is required to obtain tangible yardsticks which measure the development of organization development activity.

Based upon these findings, our efforts in the future would seem best directed towards looking at the total organization and each section upon which it is built as part of the process of identifying problems in the execution of daily business and overcoming them. This requires (a) obtaining greater insight into the changing environment and into expected adaptations which need to be made, (b) setting explicit targets and critically reviewing their achievement as closely related to business results, and (c) conducting a more active search for and introducing various techniques for problem solving and evaluation of organization development activity.

In considering the future it is often argued that Japan's groupism will gradually be dissolved, that esteem for individual autonomy and initiative will further be increased and the speed of the change of the external environment and the necessity to adapt to that change will be accelerated. Economic growth has improved markedly the standard of living and in these circumstances people tend to pursue more individually oriented goals like self-esteem, self-fulfilment and autonomy, rather than prizing conformity and being dedicated to groups.

The objective of organizational development concerns active adaptation of both the individual and the group to changes. It is through organizational development that the old and the new meet, but mutual adjustment is a slow and endless process. Organizational development is a vehicle for this process; it is an activity with a start and no end.

Epilogue

Organization Development activities in Shell Japan have been conducted in pursuit of the goal of participation in management and at the same time these activities have been recognized as helpful in developing an organizational climate where other forms of participation can function smoothly. The efforts that Shell Japan has made in the field of organization development activities and participation cannot be explained in isolation, but must be related to the change in the business environment in which the company has operated since the 'oil crisis'. Before the oil crisis the petroleum industry in Japan enjoyed rapid growth for quite some time. In those days, almost all problems encountered could be solved through an examination of matters other than those involving personnel and personal relationships. The meaning of 'corporate excellence' used to be of less significance since nobody had any doubt about the future prosperity of the company which was experiencing constant growth. However, since the oil crisis the company has been placed in a completely different business situation where everything has been turbulent in terms of crude cost, supply of and demand for oil products, a sharp decline of consumption, the competitive market situation, etc. Organization development activities in Shell Japan have infiltrated the organizations, involving an increasing number of people at all organizational levels, people who share a determination to ensure the company's activities remain competitive despite the turbulent business environment, and aspire to having a meaningful working life with Shell Japan.

The company's management philosophy, which was established in early 1976, clearly sets the direction in which people at all organizational levels should make efforts both as a group working together in Shell Japan and as individuals. It is important to note that the management philosophy was not an edict from 'top management' but rather was compiled with the participation of lower level managers as well as employees down the line. The management philosophy consists of 5 different points, but amongst others the need for participation and productivity improvement are strongly advocated as really crucial issues.

Productivity improvement requires improvement of human relations at the workplace and development of the individuals involved. The vitally important point is that effort of this kind is not regarded as a sacrifice on the part of the employee, but rather as an initiative enabling working life to be more meaningful. Why is participation important? Does participation give a feeling of involvement to the individuals concerned? Or does participation increase commitment on the part of the individuals concerned? The answers are clearly 'yes'. But what is more important is the management belief that participation brings the best solution for productivity improvement provided that the employees concerned are properly guided and oriented as a group and as individuals. This is because employees are in a position to know exactly what and how things should be carried out for productivity improvement, through their day-to-day business activities.

To cite an example, as a result of closing nine depots in 1983 as part of the rationalization of the distribution network, about 40 employees working at those depots had to move to different workplaces, leaving, in most cases, their native towns in which they had long resided. The change was carried out very smoothly because of participation in the decision, and because thorough discussions were held many times prior to the closure.

Our next proposed step in the field of organization development activities and participation is to be able to react more quickly to the changing environments. Participation is usually time consuming as compared with unilateral decision making by management. Corporate excellence should be judged not only by the quality of decisions but also by the time spent to react to changes.

Whether organization development activities and participation can function successfully or not seems to depend largely on the work ethics of the individuals concerned and their evaluation of their work. Looking back at our experience, such positive attitudes are not considered to arise as a matter of course; they are not necessarily characteristics of the Japanese business culture, but they can be fostered and built through day-to-day efforts to improve and maintain mutual trust between management and employees and good relations between superiors and subordinates. It is often said, in the companies where sound and constructive employee relations have been established, that employee relations are fragile and this is particularly so where both management and employees do not recognize that fact.

With this view in mind, the most important challenge for the future may perhaps lie in the area of overall personnel systems. We have to recognize that the value attached to work by the young generation is changing and tends to be diversified. Though one may argue about the extent to which changes take place, whatever the change in the people's values, the only solution is to continue to pursue matters so that the members of the organization can find some important meaning in their working life. To find this direction, overall personnel systems have to be reviewed periodically and be redesigned where appropriate in response to changes in people's values, attitudes, and the environment in which the company operates.

Tokyo, Japan
May, 1983

Y. Sato
Director, Personnel and Services
Shell Sekiyu Kabushiki Kaisha

People and Organizations Interacting
Edited by A. Brakel
© 1985, John Wiley & Sons Ltd.

Chapter 11

A Group in Transition

James N. Watson and Wendy A. Pritchard

The context

The aim of this chapter is to look back at the ways in which the character of the Royal Dutch/Shell Group of Companies has been changing over the last 20 years or so and to try to interpret some of the implications. Examples of these changes are described in other chapters of the book.

In simple terms we are asking questions such as the following: What has been happening to Shell companies? Why? How? Where are they now? Where may they be going?

Until about 1960 Shell's world was comparatively stable. The acquisition and trading of crude oil and its products was a relatively secure and profitable business. There was a fairly high degree of centralization in the oil business, though less in the Group than elsewhere. Shell was widely recognized as a good employer, providing desirable jobs, excellent wages, and enviable conditions of service.

Then the scene began to change. Elements of a new instability began to emerge—an instability of markets, of politico-economic factors, and of human values and attitudes. Environmental differences started to emerge in different countries, the failure of commercial ventures became more common, feelings antagonistic to big business were being exhibited by governments and members of the public. Changing attitudes began to manifest themselves in challenging or apathetic behaviour by staff and even by senior managers.

Like some other large organizations at that time, Shell turned to the social scientists for help. What was going on, especially in the countries of the developed world? Were the changes going to last? Would they spread to other countries?

Shell companies have been trying to find the answer to these questions, and others like them, for over 20 years. Looking back over these two eventful decades, there appears to be a strong case for the view that the world has lived through a discontinuity—a 'step change'—of the type that occurs from time to time in human affairs and usually ushers in a new era in one sense or another. In the years between 1960 and 1980, or thereabouts, the discontinuity (in many countries besides those of the 'developed' West) seems to have been in the general area of attitudes to authority and the sharing of decision-making power. It can hardly be a coincidence that rather violent attitudinal shifts have occurred during this same period in so many of the power relationships in our societies. Men and women, whites and blacks, parents and children, doctors and patients, teachers and pupils, management and workers—is there any area of human affairs, or any country in the world, where a relatively substantial transfer of power from the strong to the weak has not occurred? And is this not, in the long run, a discontinuous and irreversible process rather than an exponential one—more a revolution, in the words of Chapter 7 of this book, than an evolution? Figure 1 represents this idea in graphical form: the social turmoils of 1968–1970 would fit in with the steepest part of the curve.

The implications of this graph for our present purposes are that most of today's organizations were built (and many of their managers trained) in the relatively stable conditions that obtained before 1960, and the developed countries may now again be in a *relatively* stable period, post-1980, for which pre-1960 managerial attitudes and styles are quite inappropriate. The essential difference between the periods before and after the discontinuity, on this model, would be that before 1960 the notion of obedience to authority was fairly widely accepted by the haves and have-nots alike, whereas 20 years or so later it had been largely replaced by the conviction that every person has a right to share in the making of decisions that affect him or her to any significant degree. The post 1980 period, moreover, may be qualitatively different in another way—namely that uncertainty may itself be part of the 'stable' picture.

The implications of this relatively sudden change, of course, are enormous and what is nowadays referred to increasingly by sociologists as 'the new paradigm' incorporates attempts to describe these new collaborative values. The consequences for organizational change are the real heartland of organization development (O.D.). It is here, by helping managers to diagnose where change is needed in their organizations, and to plan accordingly, that the O.D. adviser earns his or her keep.

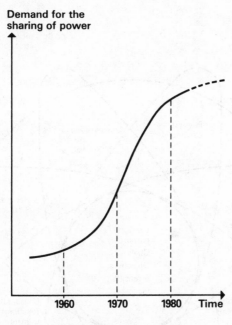

Figure 1

There are now about 50 internal Shell O.D. people around the world, as well as a number of external consultants specializing in different parts of the field. Shell companies have invested considerable sums of money in behavioural science training for managers and specialist advisers, and various kinds of O.D. work have been undertaken in different locations and cultures. Some interesting examples are described elsewhere in this book.

One of the most important insights that have been gained from these efforts is that organizations are much more than their formal structures. In the days of comparatively stable environmental conditions the two-dimensional organization chart was sufficiently definitive to be a useful guide to the nature and functioning of the organization. Those days, however, have gone. The organization chart has next to nothing to say about the organization's mission, objectives, strategies, competences, policies, procedures, processes, culture, values, and the rest, to say nothing of the informal structures and relationships that form part of its everyday reality. And yet these are key features of the organization, especially in today's conditions, and determine how it will perform its function. Shell managers, then, have discovered that the secret of improving organizational performance lies in addressing some or all of the above variables, and not merely in making structural alterations which, though almost a reflex action to change 20 years ago, is now revealed as far too simplistic a response in today's more turbulent conditions (see Figure 2).

Techno-economic sub-systems

(areas familiar in classical
scientific management)

Psycho-social sub-systems

(newer areas of management
attention)

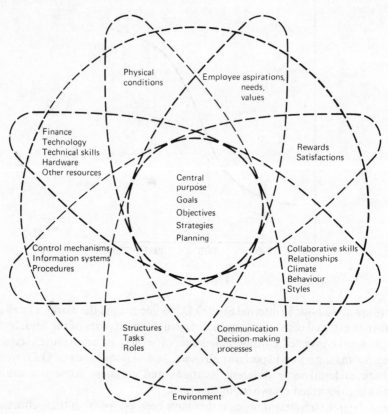

Notes
(i) No human organization can be represented adequately in a two-dimensional model. The sub-systems identified above, and the words chosen to describe them, are largely a matter of taste.
(ii) All the sub-systems interact with one another, and with the organization's environment, which invades all the sub-systems and affects the organization's central purpose, objectives and strategies.
(iii) All the boundary lines are dotted to indicate that they must be permeable if the organization is to remain healthy.

Figure 2   The socio-technical organization: its central purpose and interrelated
sub-systems

The management task, indeed, has changed in a number of important respects in the last generation or so. The mere mention of many of the variables listed above would have raised managerial eyebrows not so long ago. Mission? Processes? Culture? Values? Relationships? What do these things have to do with running a business? Even today managers are still not good at taking such things into account in their planning, though they are to a greater or lesser degree aware of their importance. Management attitudes have not yet caught up wholly with the consequences of the discontinuity.

In spite of this, people have gradually—almost painfully—become aware of a number of key things about organizations and the processes by which they change. Organizations exist in their contexts, for example, and must study their environments, communicate with them, and react to them in order to stay healthy. The environment plays a critical part in determining the central purpose of the organization, because it is the surrounding society that gives the organization its licence to operate in terms of that society's needs.

Clarification of central purpose, objectives and strategy are therefore crucial to any organization. In fact, they mould the organization's shape and character. It has long been understood that they determine techno-economic variables like tasks, technology, and structure, but it is now clear that they also have a powerful effect on vital psycho-social characteristics like styles of behaviour, communication, decision-making processes, and so on.

It follows from this that, as the organization derives its purpose and nature from an environment that is constantly and substantially in flux, its own character and sub-systems need to be flexible and responsive to outside influences. In fact, the whole idea of 'outside' and 'inside' now bears scrutiny. One of the consequences of the new paradigm has been the blurring of organizational boundaries that has occurred as the organization is perceived more and more as an integral and interdependent part of the wider world around it.

It also follows that organizations need to change—sometimes rapidly—with the passage of time, and that managers have to develop the skills that are required to change them. There is ample evidence that this is not an easy process—it usually seems easier and less risky to leave things as they are, though there may be serious hidden costs in doing so. It is also difficult as a rule to plan large-scale change far in advance: planning is (or should be) an incremental process involving many people, and it depends for its validity on what may be called 'organizational learning', the development of views fairly widely shared throughout the organization on what is happening and what should be done about it. This developing of consensus can be a slow and laborious process, and one that can easily be overtaken by events, but time and money spent on trying to improve diagnostic and consultative skills in the organization are usually good investments.

The transition in focus

Perhaps we should now turn to the question: 'Where does Shell stand in all this— if any organization so complex and multi-faceted can actually be said to stand anywhere?' The writers of this chapter would contend, on the basis of their

working experience, that there are indeed a number of elements that go to build
an identifiable corporate Shell personality and posture, unique in its totality i
not in its individual components.

Organizations develop distinctive cultures, which are a complex mixture o
factors derived from the values and backgrounds of those who create, manage
and work in them as well as from the technical, economic, and socia
characteristics of the societies in which they exist. They also develop what are
sometimes called 'distinctive competences', which is social science jargon for the
things that they can do better than other organizations. And they sometimes fai
to notice their weaknesses.

What, then, might we pick out as some of the key features of the overall Shell
culture? And what, on a total Group basis, do these mean in terms of direction ir
the future?

Size

Most striking of all to the observer, perhaps, is the fact that the Group is very big.
The strengths and weaknesses of big organizations have been widely documented
elsewhere, but at least some of them may be worth considering again here
because of their importance as determinants of the overall character of the
Group. It is obviously very important, for example, to be large enough to partake
of what are usually called the economies of scale, but these are often
accompanied by more or less hidden losses which in some cases may nullify the
expected gains. Shell companies are attracted by big projects and big markets, for
example—but do they meanwhile miss good commercial opportunities in the
small ones? How well, in any case, do they manage big undertakings, with all the
attendant complexities? There is little doubt that managers still have a lot to learn
about organizing business units on a human scale without losing the cohesion
that stems from the larger framework of the Group. Shell's collective strength,
for example, sometimes tends to overshadow its smaller companies, and its
economic power, which is clearly a potential force for good, is widely seen by the
outside world as a threat. The wide geographical base which is one of the Group's
greatest strengths sometimes has troublesome logistical consequences, and the
degree to which Group companies have achieved self-sufficiency has overtones of
incestuousness and the dangers of a closed system. It is comparatively easy for
any organization which has the size and power to influence its environment to
forget that it is the outside world that gives it its mandate to operate, and that any
feelings of immortality that it may have rest on very shaky foundations.

Complexity

The Group is also a highly complex organisation, by any standards, and the issues of complexity are different from those of size alone. There is probably no other private enterprise organization in the world that has the multi-cultural dimensions of Shell. The Group is certainly the most 'multinational' of all the organizations that today labour under the burdens of that label. Shell really does have Indian managers working in the Netherlands and Norwegians in Thailand—though not yet in very large numbers—and there are no more than one or two foreigners in the management teams of the great majority of Group companies around the world. The day-to-day decision-making, too, is very much more decentralized in the Group than in the organizations of its competitors. One must be careful, of course, not to generalize too lightly in this matter: the degree of decentralization that is appropriate in a given field of operations is contingent upon a variety of circumstances. It makes sense, for example, to decentralize to a large degree the selling of many products, but the same does not apply to major investment decisions or the management of world-wide exploration operations.

In this remarkable cultural diversity, lie weaknesses as well as strengths, of course. The complexities we are discussing here have their roots in a number of different things. The Group has learned (up to a point) to accommodate in its decision-making processes the differences of opinion that arise from different national backgrounds, but frequently as important are those that stem from different academic traditions or even from different functional cultures, in the Shell sense. And while this web of subtle cultural factors makes for richness in decision-making, it may also slow things down in a variety of ways. Whether or not the gains outweigh the losses will depend on the circumstances of the case. There is little doubt, however, that the multi-cultural decision-making capacities that the Group has acquired—sometimes painfully—over the years are now one of its most remarkable characteristics.

Another interesting aspect of the Shell culture seems to be a somewhat greater tolerance of ambiguity than is found in many other enterprises of a similar type. Although many parts of the Shell organization are quite compartmentalized (especially in the Service Companies) the boundaries between the pigeon-holes are in many cases surprisingly ill-defined—largely, one suspects, by design. Before 1960 this might have appeared to be a serious competitive weakness, but in the turbulent and complicated business conditions that exist in 1984, it is beginning to look like a positive strength. It certainly prepares the ground for consensus decision-making in a way that many other organizations have not yet matched, though again it is not easy to evaluate the benefits that may have accrued to the Group for this reason. Perhaps all we can say is that in any organization as complex as the Group a part of the secret of good overall performance seems to lie in maintaining a high level of healthy interaction between the parts without permitting this to degenerate into confusion, opacity, and stagnation.

Roots

No analysis of the culture of the Royal Dutch/Shell Group can proceed very far without dealing with its parentage. The Group is pervaded (though not controlled) by an ethic that can be seen as Anglo-Dutch, techno-economic, middle-class, ex-colonial, paternalistic—and so on *ad infinitum* without ever completing the description to anyone's satisfaction. There is still a good deal of truth, however, in the old assertion that the typical senior Shell manager is 'a cross between a Delft engineer and a Scottish chartered accountant'. There is a synergy between the strengths of the Dutch and British orientations to business, as well as many examples of conflict, misunderstanding, and unhelpful stereotyping. Those of us who have worked in Shell for a substantial number of years suspect that the view of the outside world taken by our top management is illuminated and balanced by the Group's dual parentage, although most people would agree that it is still based very largely on 'Western' values, and that these are coming increasingly under attack. Shell is a relatively comfortable, tolerant, and caring organization, but the obverse of the coin is that it can also be paternalistic, narrowly rational, and relatively poor at confronting and making capital from genuinely felt differences of opinion. Few large Western enterprises are notably efficient at acknowledging and dealing with feelings, and Shell is in general no exception, which tends to stifle some of the inputs that would otherwise be available for decision-making processes. Other characteristics that probably spring in part at least from the Group's Anglo-Dutch parenthood are a rather high business morality (though this has not always been interpreted and applied as well as it may have deserved) and a caution in making judgements that can oscillate from commendable to excessive.

Complacency

The Group also bears the marks of its years of great success. Shell people, by and large, are highly competent, and are accustomed to thinking of themselves as such. The dangers, of course, are of arrogance and closed thinking, and one of the Group's key tasks today in the field of management training is to find ways in which pride in the past can be reconciled with humility and the habit of learning, both from personal experience and from the experience of others inside and outside the Group.

Shell managers, like any others who have developed a repertoire of successful action in the past, are taken aback if they find that a well-tested response no longer has the desired effect, and in general they need imaginatively designed opportunities to learn and practise new skills for the planning and management of change. Here again the central difficulty seems to be crossing the threshold between what can be achieved by expert, objective-centred direction, and what requires the making of a step into the unknown. In today's conditions the manager who insists on having a guaranteed outcome before embarking on change will make no change at all. The problem can be seen as part of the wider issue of where to find solid ground which can form a foundation for business planning. The 'one-line forecasts' produced by the old extrapolative methods are now seen as naive, and 'goal-centred' planning techniques have fared no better because the goals require constant revision. Even the current Shell scenario-based approach has its critics (though others would contend that the main problem lies in the fact that scenarios are not being properly used).

About the only thing that seems clear is that managing a business—or indeed being concerned with the survival of any organization—is a cockleshell voyage, with a handful of others, in a turbulent ocean full of surprises. Not all of these, mercifully, are unpleasant.

Rational bias

The sacred cow that has recently died was called 'scientific management'. It did not die because it was scientific, of course, but because its uncompromising rationality left no room for judgements and choices that took non-rational criteria—like values, feelings, prejudices, and so on—into account. It takes more than expert prescriptions to make the world—in the shape of what other people do—go round, and managers must work together with others who want to share in creating the future. Tomorrow, in short, is manufactured today.

The legacy of Shell's special brand of scientific management is still visible in many ways. There are many inappropriate kinds of behaviour that are having to be unlearned, so to speak, and in some cases it is not clear what should replace them—if anything. At the heart of the scientific management paradigm is the authoritarian stance that believes in the superior powers of top management and in the reductionist approach that calls for the repeated division of tasks in pursuit of economies of scale. Top management does have a crucial job to do, of course, but in today's conditions the nature of the job has changed in many ways. The days when the manager sat alone in his office, making decisions that were based almost entirely on technical and financial criteria (and were then implemented by subordinates more or less without question), have gone for ever, certainly in the developed countries. The skills that are now at a premium are those that come closest to the real meaning of the word 'managing'—interpreting environmental factors, clarifying tasks, setting standards, developing criteria, building an organizational climate in which people can make use of their talents and skills, integrating the resources and strengths of the organization, and so forth. Even at lower levels of management, where the requirements for deep technical knowledge still resides, there has been a growth of 'technical obsolescence', the gradual cessation of learning that occurs because the real cutting edge of the business is moving progressively downwards. In Shell terms this means a general shift in the locus of decision-making to lower levels and out to the Operating Companies.

There has also been a change of emphasis, in many parts of the Group's business, from technical to commercial criteria. The developed world, in particular, is littered with 'product mountains', and has therefore become more of a buyers' market than it was. There are numerous examples of areas in which Shell companies are technically strong but short of commercial competence, and where managers must learn to make greater use of 'right-hemisphere' brain functions like intuition and the capacity for holistic perception. In order for this to happen, of course, the Shell culture has to change in the direction of encouraging greater participation and rewarding (or at least not punishing) the taking of reasonable risks.

Another area where there is a lot of room for managers to develop their abilities is in what are usually called 'social' or 'interpersonal' skills. People do not automatically collaborate well with others: the 'socialization' process can be nearly as painful for managers as for children. And as the making of good decisions comes to depend more and more on the abilities of people to work together new decision-making structures emerge. Shell companies have been familiar for many years with a variety of non-hierarchical structures—project organizations, task forces, semi-autonomous groups, regional/functional/product matrices, and so on—which have come into being because the existing structure is too slow-moving, too compartmentalized, or in some other way insufficiently flexible for the task in question, but it is only in recent years that managers have begun to look seriously at the uses of networks. One distinguishing feature of a network is that the locus of power can move from one point to another according to the needs of the moment and the capabilities of the individual people concerned, and it is possible to contend that Group structures, and even the Group itself, exhibit this feature from time to time. It may be that this will have to develop further in this area in order for Shell companies to survive, in which case managers who understand such structures and feel comfortable with them will be at a premium.

A final point that seems to need making here is that the people who work in an organization are more profitably regarded as people that as 'assets'. A company, after all, is a 'company of people' who have come together for some common purpose, and assets are things they make use of. This is much more than a piece of pedantry: it is a management perspective that is still rather unfamiliar in many organizations. To embrace this perspective is to arrive at a different view of many important dilemmas—the key one being whether or not to hire people (and pay them) for what they are rather than for what they do. Treating people as members of the company rather than as disposable assets is consistent with the general posture of Japanese business as well as with the trend of employment legislation in an increasing number of countries, and there are signs that it works.

Developing capability

At this point the reader might ask: 'If I accept for the moment that all these changes are taking place in the world, and that Shell companies are responding to them in the ways described above, what can be done to increase the Group's capability to adapt in the future, and how can the O.D. consultant help?' There are many ways to respond to such a question, depending on one's overall view of the world, where one sits on the optimism—pessimism continuum, and (clearly) what one thinks of O.D. consultants.

The question addresses a complex issue, so our first step should be to try to extract its essentials. The question could be re-stated as follows: 'How can a very large assembly of very different people articulate a continuing joint purpose and plan to work together to achieve it?' Reduced still further, we come to *the articulation of a purpose* and *the planning for its achievement*. In its final distillation, perhaps, this leaves us with two simple words: *'purpose'* and *'planning'*, the second, hopefully, being derived from (and consistent with) the first.

And here, at last, we seem to be near to the limits of linguistic analysis. 'Why do people associate together?' would be another way of addressing the notion of purpose, and the concept of planning would become something like: 'What choices should those people be making in the world as they see it?' If we now come back to the initial idea of the organization interacting with its environment, we can see that both the formulation of purpose and the consequent planning of action depend for their quality upon a continuous process of organizational learning. In the sequence purpose → objectives → strategy → organization, in fact, all four stages are being refined continuously as the organization make use of what it learns.

The continuing process of organizational change (to adapt a well-known learning model proposed by David Kolb, Massachusetts Institute of Technology) can be thought of in terms of perceiving the present reality in which the organization finds itself (in terms both of its own characteristics and of those of its environment), describing it in some detail, forming hypotheses about why things are as they are, validating these, building a vision of how the reality could be improved, planning the necessary change, and implementing it to create the new reality.

For those who prefer a visual model, the process can be represented as in Figure 3. It follows from all this that the performance of the organization will be profoundly influenced by its ability to learn, and that one way of looking at the work of the O.D. consultant is in terms of how he can help the organization to improve its learning capability.

For an organization to learn it is necessary for its individual members to be learning, and it is perhaps here that the insights of the O.D. consultant can be enormously valuable. Managers are accustomed to think of the output of the

STRATEGIC PLANNING:
A Continuous Interactive Learning Process

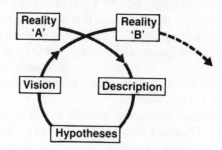

Figure 3   Strategic planning: a continuous
interactive learning process

planning process in terms of the content of the plans themselves, but the learning of which we are speaking now arises largely elsewhere—namely, in the way that people actually experience the planning process itself. The O.D. consultant can, amongst other things, help the organization to design the planning process so that it may make the most of its learning investment as well as produce the plans it requires. The consultant's skill, applied in the minutiae of planning, can help the people involved in the process to develop a common language as well as to extend their understanding of the nature and contexts of the issues at stake.

It cannot be stressed too strongly that the O.D. consultant is not the arbiter of change: he is one of the 'company' of people (whether as an internal or an external resource) who are individually and jointly concerned with improving organizational performance, and the criteria against which that improvement is to be judged are not his, though his skills may well be very helpful when the criteria are being drawn up, and his opinions no less worthy of attention than those of other people. In terms of his skills, they should be useful in the continuous processes of describing the present organizational reality and assessing its overall health and the health of its subsystems (Figure 2). They can be of assistance when purpose (mission), objectives, and strategy are being shaped and re-shaped in the heat of the operational furnace, and they can help to provide interpersonal and interfunctional synergy when the work of the organization is being re-planned (with all the consequences of that re-planning for organizational structure, relationships, procedures, and the rest). If he is a good practitioner he will see a large part of his function to be the transferring of his skills to others within the organization, and this should in theory reduce the demand for O.D. consulting work in Shell as we see it today. The world being what it is, however, it looks as if the Group may need to regard transition as a continuous process and so may be able to make good use of the values, insights, and skills of its O.D. people for a long time to come.

People and Organizations Interacting
Edited by A. Brakel
© 1985, John Wiley & Sons Ltd.

Chapter 12

The Cultural Perspective

Geert Hofstede

Shell culture versus national cultures

In the literature about organizations, the word 'culture' is gaining popularity. Not in the old-fashioned sense of art and education, as a synonym for 'civilization' (this is 'culture' in the narrow sense), but in the broader scientific, anthropological sense, incorporating all forms of collectively-learned human behaviour—even whether, when and how to burp or to blow one's nose. Elsewhere (Hofstede, 1980) I have defined 'culture' in this broad sense as the 'collective programming of the mind' which distinguishes the members of one group or category of people from another. This assumes that culture is primarily carried in the minds of people, even if it becomes visible in their behaviours and in the products of their hands. We can attribute different 'cultures' in this sense to the inhabitants of different countries but also within these countries to people from different regions, generations, social classes, occupations, religions, and even families. The mental programmes of each individual can be conceived as integrating the influences of all these layers of culture plus unique personality characteristics, into a unique whole. We can also attribute different cultures to different organizations and even to different parts of organizations, because organizations and departments also, wittingly or unwittingly, programme their members.

The definition of 'culture' as 'programming of the mind' implies that culture consists of learned characteristics: it is not transferred in our genes ('genetic') but is passed on by parents to children, by people to other people; it represents the collective memory of the people who carry it (it is 'memetic' as opposed to 'genetic'). If a new-born child is adopted in a foreign country, it acquires none of the culture of its natural parents and all of the culture of its foster parents. Growing up in a specific country, region, generation, social class, and family implies being programmed by the people in that country, etc., but also by the physical environment which is partly the heritage of earlier generations, and via the language, the stories, the songs, the religious beliefs, the traditions, the fears, the duties, the foods, and whatever else makes human social life. The new-born child is culturally unprogrammed, so the first programming is always done in the family: next comes the day nursery, kindergarten, all kinds of schools, whatever exists in the particular case; then there are the peer groups and street corner societies; then there is the work environment.

Organizational cultures like Shell's are established early in the life of the organization. The idiosyncracies of the founders become myths to later generations, not necessarily true but expressing the unique identity of this organization in symbolic terms. Organizational cultures also reflect the kind of activity an organization is in: the cultures of a police corps, a hospital, and an oil company differ predictably. But different police corps, different hospitals, different oil companies also have their own distinctive cultural characteristics which survive over time. New organization members are selected, sometimes self-selected, to fit the organizational culture: recruiting departments are gatekeepers of culture. Once on board, new members are 'socialized' to 'the way we do things here', which is the organizational culture. They learn the organizational language, which words to use and which words to avoid when and where; the proper patterns of behaviour for people in different roles; the social networks, whom to pay attention to and whom to ignore; the meaning of status symbols; of being invited or not invited at meetings; of being on the distribution list of memos and reports; of being selected to training; of being promoted at what age. They learn the myths, the heroes, the enemies, the way to dress when and where. In short, on top of whatever mental programming they acquired before, they receive a dose of organizational programming, which is the essence of the organizational culture.

Within any culture—national, organizational or other—countercultures may arise. Countercultures typically deviate from the mainstream culture in one or a few explicit respects, but they continue to share many other characteristics with the mainstream culture, which often go unnoticed. Early interventions by process consultants in Shell could be interpreted as countercultural, a concern for individual creativity being their deviant characteristic; this counterculture introduced new behaviours and new elements of company language. However, those propagating the counterculture built on an individualism already present in the mainstream, on a work ethic, career ambitions, a status hierarchy, a set of corporate beliefs, so they shared many cultural elements with the mainstream. There is a Law of Conservation of Culture, which means that unless we replace all people in the system high and low, cultural revolutions will always be much more gradual, partial, and marginal than the revolutionaries would like them to be.

A work organization like Shell is not a total institution (like a prison or asylum); it always only partly incorporates its members. So, in spite of sharing the organizational culture, members continue to carry their own national, regional, generational, occupational, family, and other cultural layers. Especially within a multinational, multi-divisional entity like Shell, the range of culturally-determined mental programmes found among employees is vast, and if an individual moves from one unit to another, he or she is likely to experience a culture shock. This applies in particular for international moves—say, if an Englishman moves to the Netherlands.

A very important role in cross-cultural communications is played by national languages. In spite of the existence of a common Shell jargon, real communication presupposes a profound understanding of the local language, beyond the touristic level. And language proves to be a biased, not a neutral vehicle for our thoughts: languages contain thought patterns adapted to the mental programming of their native speakers. One cannot learn a language without learning about a culture as well, and vice versa: one cannot develop empathy with another culture without a grasp of its language.

Dimensions of national cultures

From the sources of differences in mental programming referred to, the nation is the most powerful: more powerful in most respects than social class, generation, occupation, religion, family, or organization. Also, national patterns of mental programming tend to be extremely stable over time. This is because the educators transfer the values and behaviours with which they were programmed themselves, and also because what is in the minds of the people has become crystallized in *institutions* common to the members of a nation: a government system, a legal system, an educational system, an army, patterns of religious practice, family structures, industrial relations, architecture, literature, and even scientific theories. All these do reflect something of the particular mental programming of the country. National differences in mental programming have become more and more important because an increasing number of activities in our world demand the co-operation of people from different nations: in supranational bodies like the United Nations or the European Common Market; in bilateral co-operation projects like those for development aid to the Third World; in multinational corporations like Shell; and in international religious, humanitarian, and scientific bodies. We may even say that the survival of mankind largely depends on the effective co-operation of people with different mental programmes rooted in their different national origins.

My own research over the past fifteen years has been largely devoted to national differences in mental programming (Hofstede, 1980). I studied in particular the distribution of *values* from one country to another, as one aspect of national cultures. Values can be defined as 'broad preferences for one state of affairs over others': they indicate what we like and what we dislike, what we call 'good' and what we call 'evil', even what we consider as 'rational' or 'irrational'. Values are linked to culture not in the sense that all members of a cultural group will hold exactly the same values, but that the *distribution* of values among the members of a culture is typical for that culture: the link is statistical, not absolute.

In my research, I compared the distribution of certain work-related values within matched samples of people from at first 40 and later over 50 different countries. I found that the value patterns dominant in these 50-odd countries varied along four main dimensions which I called: (1) individualism versus collectivism; (2) large or small power distance; (3) strong or weak uncertainty avoidance; and (4) masculinity versus femininity. All four are related to some very fundamental issues in human societies, but issues to which different societies can produce different answers. They are the kind of issues which anthropologists explore in small non-literate societies in different parts of the world, but transferred to the scale of the nation state. They are so fundamental that they occur in *any* human society, whether primitive or modern.

Individualism—collectivism

The first dimension is 'individualism versus collectivism'. The fundamental issue involved is the closeness of the relationship between one person and other persons. At one end of the scale we find societies in which the ties among individuals are very loose. Everybody is supposed to look after his or her own self-interest and maybe the interest of his or her immediate family. This is made possible by a large amount of freedom which society leaves individuals. At the other end of the scale we find societies in which the ties between individuals are very tight. People are born into collectivities or in-groups which may be their extended family (including grandparents, uncles, aunts, and so on), their tribe, or their village. Everybody is supposed to look after the interest of his or her in-group and to have no other opinions and beliefs than the opinions and beliefs in their in-group. In exchange, the in-group will protect them when they are in trouble. We see that both the individualist and the collectivist society are integrated wholes, but the individualist society is loosely integrated, the collectivist society tightly integrated.

All 50-odd countries which I studied can be placed somewhere along the individualism–collectivism scale. On the basis of the answers of my samples of respondents, I calculated for each country an 'individualism index' score. The score runs from near 0 for the most collectivist society to near 100 for the most individualist country. It appears that the degree of individualism in a country is strongly related to that country's wealth. All wealthy countries are on the individualist side and all poor countries are on the collectivist side. Very individualist countries are both Great Britain and the Netherlands, but also the United States; very collectivist Colombia, Pakistan, and Taiwan. In the middle we find, for example, Japan, India, Austria, and Spain.

Power distance

The second dimension is 'power distance'. The fundamental issue involved is how society deals with the fact that people are unequal. People are unequal in physical and intellectual capacities. Some societies let these inequalities grow over time into inequalities in power and wealth; the latter may become hereditary and no longer related to physical and intellectual capacities at all. Other societies try to play down inequalities in power and wealth as much as possible. Surely, no society has ever reached complete equality, because there are strong forces in society that perpetuate existing inequalities. All societies are unequal, but some are more unequal than others. This degree of inequality is measured by the power distance scale, which also runs from about 0 (small power distance) to about 100 (large power distance).

In organizations, the level of power distance is related to the degree of centralization of authority and the degree of autocratic leadership. The way the power distance dimension was measured shows that things like centralization and autocratic leadership are rooted in the 'mental programming' of all members of a society, not only of those in power but also of those at the bottom end of the power hierarchy. Societies in which power is distributed very unequally can remain so because this situation satisfies a psychological need for dependence among the people without power. Societies and even corporations will be led as autocratically as their members will permit. The autocracy is both in the members and in the leaders: their value systems usually represent one integrated whole.

The research shows that Asian, African, and Latin American countries have large power distance index scores, but that also France and Belgium, Spain, and Italy score fairly high. Germany, the Nordic countries, the Anglo countries, and the Netherlands score fairly low. There is a global relationship between power distance and collectivism: collectivist countries nearly always show large power distances, but individualist countries do not always show small power distances. The Latin European countries, France, Belgium, Italy, and Spain show a combination of large power distances plus individualism. The other wealthy Western countries all combine smaller power distance with individualism. All poor countries are collectivist with large power distances.*

*Except Costa Rica which is collectivist with a fairly small power distance.

Uncertainty avoidance

The third dimension is 'uncertainty avoidance'. The fundamental issue involved here is how society deals with the fact that time only runs one way. That is, we are all caught in the reality of past, present, and future and we have to live with uncertainty because the future is unknown and will always be so. Some societies teach their people to accept this uncertainty and not to become upset by it. People in such societies will accept each day more easily as it comes. They will take personal risks rather lightly. They will not work so hard. They will be relatively tolerant of behaviours and opinions different from their own because they do not feel threatened by them. I call such societies 'weak uncertainty avoidance' societies.

Other societies teach their people to try to beat the future. Because the future remains essentially unpredictable, in those societies there will be a higher level of anxiety in people, which becomes manifest in greater nervousness, emotionality, and aggressiveness. Such societies—I call them 'strong uncertainty avoidance' societies—also create institutions to promote security and avoid risk. We can create security in three ways. One is technology, in the broadest sense of the word. Through technology we protect ourselves from the risks of nature and war. We build houses, dykes, power stations, intercontinental ballistic missiles which are meant to give us a feeling of security. The second way of creating security is law, again in the broadest sense of the word. Through laws and all kinds of formal or informal rules we protect ourselves from the unpredictability of human behaviour. Having many laws and rules implies an intolerance of deviant behaviours and opinions. Where rules cannot be made because the subject is too fuzzy we can create a feeling of security by the nomination of experts. Experts are people whose word we accept as a kind of law because we assume them to be beyond uncertainty. The third way of creating a feeling of security is religion, once more in the broadest sense of the word. I include in it secular religions and ideologies, such as Marxism, dogmatic Capitalism, or movements that preach an escape into meditation; I even include science in it. All human societies have their religions in some way or another. All religions, in some way, make uncertainty tolerable, because they contain a message that is beyond uncertainty. It helps us to accept the uncertainties of today because we interpret them in terms of something bigger and more powerful that transcends the personal reality. And in strong uncertainty avoidance societies we find religions which claim absolute truth and which do not tolerate other religions. We also find in such societies a scientific tradition looking for ultimate, absolute truths, as opposed to a more relativist, empiricist tradition in the weak uncertainty avoidance societies.

The uncertainty avoidance dimension implies a number of things, from aggressiveness to a need for absolute truth, which we do not usually consider as belonging together. They appear to be statistically associated in the logic of culture patterns, but this logic differs from our own daily logic. Without research

I would not have found that on the level of societies these things go together.

On the uncertainty avoidance index we find the Latin countries, both Latin-European and Latin-American, scoring high; the Asian and African countries medium to low, except Japan and Korea, which score high; in Europe, Germany, Austria, and Switzerland score fairly high, the Nordic and Anglo countries and the Netherlands score lower. This is illustrated in Figure 1 which plots power distance index scores (horizontally) against uncertainty avoidance index scores (vertically).

Masculinity–femininity

The fourth dimension is 'masculinity versus femininity'. The fundamental issue involved is the division of roles between the sexes in society. All societies have to deal with the basic fact that one-half of mankind is female and the other male. The only activities that are strictly determined by the sex of a person are those related to procreation. Men cannot have babies. However, human societies through the ages and around the globe have also allocated other roles to men only, or to women only. This is called the social, rather than the biological, sex role division. All social role divisions are more or less arbitrary and what is seen as a typical task for men or for women varies from one society to the other. The fundamental difference is whether societies try to *minimize* or *maximize* the social sex role division. Some societies allow both men and women to take many different roles. Others make a sharp division between what men should do and what women should do. In this case, the distribution is always so that men take the more assertive and dominant roles and women the more service-oriented and caring roles. I have called societies with a maximized social sex role division 'masculine' and those with a relatively small social sex role division 'feminine'.

In masculine societies, the traditional masculine social values permeate the whole society—even the way of thinking of women. They include the importance of showing off, of performing, of achieving something visible, of making money, of 'big is beautiful'. In more feminine societies, the dominant values—also among the men—are closer to those traditionally associated with the feminine role: not showing off, putting relationships with people before money, minding the quality of life and the preservation of the environment, helping others, in particular the weak, and 'small is beautiful'. In a masculine society the public hero is the successful achiever, the superman. In a more feminine society public sympathy goes to the anti-hero, the underdog, the schlemihl. Individual brilliance in a feminine society is suspect. In Figure 2, masculinity index scores (horizontally) have been plotted against individualism index scores (vertically). We see that the most masculine country is Japan; also quite masculine are the German-speaking countries Germany, Austria, and Switzerland. Among the one-third most masculine countries are some Latin countries, such as Venezuela, Mexico, and Italy; also, most Anglo countries, including both Great Britain and

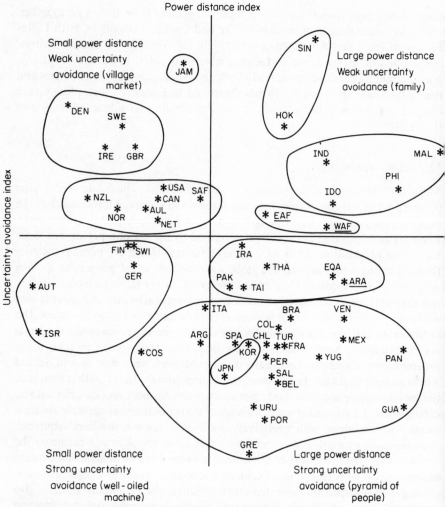

Figure 1 A power distance × uncertainty avoidance plot for 50 countries and three
regions

Country abbreviations:

ARA	Arab countries (Egypt, Lebanon, Lybia, Kuwait, Iraq, Saudi Arabia, U.A.E.)	CHL	Chile
		COL	Colombia
		COS	Costa Rica
ARG	Argentina	DEN	Denmark
AUL	Australia	EAF	East Africa (Kenya, Ethiopia, Zambia)
AUT	Austria		
BEL	Belgium	EQA	Equador
BRA	Brazil	FIN	Finland
CAN	Canada	FRA	France

GBR	Great Britain	PAN	Panama
GER	Germany	PER	Peru
GRE	Greece	PHI	Philippines
GUA	Guatemala	POR	Portugal
HOK	Hong Kong	SAF	South Africa
IDO	Indonesia	SAL	Salvador
IND	India	SIN	Singapore
IRA	Iran	SPA	Spain
IRE	Ireland	SWE	Sweden
ISR	Israel	SWI	Switzerland
ITA	Italy	TAI	Taiwan
JAM	Jamaica	THA	Thailand
JPN	Japan	TUR	Turkey
KOR	South Korea	URU	Uruguay
MAL	Malaysia	USA	United States
MEX	Mexico	VEN	Venezuela
NET	Netherlands	WAF	West Africa (Nigeria, Ghana, Sierra Leone)
NOR	Norway		
NZL	New Zealand	YUG	Yugoslavia
PAK	Pakistan		

the United States, and some of their former colonies like the Philippines and Jamaica.

On the far end towards the feminine side we find the four Nordic countries and the Netherlands. Among the one-third more feminine countries we also find Yugoslavia and France and a number of mostly smaller Latin countries, like Portugal, Chile, Uruguay, Guatemala, and Salvador.

The position of a country on the four scales should be seen as an equilibrium established over a long period of history among elements which are universally human. For example, the social roles I identified with 'masculine' and 'feminine' societies are obviously present in all societies; the 'masculine' and 'feminine' feelings and behaviour are even present in every human being, regardless of his/her sex. The Chinese call this the 'yang' and 'yin', the opposites that presuppose each other. The position of a country on the scale indicates that the equilibrium between 'yang' and 'yin' forces tends to be found in this society at a certain point.

The cultural choices represented by the scores of a country on the four dimensions help determine the fate of nations at different points in time. What is functional at one moment in time may be dysfunctional in another. For example, the same cultural choices that led Germany, Japan, and Italy to military aggression in the Second World War, a combination of stong uncertainty avoidance and strong masculinity, also help explain their remarkable recovery and economic success after the war. A nation's strong points are also its weak points. You cannot have your pudding and eat it.

So far I have painted a static picture of national cultures. Measures over time indicate that there are shifts. If countries become wealthier, they shift towards

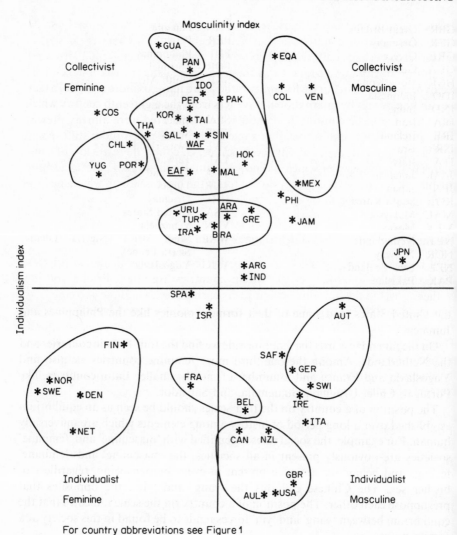

Figure 2   An individualism–collectivism × masculinity–femininity plot for 50 countries and three *regions*

greater individualism, without, however, all becoming equally individualist. There has been over the past two decades a trend for power distances to be reduced, but mainly in those countries in which they were already relatively low. There seem to be world-wide waves of uncertainty avoidance which have accompanied the rhythm of World Wars, and we are at present experiencing a rising tide of uncertainty avoidance which some people call 'doomsday thinking'. Finally, it seems that masculine countries tend to become even more masculine and feminine countries even more feminine. Throughout these changes, relative differences between countries remain remarkably stable. There is no sign of convergency between cultures, such as was the common belief in the 1950s when the European Common Market was founded. Increasing international contact seems to confirm us in our own identity rather than make us more similar. In fact, we can find quotes by international travellers from the eighteenth century which show that the basic cultural differences which I pictured were already present then, and there are indications that some of them are much older still—going back as far as the Roman and Chinese Empires. Of course there are lots of value changes in our societies which we notice—but I believe these are at a more peripheral, specific level and they do not touch the basic issues on which the four dimensions are founded.

The merger of British and Dutch cultures within Shell

Shell is, together with Unilever, one of the few examples in the world of a successful bi-national merger. Its parent countries are Great Britain and the Netherlands. On the four dimensions in my earlier research, these two countries rank as shown in Table 1. We see that Great Britain and the Netherlands score virtually identical on individualism (very high) and power distance (fairly low). They are reasonably close on uncertainty avoidance, although the British are more comfortable with uncertainty than the Dutch. They are wide apart on the masculinity–femininity dimension, Great Britain scoring quite masculine, the Netherlands very feminine.

Table 1   Rank orders for Great Britain and the Netherlands on four dimensions of national culture, among 50 countries around the world

	Great Britain	Netherlands	Difference GB − NL
Individualism	48	46	2
Power distance	11	14	− 3
Uncertainty avoidance	7	18	− 11
Masculinity	41	3	38

(1 = lowest rank; 50 = highest rank)

Wide disparities in a business relationship on the individualism–collectivism dimension are difficult to bridge, as joint ventures between Western and Third World partners show. The relationships between business partners are of a very different nature in the two types of culture: calculative, contractual, and exchangeable for more advantageous deals elsewhere, if possible, on the individualist side; moral and based on life-long person-bound loyalty and mutual obligations and favours on the collectivist side. Since Britain and the Netherland are both very individualist, this type of misunderstanding will not occur in Shel (but it could between Shell and its venture partners in the Third World).

Wide disparities on power distance and/or uncertainty avoidance (see Figur 1) also tend to make international co-operation precarious. This is because the lead to different implicit models of what an organization should be and how i should function. Organizations are devices to distribute power and they also have as a main task to avoid uncertainty, to make things predictable. We have countries with large power distance and strong uncertainty avoidance, like France; with small power distance but strong uncertainty avoidance, like Germany; with small power distance and weak uncertainty avoidance like Britain; and with large power distance but weak uncertainty avoidance, like India and Indonesia. Professor O. J. Stevens of INSEAD once did an interesting experiment. He gave the same description of an organizational problem to a group of French, a group of German, and a group of British management students. The problem described a conflict between two departments. The students were asked to determine what was wrong and what should be done to resolve the problem. The French in majority referred the problem to the next higher authority level. The Germans suggested the setting of rules to resolve such problems in the future. The British wanted to improve communication between the two department heads, for example by some kind of human relations training. Stevens concluded that the dominant underlying model of an organization for the French was a *pyramid of people*: a hierarchical structure held together by the unity of command (large power distance) as well as by rules (strong uncertainty avoidance). The model for the Germans was a *well-oiled machine*: the exercise of personal command was largely unnecessary because the rules settled everything (strong uncertainty avoidance, but smaller power distance). The model for the British was a *village market*: no decisive hierarchy flexible rules, and a resolution of problems by negotiation (small power distance and weak uncertainty avoidance). A discussion with an Indian colleague led me to believe that the underlying model of an organization for the Indians and Indonesians is the *family*: undisputed personal authority of the father-leader but few formal rules (large power distance but weak uncertainty avoidance).

This analysis shows why, for example, a merger between a British partner (village market model) and a French (pyramid model) is unlikely to succeed: they hold profoundly different conceptions of what an organization is and should be However, Britain and the Netherlands are close enough together on both power distance and uncertainty avoidance to allow both British and Dutch people within Shell to hold the same implicit organization model—and it should be no surprise this is a *village market* model. Even in comparison with a fully Dutch corporation like Philips, and certainly in comparison with a U.S. company like IBM, Shell comes across as a village market with two central offices rather than one headquarters, and much debate between the two, without strong hierarchical lines of command, full of multiple reporting relationships, with a wide tolerance for sub-units and even individuals doing their own things, and with considerable openness to the outside world (see Watson and Pritchard's comments in Chapter 11 on Shell's tolerance for ambiguity).

A wide gap on the masculinity–femininity dimension is evidently not dysfunctional, as witnessed by the long-term success of the Shell and Unilever mergers. We should consider these mergers as marriages and they could also be seen as applications of Brakel's 'skating model', explained in Chapter 1. They represent the harmonious integration of complementary elements (the 'yang' and 'yin' of Chinese philosophy) equally necessary for the success of an organization. The masculine orientation focuses on the task, on achievement, and competition; the feminine orientation focuses on the maintenance of relationships, on people, and on social responsibility. Both the task and the relationship focus are essential for the long-term survival of an organization. I do not want to suggest that necessarily inside Shell, all British take the more task-oriented roles, and all Dutch the more relationship-oriented roles. It is quite possible that on the Dutch labour market, because of selective and self-selective hiring, Shell attracts a 'masculine' subset of the Dutch population, and on the British labour market a relatively 'feminine' subset of the British population.

Cultural choices in this volume

In addition to Great Britain and the Netherlands, the authors in this volume write about Canada, Norway, and Japan. In my national cultures research, Canada scores fairly similar to Great Britain; Norway rather similar to the Netherlands. Only Japan scores very differently, half-way between individualism and collectivism, half-way on the power distance scale, but very high on both uncertainty avoidance and masculinity. Hattori's contribution in Chapter 10 not surprisingly reflects considerably different values and practices.

Leaving Japan aside until later, the contributions in this volume all reflect a cultural choice for strong individualism, (ID), small power distance (PD), and weak uncertainty avoidance (UA). Langstraat and Roggema in Chapter 4 go 'from vertical to horizontal' with a reduction in the number of hierarchical levels (reducing PDs). Roggema and Voors in Chapter 2 set out to change (p. 18) 'the autocratic leadership on board and the caste-like division between officers and ratings (which) are at odds with societal values around consultation and participation' (these are the societal values of low PD societies). They defend (p. 20) an open-ended change strategy reducing the role of experts and involving the crew of ships in action research (a weak UA approach). Greeve's (Chapter 5) 'participative re-design' in research is a weak UA change strategy towards a small PD solution. Cormack and Wallace (Chapter 7) show the use of participation (small PD) even in crisis reform (crisis situations tend to strengthen uncertainty avoidance tendencies!). Halpern from Canada in Chapter 8 (p. 117) refers to the minimizing of status differentials (small PD) and several uncertainty increasing (weak UA) steps: 'minimizing formal rules in the contracts', 'the principle of incompletion', and 'the use of experimentation (p. 137ff.). Gjemdal from Norway starts Chapter 9 by referring to the lack of large class differences in his country and the abolition of nobility (small PD in the surrounding society).

Chapter 10, by Hattori from Japan, reflects the situation of the local subsidiary of a multinational with a foreign organization culture; its managers are at the crossroads between Shell culture and Japanese culture. 'Family training' (p. 200) and 'high spirited morning greeting' (p. 203) are Japanese and more collectivist elements; the rejection of 'irresponsible criticism to superiors among subordinates' (p. 202) reflects a higher power distance choice which we find nowhere in the other chapters; a 'disciplinary morning gathering' (p. 203) fits a culture with tight uncertainty-avoiding social rituals. This is the Japanese way in Shell Japan. On the other hand, the use of the (U.S.) 'managerial grid' package for training (p. 192) with such elements as increasing candour in communications represent an inroad of more individualistic, smaller PD ways which represent the Shell way crossing the Japanese way; but Shell Japan is wisely careful not to introduce foreign methods which would hurt the precious interpersonal harmony, like direct feedback on the other person's management style (p. 193).

The masculinity–femininity rift is evident in some of the chapters: Britain and Japan being positioned on the masculine side, Canada in the middle, and the Netherlands and Norway on the feminine side. Masculinity and individualism interact so that in Japan we do find the masculine work orientation, but group competition instead of individual competition as is the pattern in the United States and Great Britain. The difference between O.D. interventions in masculine and in feminine style is evident by comparing Cormack and Wallace's tough approach based on the survival of the fittest, with the Dutch and Norwegian O.D. contributions, such a Greeve's in Chapter 5 and Gjemdal's in Chapter 9 with their emphasis on co-operation and relationships.

Conclusion: opportunities for synergy

The idea of a broad cultural diversity existing within the organization is widely accepted among Shell managers. In Shell's 'village market' culture, such diversity is seen as a source of enrichment rather than a threat. This point merits making, because not all large multinational corporations are so tolerant about the idea of cultural diversity. Some foster a corporate philosophy of 'aren't we all the same?' in which mentioning cultural diversity is felt to be subversive. Of course, cultural diversity exists within such corporations as much as elsewhere, but it is banned to the realms of corporate folklore.

Shell's openness to cultural diversity is based upon its own bi-cultural origins, and the predominance of its international operations over its home operations. Shell serves as an unplanned laboratory for cultural synergy: for obtaining a result from the co-operation of different cultures that is more than the sum of the individual contributions. Often, of course, cultural diversity leads to cultural friction losses, so that the total result is less than the sum of the individual contributions. International mergers—or even national ones—may result in intolerable cultural friction losses, and be disbanded for that reason.

Cultural synergy is an appealing concept but difficult to bring about. It demands, first of all, some over-arching values or over-arching identity which unifies people in spite of cultural differences. These can be supplied by a strong and distinct corporate culture. In a study of successful and less successful U.S. corporations, Deal and Kennedy (1982) pointed to 'a strong culture' as the decisive factor of success. Strong culture corporations, they claim, are 'not merely organizations, but successful human institutions'. There is no doubt that Shell is a strong culture corporation, so that it is in a position to tolerate and even enjoy cultural diversity inside.

Cultural synergy does not come by itself. Mungall's intervention, described in Chapter 3, is an example of how different organizational cultures, which had led to considerable friction losses, were finally integrated, at least for one project. The idea that culture can be made to work for us is relatively new in the management and organization literature, although it may correspond to what many wise managers and consultants have done for ages, without using the label 'culture'. But now that we have the label and learn more about the phenomenon, we can more consciously intervene. One example consists of Halpern's 'culture-building workshops' with new personnel of the Canadian chemical plant, described in Chapter 8 (p. 134). What we should still know more about is:

● How do we diagnose national, organizational, departmental, and group cultures?
● What combinations of cultures are likely to produce synergy, and which will lead to friction losses or worse?
● What measures can we take to turn friction losses into synergy?

With the increasing need for co-operation among culturally diverse groups, there is a case for establishing a science of 'organizational anthropology' to answer the above questions, as a logical complement to microeconomics, organizational psychology, and organizational sociology. It will help us to move our organizations, including Shell, in directions where we want them to go.

References

Deal, T. E. and Kennedy, A. A. (1982) *Corporate Cultures: The Rites and Rituals of Corporate Life* (Addison-Wesley, Reading, Mass.).
Hofstede, G. (1980) *Culture's Consequences: International Differences in Work-Related Values* (SAGE Publications, Beverly Hills and London).

People and Organizations Interacting
Edited by A. Brakel
© 1985, John Wiley & Sons Ltd.

Chapter 13

Managing Diversity

Aat Brakel

The emphasis in the title of this book is on 'interacting', which presupposes the collaboration of interest groups. This presupposition may render the title normative rather than pragmatic; on the whole contemporary organizational practice is predominantly of the preactive mode. The task here is to find out where the best waves are going to come in, and to ride in on them—keeping others off. One must diagnose opportunities and seize them with all the arts of the calculable: economic models, technical forecasts, operations research, and the like (Trist, 1980). Looking at this *preactive* mode as an attitude to the future, the implication is that the environment is considered manageable under one's own steam.

The *interactive* mode could be considered as a higher level of complexity; the environment is seen as turbulent and unpredictable to the extent that some sort of open-ended unfolding process among interested parties may be required. In addition to the calculable, other sides of ourselves are increasingly coming into demand: the entrepreneurial hunch, intuition, and imagination.

After having made a survey of organizational developments in the preceding chapters, the question now is whether there is a thread running through the various chapters which would allow listing common elements as possible guidelines to the future. We might also find a 'step-change'—a discontinuity rather than a continuous thread.

What about calculation and imagination? One might expect a mixed bag of experiences, and discovering tracks along which a number of organizations move towards the century's end may well be of learning value.

With this objective in mind, a framework will be used to order the variety of data presented and subsequently assess the various change processes. Some thought will also be given to more general use of the model.

In the first chapter we developed 'a way to look at things' in order to get into the habit of doing a number of things at the same time; complementarity was introduced in order to emphasize the 'and/and mode' of approaching people and organizations rather than the 'either/or mode'. The theme here is 'two descriptions are better than one', which refers to the bonus of knowing what would follow from combining information from two or more sources. In such instances the resultant information is quite different from what was in either source separately (Bateson, 1979, p. 21).

The principle of combining information finds application in Shell's performance and potential appraisal system in which complementarity of qualities is the basic concept. A simple and clear example of a complementary entity is the human body: one part needs another one, and vice versa, in order to be useful and make sense. So it is with human qualities: they are all closely interrelated. For a basic quality of an individual there is an implicitly linked complementary quality which must also be present if the former has been rightly ascribed. This can be illustrated by taking the two following characteristics: imagination and sense of reality. If a person were promoted to a job of wider scope and increased responsibility, he or she will need to apply more imagination, but this increased imagination can only be of value if it is complemented by a commensurate increase in the application of his or her sense of reality. The bonus of understanding behaviour according to a complementary mode of thinking is that a closer and more authentic approximation of human behaviour is obtained than when only using single and unrelated categories. We tend to get a portrait rather than a snapshot: it is a difference in dimension and depth.

It may be worthwhile to mention in passing that a certain definition of complementarity was also introduced into physics. According to Heisenberg's uncertainty principle we cannot measure accurately both the position and the momentum of a moving particle at the same time. The more precisely we determine one of these properties, the less we know about the other. Accuracy of measurement was a presupposition for objective knowledge required by classical Newtonian physics; the uncertainty heralded the advent of the New Physics. Niels Bohr introduced complementarity into quantum physics in 1927 in order to explain the wave–particle duality of light. *Both* wave-like and particle-like characteristics are necessary to understand light (Zukav, 1979, p. 116).

Returning now to organizations: the value of combining information is obtained from complementary relationships like micro and macro aspects, or people and tasks, representing the social, resp. technical, system. In the first chapter the combination was represented in 'the skating model'. There are supposed to be a large number of similar organizational relationships, like quantity/quality, closed/open, rigid/flexible, authoritarian/participative, equalization/variation, out there/in here, rational action/empirical system, etc.

Of fundamental importance is that the organization we experience transcends these categories; it is all these, and more. That what I have 'between my ears' is always more than I am able to say or write in words. Russell and Whitehead found an expression for this type of difference in the theory of logical levels (Watzlawick et al., 1974, pp. 6–10). Going from a single category (like 'technical system' or an individual's 'flexibility') to a larger whole (like resp. 'organization' or 'human behaviour') is like going from member to class of members; it means moving up the hierarchy of logical levels. It entails a jump or discontinuity. If two single elements are combined in a complementary relationship we move from one logical level to the next higher one. The complementary mode as a tool for understanding organizations results therefore in a closer approximation of the thing called 'organization' than summing up of single elements would provide. It relates to *two* hands required for clasping.

Let us now look at the combination of the technical and social system; with the skating analogy we expressed the meta level. If we draw a straight line with each system represented at an end-point, the complementary whole would be perceived outside the dimension of the paper.

●————————————————————————————●

Another important distinction in organizational life is that between 'corporate structure' and 'individual'. There is a dynamic balance between system and person, or management and manager. As indicated above, an organization is both. If we put the 'corporate' and the 'individual' at the end points of a straight line, the organization as experienced is beyond the composing elements and again outside the paper's plane.

It is then only a small step to combine the two lines to form a cross which results in four quadrants with complementary aspects in each, as presented in Figure 1. The 'four quadrant model' thus obtained is supposed to be a steady-state model; the quadrants are interdependent and they form each others' contexts. The meaning of the elements of one quadrant is determined by the meaning of those of the other three. In the figure a number of elements have been listed in each quadrant; these elements are not exhaustive, they are intended as 'trigger elements', to exemplify others that would fit in with the cluster.

The corporate/hard quadrant (CH) contains elements related to the total system of a technical/economic nature. The business objectives and policies of the enterprise belong here, also the formal organization structure, the planning system to ensure the continuity of the business, and 'management', the entity that transcends the individual manager.

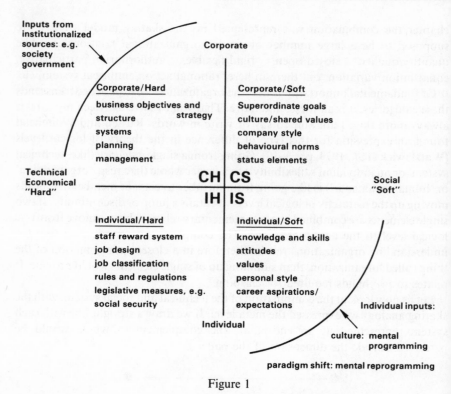

Figure 1

The corporate/soft quadrant (CS) embraces elements related to the total system of a social nature. The mission or superordinate goals belong here, so would certain ethical principles. Shared values and beliefs, particular ideologies, styles of communication, and in-company behaviour ('the way we do things here'), traditions and symbols like the number of windows in a manager's room, are found in this quadrant.

The individual/hard quadrant (IH) has elements through which the system personalizes. In a job design or job classification the system becomes very 'real' for an individual. In personal rewards and in rules to regulate behaviour the system is no longer distant and macro, but takes on micro proportions. This also pertains to certain legislation as far as it influences the individual. In all these aspects 'the system becomes a person'.

The individual/soft quadrant (IS) contains elements relating to the individual of a social nature. Personal know-how and skills, motivation, values and preferences, job expectations, ambitions and the like, fit in here.

The four quadrants we have arrived at, and more specifically their interdependence, are now suggested as a framework for ordering the data contained in the chapters and also for interpreting the change activities. Central in the model is the view that an organization is 'a lot of things all at the same time'. If that is so, change should relate to that 'all' which is represented in the model in the four quadrants with complementary relationships. This suggests a condition for organizational change: representation of activities in all four quadrants and with this condition in mind we shall consider the events described in this book.

We still have to answer the question: In what ways will 'culture' or 'mental programming' fit in the four quadrant model? On the subject of organization and its environment, it was suggested on pp. 9/10 (Chapter 1) that the social system of an organization acquires characteristics that correspond with those of the surrounding society mainly through the organization members who not only play the role allotted to them but also bring themselves—their 'societal selves'—into the organization. It is conceivable, therefore, that the phenomenon of mental programming is introduced into the model either through the individual/soft quadrant or through the corporate/hard quadrant in the case where values and ideas have become institutions or law.

In the next section the contents of the various chapters will be assessed using the framework of Figure 1. As explained above, the assumption is that in the case of a complete change process all vital organizational elements would be involved through representation in all quadrants of the model.

Assessment of chapters

Chapter 2. Project with the long breath

The chapter gives an account of a well-balanced change process in which the various elements of the four quadrants are present.

The objectives that refer to changes in society at large and in the company itself, and the creation of a less segmented structure between deck and engine room, fit in quadrant CH.

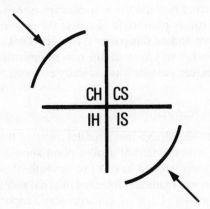

In the sphere of job design, the job content of the ratings as described in the chapter would fit in quadrant IH; its reflection in individual skills and attitudes in quadrant IS. Obtaining crew stability as a corporate policy would belong in quadrant CS. Individual consequences, e.g. in a certain duration of affiliation between seafarer and a specific ship, fit in quadrant IS.

For quick overview the model is repeated in reduced form. It will be clear that the allocation of specific events to a particular quadrant can only be done in a global sense in order to avoid excessive detail.

Chapter 3. The North Sea project

This account shows a structural change (CH) in the introduction of an integrated project organization. The sensing diagnoses made by the consultant indicate task integration (IH) and a number of CS and IS elements shown by the development of a different co-operative climate and the improvement of individual job satisfaction.

This change process is of much smaller scope than the previous one; however, similar aspects are coming to the fore upon assessment using the model.

Chapter 4. From vertical to horizontal

The structural change of setting up a number of autonomous production units refers to the CH quadrant. The manager of such a unit is head of a multi-functional co-ordination team, which is meant to optimize the various needs (e.g. production and technical maintenance) and relationships (CS). In a number of cases reporting lines and job designs were adapted (IH), while in the multi-functional working environment, as compared to the originally segregated set-up, changes in individual values and attitudes are noticeable (IS). It will be clear that the description shows a complete change in a well-balanced way.

It is worthwhile observing that according to the Managers' Epilogue further adaptations were required because the new concept of organization did not fit into the conventional career pattern. In this case the organization was changed again in order to accommodate this pattern. In Shell Tankers' case (Chapter 2) the approach was the other way around: the new organization was retained and the educational and career pattern was radically changed.

Chapter 5. Redesign in research

A number of participative redesign meetings described in the chapter resulted in the proposal that the management of a pilot plant should be given to project teams and that these teams should have a fair amount of autonomy (1976). In mid-1978 an evaluation was made and it turned out that success in developing the proposals was very limited. Lack of management support was quoted as a reason; more successful change processes mentioned in other chapters indeed show a much more positive and stimulating support of management. Another reason may be that the setting up of a project team in the context of a conventional line-staff structure has been underestimated. The chapter mentions a fair amount of autonomy for project teams. What is 'a fair amount of autonomy'? Other chapters that describe successful changes show pronounced attention, e.g. for new organization characteristics, feedback sessions, writing job descriptions, and distributing responsibilities and authorities for the new situation. It would appear that the success of an intentional redesign hinges on clear decisions and descriptions concerning responsibilities and authorities, especially in multi-functional teams where team members operate in a new management structure.

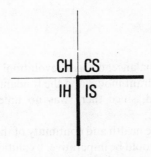

Using the model of Figure 1 it emerges from the chapter that activities remained on the social side and never became 'hard' in the sense that structures or design proposals were firmly agreed upon between interested members or parties, including clear arrangements on responsibilities and autonomy. The chapter shows an intervention that became blocked in the IS quadrant without reflections in the other quadrants and consequently no permanent adaptation of the organization.

Chapter 6. *Organization development on the shop floor*

In order to alleviate a number of problems a blueprint of a new organization structure was produced, which fits in the CH quadrant. Detailing of the blueprint in terms of job designs and daily operations was done by the work-force in joint consultation sessions. These activities fit in the IH and IS quadrants. There are indications in the chapter that the climate of co-operation and the style of working together had improved, which fit in the CS quadrant. The chapter suggests—all things taken together—that elements of the change process are represented in all quadrants of the model, which points towards complete change.

Chapter 7. Evolution, revolution, and the battle for survival

This intervention starts in the CH quadrant of the model—and remains there. The revolutionary process, called 'puntuated development', excludes evolutionary balancing; that is to say, it is not possible to pinpoint a number of more or less simultaneous or consequential events that would fit in the other quadrants.

The process was out of balance: it was a revolution! The four quadrant model was reduced to a one quadrant model and the fundamental complementarity of the model was suspended, since there was no time for balancing the vital organizational elements.

We speculate that for the health and continuity of the organization a return to the four quadrant model would be imperative. Evolution should be the following phase with a restored balance and preferably sustaining activities with elements that would fit again in the model.

Chapter 8. Shell Canada: the Sarnia Chemical Plant

This chapter's description of events leading to an organization design based on quality of worklife principles starts with a Philosophy Statement related to work

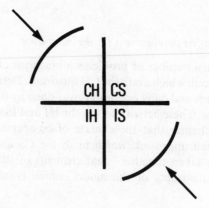

design which is clearly an element of the CH quadrant and also reflects developments in society at large. The alternative organization design fits in here as well, which has spin-offs in IH (the remuneration programme) and IS (training activities). Aspects like team norms relate to the CS quadrant. It is interesting that the support systems for sustaining the change process appear also to be related to the various quadrants of the model. The chapter mentions the 'principle of incompletion', which expresses the notion that a design is never complete. One is continuously learning which relates to the various perspectives of the model.

Both the implementation of the design philosophy in the new plant design and the support systems are in terms of the four quadrant model to be considered as well-balanced and ongoing change processes that cover the total system of the organization.

Chapter 9. Development in Norske Shell's organization

The Working Environment Act mentioned at the beginning of the chapter can be regarded as a societal input on a legislative basis which enters the model through the CH quadrant. Results from behavioural science as an initiating element of O.D. would also fit in the CH quadrant. The values and attitudes of the young can be located in the IS quadrant. The O.D. process described in its institutionalized form would belong in the CS quadrant. Individual aspects of the O.D. groups are IS elements.

The various statements issued as shown in the Appendices refer to the CH quadrant. In the section 'Results', items are given, e.g. a participative management style and a certain climate of co-operation, which fit in the CS quadrant. In the restructuring of one's own departments and the setting up of partly autonomous groups the types of elements of the IH quadrant come to the fore. Also, this chapter shows a development that embraces all parts that make up the organization; it is complete adaptation on a continuous basis.

Chapter 10. Working life in Japan

A number of elements that belong to the cultural context of the organization are mentioned at the beginning of the chapter, e.g. the relationship between individual and group, life-long employment, in-house unions, and remuneration based on capability.

These elements enter the model and appear to influence it to the extent that borderlines between quadrants become blurred. It emerges from the chapter that separation between the quadrants individual/soft and corporate/soft—obvious in Western thinking—is much less pronounced. Indications of the importance of the work-place in relation to the individual are the apparent ease of having a family training on Friday evening and Saturday morning, and the weight attached to a high-spirited morning greeting and disciplinary morning gathering. Also, the division between the quadrants individual/hard and individual/soft is different since, for example, additional knowledge is rewarded irrespective of job availability.

The partitions between the IH, IS, and CS quadrants appear at least partly permeable. A quality emerges from the chapter which is different from what is common in the West European sense and which distinguishes itself from the other chapters we have looked at so far.

The complementarity of elements, which is a fundamental characteristic of the four quadrant model, is in the Japanese case noticeable to a limited extent. For instance, in the relation between individual and group there appears to be superordination of the latter rather than interdependence of both.

Although elements of all four quadrants are to be found in the chapter, pointing to a successful and complete organizational adaptation, we have to exercise restraint in drawing conclusions because of the different *meaning* attached to some elements. This would also indicate that, for example, introducing the Japanese quality circle concept into Western industries to improve efficiency or for any other laudable reason, requires adequate attention to roots and contexts, and not mere copying.

The above short summaries indicate that the four quadrant model (Figure 1) gives a unifying perspective and provides an effective way to look at the various change processes. Adaptations are apparently successful when all the vital components of an organization become involved, which finds expression in representation of these elements in all quadrants of the model. This is the case with most of the chapters; the exceptions are Chapters 5, 7, and 10. In Chapter 5 the process did not reach completion. Chapter 7 showed a revolutionary process concentrated in one quadrant only. In Chapter 10 only a tentative conclusion was given because of the different meanings given to a number of elements as compared with what is customary in the Western world.

The model offers a perspective on organizations based on complementary viewpoints. It puts elements into each others' contexts and stresses their interdependence. It thus becomes an exercise in thinking at different logical levels when trying to approach the organizational reality we experience.

Apart from the processes, the case histories also reveal the following factors.

(1) Most chapters show clear *objectives*, i.e. at the outset there is a vision of where one wants to be. The spectrum varies from broad objectives encompassing societal developments in the Shell Tankers' case, to much more specified and localized objectives e.g. in the North Sea case and the workshop case.

(2) The *initiation of projects* is, in most chapters, done by management through *workshops*. Management gives a certain direction which may well be in the form of a blueprint, followed by further workshops down the line who fill in the details of the blueprint. We find this approach in Chapters 2, 4, 5, and 6, and also in Chapter 3, although the type and scope of the problem gave the O.D. consultant a more pivotal role than in the other instances. In Chapter 7 top management assisted by the O.D. consultants takes and keeps the initiative during the revolutionary phase of the process.

(3) The majority of chapters shows *evolutionary developments*, which take time. Since some managers often want results yesterday, this time requirement can be conflicting, although there will be agreement on the statement that balanced development needs time. Growth has its own regularities. We see this development over a period of time in most processes. It is important to realize this, the more so since change requires sustenance and thus more time. Halpern (Chapter 8) observes: 'a tendency for varied and unrealistic expectations to emerge, primarily related to the time required to meet stated objectives. Not having achieved "instant Utopia" leads to considerable frustration. There is a need to deal with "realism" and somehow to get the understanding across that people are involved in an evolving, growing, developmental situation, that espoused objectives are long-term targets and, indeed, some may never be realized to everyone's satisfaction.' But if survival is the objective, there is no time and a revolutionary approach the line of march, as described in Chapter 7.

The cultural element

The chapters show a certain 'national variable' which we become particularly aware of when studying the Japanese case in between the others. We 'know' that national traditions, legislation, relations between management and unions, and so on play their part in the various countries. In the Western world these aspects often have a certain familiarity. But with the Japanese case we see another world, which is no longer familiar to us. Broadly speaking we have just begun to look at cultural pluriformity and diversity because so far a cultural perspective of organizations has often been perceived as rather unnecessary, or irrelevant, and could be taken for granted. But in 1984 things have become more sensitive, and a heightened awareness of managers for cultures' consequences has become a vital condition for success in a number of situations, which vary greatly. Culture was defined as a programming of the mind, shared with some but not all other people; these situations therefore vary from the way of life in a strange and far-away country to different values and beliefs my next-door neighbour may hold on issues in our daily life. The cultural element in this broad sense requires awareness of the context in which we are operating; also, to develop an ability to look at things in a different context. This may sound simple enough, but a fish only 'knows' water when out of the bowl, and a different context is somewhat like we 'fish' trying to describe what it will be like when we evolve to walk on land. If internationalization of business is a line of march, empathy for cultural variables is a prerequisite. Empathy can be supported by understanding, which is what these paragraphs endeavour to stimulate.

Hofstede in Chapter 12 shows the cultural choices that becomes apparent in the various chapters. He bases his contribution on extensive research, which revealed four main dimensions on which country cultures differ, namely power distance, uncertainty avoidance, individualism, and masculinity. He shows that—apart from Japan—the contributions reflect a cultural choice for strong individualism, small power distance, and weak uncertainty avoidance. Hattori's contribution from Japan reflects considerably different values and practices, which is in accordance with the different position of Japan on the various scales and our considerations on the basis of the four quadrant model. Hofstede provides an interesting and challenging perspective on cultural diversity; his maps may well be of use in personnel planning activities and may provide food for thought and discussion when transferring managers from one country to another.

Also of interest are his thoughts on the merger of British and Dutch cultures within Shell. The rank orders for Great Britain and the Netherlands on the four dimensions of national culture show that both countries are close together on individualism, power distance, and uncertainty avoidance, but wide apart on the masculinity–femininity dimension. This dimension may be assumed to provide the elements of a complementary relationship. The crux of the matter is the over-arching combination which in Shell is apparently effective. The line of thought of Hofstede's conclusion points towards 'opportunities for synergy'; he stresses the increasing need for co-operation among culturally diverse groups.

In Shell's cultural diversity lie weaknesses as well as strengths, which is to be expected in an organization as complex as the Group. Pritchard and Watson elaborate on this and related subjects in Chapter 11. In their listing of key features of the overall Shell culture and their meaning in terms of direction in the future they point to the need for crossing the threshold between what can be achieved by expert, objective-centred direction, and what is required to take a step into the unknown. This problem can be seen as part of the wider issue of where to find solid ground which can form a foundation for business planning. In addition to the *traditional competences* based on rationality the writers point to *other competences* such as intuition and use of non-rational criteria like values, feelings, and prejudices.

We think that the transition from traditional scientific management criteria to a mix of rational and non-rational criteria in management decision-making would constitute a paradigm shift, very much like the one described in Chapter 11 concerning attitudes to authority. If a manager has been educated to be first of all a rational manager in the enlightened traditions of our educational systems, the paradigm shift would mean mental *re*-programming in order to see more than the rational side only. It is basically a cultural change involving an additional perspective on the organizational world. The resultant total perspective is more complete and richer than the rational perspective on its own. It is here that we find the vitality and *élan* required for a creative and innovative look at the world around us. We shall see in the next section that this paradigm shift may well be on the way.

A final view

We have addressed the question of adaptation of organizations and considered a number of events which we tried to put in a certain order. We do not think it is possible—even desirable—to write down a number of hard and fast conclusions: we have to take too many things into focus at the same time. We therefore discuss a connecting pattern; the message here is to combine information from various sources. Information in the traditional sense of $1 + 1 = 2$, *and* in another sense in which $1 + 1$ equals more than 2.

Why do people—managers—start a change process? Obviously because of some rational argument—examples of which are provided in the above chapters. But there is more than that. If we read through the chapters, and more particularly through some of the Epilogues, we also encounter more or less explicit visions of things to come. 'The new organization we are looking for' is a recurring theme in, for example, the chapters on tankers and chemicals, and those from Canada, Norway, and Japan. This theme contains the hopes, aspirations, and also the anxieties and fears of managers who distinguish the contours of something new on its way.

Managing change apparently requires a two-fold, i.e. combined, approach: technical competence *and* imaginative vision. To the extent that we distinguish both elements it is the paradigm shift mentioned at the end of the previous paragraph on its way. Imaginative vision requires the ability to combine information from different sources, put things in another context, paint the contours of a future picture, working towards it with knowledge, common sense, stamina and gut-feel. Through the ability to combine, *we make a difference*. Although this may well be half the truth.

In Shell companies the helicopter viewpoint is considered to be the essential quality to advancement. This 'helicopter quality' has been defined by Muller (1970) as a man's ability and urge to

(a) look at problems from a higher vantage point with simultaneous attention to relevant details and to shape his work accordingly on the basis of a personal vision; and

(b) place facts and problems within a broader context by immediately detecting relevant relationships within systems of wider scope.

This quality was found to have the highest relevance to ultimate career potential. It combines overview and relevant detail. But overview does not stop at the gate of the enterprise; it includes the environment and the context within which things happen. From an open systems perspective we may even say that the environment is very much part of the total organization.

We have seen quite a contextual variety in a number of chapters, e.g. quality of worklife aspects in Canada, legislative measures in Norway, the ancient culture of Japan, technical and educational aspects of the national schooling system in the Shell Tankers' case, and the various aspects assembled by Hofstede; all these are environmental elements that impinge on the organization and are part of it.

Here we find the other half of the truth: we have to make a difference *within a certain context*. A difference cannot be made on one's own or in a vacuum. Bateson notes that it takes at least two somethings to create a difference (Bateson, 1969, p. 68).

The Dutchman Zijlker discovered crude oil in 1880 on North Sumatra, then part of the Dutch East Indies. He was an entrepreneur, a pioneer, who created himself a context that became Royal Dutch. That is what is required of the manager nearing the year 2000: be a pioneer who creates himself a context. Even if—as will often be the case—a context already exists. The chapters point out that a *difference is made by interaction*.

Interaction takes interest groups into account and embraces new information from different origins. The manager's mental focus has to alternate between his inner and outer worlds. In fact, it has to be the focus of all organization members, which then makes the organization a centre of learning (Juch, 1983, p. 174). It transcends traditional and hierarchical models to a meta model of organizations, in which participative approaches also have their place. Bureaucracy has been called the enemy of innovation. One of the reasons for alternative and new forms of organization is the loosening of creativity, giving talent a chance through the whole organization.

People who want to make a difference should not become reduced to mediocrity by an organizational harness. Top managers may have the stature and the power to make decisions, irrespective of structure. But top managers are few; talented people—as a general rule—are more in abundance and cannot be creative in stifling circumstances.

The case histories show the development of a variety of structures that differ from traditional ones. Apparently, the existing structures were experienced as insufficiently flexible for the tasks in question; in general the new structures allow more elbow room and more experimentation to satisfy existing needs. At the same time these structures with increased flexibility make our organizations attractive for innovative and entrepreneurial talent.

The organizational image that corresponds with the proposal to make a difference by interaction is quite varied and not very determinate. We noted that an organization is many things at the same time. 'Organization' is basically a notion that conveys a *connecting pattern* and 'managing diversity' means the ability to think and act in terms of such a connecting pattern. The language we used for this pattern is of a complementary nature.

Orwell invented 'doublethink' for his prophecy *Nineteen Eighty-Four*; we only borrow his term—not the content—and would use it anew in order to express over-arching ideas. It comes close to what we mean by 'combining information'. 'Doublethink' would then be more appropriate to discuss people and organizations interacting than 'singlethink'.

References

Bateson, G. (1979) *Mind and Nature* (London).
Juch, Bert. (1983) *Personal Development* (Chichester).
Muller, H. (1970) *The Search for the Qualities Essential to Advancement in a Large Industrial Group*. (The Hague).
Trist, E. (1980) The environment and system-response capability, *Futures*, **April 1980**.
Watzlawick, P., Weakland, J. and Fisch, R. (1974) *Change* (New York).
Zukav, G. (1979) *The Dancing Wu Li Masters, An Overview of the New Physics* (London).

People and Organizations Interacting
Edited by A. Brakel
© 1985, John Wiley & Sons Ltd.

Biographical Notes of Authors

Jan Boeseman (1943)

Joined Shell in 1974 and worked in Personnel in the Netherlands and the Middle East. At present with Shell Gabon in Africa. Graduated from Leyden University in 1973 in organization sociology.

Aat Brakel (1925), editor

Worked in Shell 1951–1983 in Venezuela, British Borneo, the Netherlands, and the United Kingdom in Oil Exploration, Chemicals, Personnel, and Organization. At present independent consultant. Holds a Master's degree in chemical engineering and a Doctorate in sociology from Dutch universities.

David Cormack (1944)

Worked originally in the textile industry in the United Kingdom. Joined Shell Chemicals U.K. Ltd in 1976 as Organization Development Consultant. Since 1981 O.D. manager for Shell International Petroleum Company. Has a Doctorate from Leeds University.

Lars Gjemdal (1931)

Held several positions in the Norwegian Army before joining Shell in 1970. Worked in Training, Organization Development, and Personnel. At present with the Central Personnel Department of Norske Shell in Oslo. Graduated from the Norwegian Army Staff College in 1965.

Kees Greeve (1933)

Joined Shell in 1955 and worked as a mechanical engineer in some of Shell's research institutions. Head of Management Services of Shell's Research Laboratory at Amsterdam from 1967 to 1980. Since 1980, Head of the Organization Effectiveness Unit of Shell's Refinery and Chemical Plants in Pernis near Rotterdam, the Netherlands.

Norman Halpern (1934)

Is currently Consultant, Organization Effectiveness with Shell Canada. He joined Shell in 1955 following graduation as a chemical engineer from McGill University in Montreal, and has worked in a number of senior technical and line management positions before assuming his present assignment. He also holds Master's and Doctorate degrees in Adult Education from the University of Toronto. He has been a consultant for a number of socio-technical systems designs within Shell, including the Sarnia project described in this book.

Osamu Hattori (1936)

Joined Shell Japan in 1961 and worked in Personnel on training matters and in Marketing as sales representative. Currently Functional Adviser dealing with planning and career development of staff. Graduated from Tokyo University of Education in English Literature (1961).

Geert Hofstede (1928)

Dean, Semafor Senior Management College and Director IRIC (Institute for Research on Intercultural Co-operation), both at Arnhem, the Netherlands. Was chief psychologist in the international staff of IBM Europe, and Visiting Professor/Scholar at IMEDE, Lausanne, INSEAD, Fontainebleau, European Institute for Advanced Studies in Management, Brussels, and IIASA, Laxenburg, Austria. Author of (among other publications) 'Culture's Consequences' (SAGE Publications, 1980, 1984). Holds a Master's degree in mechanical engineering and a Doctoral degree in social psychology from Dutch universities.

Arie Langstraat (1950)

Became an organizational consultant with Shell Netherlands Refinery in 1976. Joined Shell's Regional Centre for Training and Organization Consultancy in the Netherlands in 1980. In 1984 he joined the Dutch government's Finance Department. Graduated from Leyden University, the Netherlands, in organization sociology in 1976.

Donald Mungall (1949)

Worked with local government in the field of organization development in London prior to joining Shell in 1977. Was O.D. adviser with International Trading, Coal and Marketing organizations in Shell International Petroleum Company. Has presently responsibility as O.D. manager of Shell U.K. Ltd for managing O.D. contributions to Shell U.K. Exploration and Production, Shell Chemicals U.K. and Shell U.K. corporate functions. Has a BA degree from Heriot-Watt university, Edinburgh, and a MA in organizational psychology from Lancaster university.

Wendy Pritchard (1946)

Worked for Rank Xerox U.K. Ltd from 1969 to 1974, latterly as O.D. Manager. Since 1974 she has been with Shell International, initially as O.D. Adviser and then O.D. Manager for the London Service Companies, and now as O.D. Adviser to Group Operating Companies worldwide on organization development and effectiveness matters. Has a MSc in occupational psychology.

Jacques Roggema (1939)

Joined the staff of the Work Research Institute in Oslo, Norway, in 1960 and became intimately involved in organizational change projects in the Norwegian Merchant Navy. Until recently he spent a substantial part of his time as an independent organization consultant working for Shell in the Netherlands. Works at present for local government. Has a Doctorate in psychology from the State university of Groningen, the Netherlands.

Philip Sadler (1930)

Principal of Ashridge Management College since 1969. He has served on various government committees. His current appointments include serving as a Vice-President of the Society for Strategic and Long Range Planning. He is co-author of *Organisation Development* and *Case Studies in the Printing Industry*. He holds a BA in sociology of the London School of Economics (1950).

Jeroen van der Veer (1958)

Joined Shell in 1973 and worked in the Netherlands as technologist and engineer in refining. Manager of a unit involved in cavity wall insulation and double glazing. Manager, Supply, Planning and Economics of Shell's refinery at Curacao (Dutch Antilles) 1978–1981. At present LPG Manager of Shell U.K. Holds Masters' degrees in mechanical engineering and in business economics from Dutch universities.

Theo Voors (1930)

Worked for 20 years as instrument engineer in Shell Companies in Nigeria, the United Kingdom, and Iran and became engaged in management training and O.D. projects in 1973. In 1980 he became head of training and development of Shell's companies at Pernis near Rotterdam, the Netherlands. At present he is Manager Training and Development of the Petromin-Shell refinery in Al-Jubail, Saudi Arabia.

Brian Wallace (1938)

Managing Director of Organization Dynamics Ltd (ODL), a firm of external consultants specializing in organization development. A graduate mathematician he spent a number of years in the aircraft industry, before becoming an internal O.D. consultant, initially with ICI and then with Shell. He formed ODL in 1976 and since that time has built a team of consultants with a wide-ranging portfolio of clients—spanning major multi-nationals (e.g. Shell), medium-sized manufacturing companies (e.g. LRC Products) through to entrepreneurial concerns in the computer industry (e.g. Research Machines).

Jim Watson (1924)

Was with Shell from 1952 until his retirement in 1983 and has worked as a technologist, an administrative manager, and a specialist in various aspects of personnel affairs. In 1974 he was appointed Head of Human Systems Development in Shell International Petroleum Company Limited, and was responsible for advising Shell companies around the world on the use of organization development techniques in management.

Index

DATE DUE

DEC 1 9 1992			